BEARING WITNESS

· ·

Amalia Amaki, *Fan Series: Overcome Evil with Good*, 1995, photographs, buttons, beads, and jewelry fragments (in a case), 20″ × 15″.

BEARING WITNESS

· ·

Contemporary Works by African American Women Artists

JONTYLE THERESA ROBINSON, CURATOR

Contributions by

MAYA ANGELOU · TRITOBIA HAYES BENJAMIN

PEARL CLEAGE · JOHNNETTA BETSCH COLE

M. AKUA McDANIEL · JONTYLE THERESA ROBINSON

BEVERLY GUY-SHEFTALL · LOWERY STOKES SIMS

JUDITH WILSON

SPELMAN COLLEGE AND RIZZOLI INTERNATIONAL PUBLICATIONS, INC.

PRESENTED BY:

 AT&T

TRAVELING EXHIBITION TOUR ORGANIZED BY EXHIBITSUSA

FOR TOUR INFORMATION THROUGH 1999, PLEASE CALL 1-800-473-EUSA

THE EXHIBITION WILL BE AT THE FORT WAYNE MUSEUM OF ART FEBRUARY 1–MARCH 30, 1997

ADDITIONAL FUNDING PROVIDED BY THE ATLANTA COMMITTEE FOR THE OLYMPIC GAMES, CULTURAL OLYMPIAD

First published in the United States of America in 1996 by
Rizzoli International Publications, Inc.
300 Park Avenue South, New York, New York 10010

Library of Congress Cataloging-in-Publication Data
Bearing witness : contemporary works by African American women
   artists.
        p.   cm.
     Includes bibliographical references and index.
     Contents: The visual education of Spelman women / M. Akua McDaniel
— Passages / Jontyle Theresa Robinson — Warrior women / Beverly
Guy-Sheftall — Triumphant determination / Tritobia Benjamin —
African American women in the arts / Lowry Sims — Hagar's daughters
/ Judith Wilson.
     ISBN 0-8478-1962-0 (HC). — ISBN 0-8478-1963-9 (PB)
     1. Afro-American women artists—Exhibitions.   2. Art, Modern—20th
century—United States—Exhibitions.
N6538.N5B43   1996
704'.042'08996073—dc20   96-4294
                                              CIP

DESIGN BY ABBY GOLDSTEIN

PRINTED IN SINGAPORE

DEDICATION

This catalogue and exhibition are dedicated to all African American women artists past and present.

ACKNOWLEDGMENTS

. . . .

SO MANY wonderful individuals brought this catalogue to fruition. For their assistance I will be eternally grateful.

To my wonderful colleagues and friends of Spelman: Johnnetta B. Cole, President, Glenda Price, Provost; Billie Sue Schulze, Vice President for Institutional Advancement, Spelman College Women's Research and Resource Center; Tamara Plummer, Tony Bingham, Audree Irons, Charles Bullock, Delilah Wynn Brown, Floyd Coleman, Cynthia Cooke, Johnnie Davis, James Adair, Harold Rhynie, Clayton Bass, Everett Freeman, Tina Dunkley, DeJay Bird, Emily Hanna-Vergara, Arturo Lindsay, Lev Mills, Tuliza Fleming, John Bowden, Richard A. Long, Jo Moore Stewart, Andrea Barnwell, Alexander O'Neill, Haas & Martin, Deni M. McHenry and ExhibitsUSA, Delta Sigma Theta Sorority, Inc., and Jacquelyn S. Marshall.

Thanks to the consultants to the exhibition: June Kelly, Alvia Wardlaw, Peg Alston.

Very Special Thanks to Akua McDaniel and Beverly Guy-Sheftall for their support from Beginning to End.

Sincere thanks for invaluable and immeasurable assistance to Manuela Soares, editor, and Abby Goldstein, designer of the catalogue.

I am profoundly grateful to my Spelman and Clark Atlanta University students: Kimberly Brown, Libya Doman, Dawn Glover, Wendi O'Neal, Kakuya Shakur, Niambi Sims, Miesha Hardison, Anne Collins Smith.

A special thanks to my family: Freddie A. Robinson, Earl Robinson and Dana McGee, Salim Ibn Malik, Dorothy Grovey Ellis, Nell and Claude Cole, Jonnéllè Cole-Hollins, Aysha and Briana. And thanks to my neighbors and friends: Giselle, Clyde, Matthew, and Julian Clark; Martine, Earl, and Vanessa Ford; Elizabeth Cook, and Anna.

Thanks to Spelman student Ariel Brown, my research associate, who is intelligent, lucid, considerate, and gave invaluable assistance in writing the biographies.

To my daughter, Prajjon Nicolle Robinson, who at age four already understands how important books are and entertained herself for long stretches of time while I worked on this project.   Jontyle Theresa Robinson

Philemona Williamson, *Curiosity's Path*, 1995, oil on linen, 48″ × 60″.

CONTENTS

· · · · · · · · · · · · · · ·

Emma Amos, *Have Faith*, 1991, silk collagraph, copper, 32″ × 41″.

PREFACE

· · · · · · · · · · · · · · · · ·

JOHNNETTA B. COLE

Spelman College President

ONCE THE idea was born, it was as if history and destiny had finally collaborated to will *Bearing Witness* into being. This exhibition of the works of twenty-five contemporary African American women artists is a powerful statement. Like all art of consequence, it is also filled with questions. Among the queries is this: why has it taken so long for these exquisite works by black women to be assembled in a major exhibition?

Bearing Witness first appeared at Spelman, a college where African American women fall deeply in love with their own possibilities. The exhibition was mounted in the museum of the Camille Olivia Hanks Cosby Academic Center, a building that magnificently expresses African American philanthropy, design, and construction.

And the world came to see *Bearing Witness*. This tour de force of womanist artistry touched people from many nations who gathered in Atlanta for the centennial celebration of human spirit and determination that is the Olympics.

From the opening on the Spelman campus, this collection of sixty works of art—from painting to fabric art to massive sculpture pieces—will travel to some of America's most prestigious museums. Wherever these works of our sister artists are shown, they will say so much that is both urgent and everlasting, elegant and disturbing, sad and hopeful. There is so much in *Bearing Witness* that we must see, and that we must hear.

Carrie Mae Weems, from the installation *From Here I Saw What Happened and I Cried* (10 works), 1995, installation of monochromatic color photographs with sand-blasted glass, 42″ × 33½″.
Courtesy: P. P. O. W. Gallery, New York, New York

FOREWORD

. . . .

MAYA ANGELOU

SHOULD AN off-earth visitor arrive wishing to know something of this spinning mote of matter which is the human home, I would direct the questioner to African American Women's art.

If the visitor sought to understand the depth of strength in the human heart, I would direct the quester to search in African American Women's art.

If the quester became interested in the artful resilience displayed by African Americans in their centuries-long sojourn over the planet, I would first say to the inquirer that African American art and culture are not separate nor can they be separated. Each form enriches the next, so even as we sing, we dance; even as we sculpt, we draw; as we sing praises to Heaven, we sing the blues about life here below. And at our best, we accept art in our lives, and we are indebted to the art of living for we have survived with passion, compassion, humor, and style.

The seeker should pursue answers on African American survival in the words of Margaret Walker, Gwendolyn Brooks, and Mari Evans; in the choreography of Katherine Dunham, Pearl Primus, and Judith Jamison; in the vocal genius of Billie Holiday, Aretha Franklin, and Leontyne Price; in the compositions of Mary Lou Williams, Undine Moore, and Margaret Bond; in the dramatic art of Diana Sands, Louise Beavers, and Alfre Woodard; in the mental clarity of Mary McLeod Bethune, Ida Wells Barnett, and Dorothy Height.

The curiosity of the unearthly inquirer would be piqued to see this frail, shattery, flabby creature; this human who was enslaved by fellow humans who themselves worshipped liberty withstand the greed and cruelty of slavery to survive as a celebration of life.

I would point the querist to the graphic art of the African American women shown in this catalogue. The art was evoked, defined, and praised in our great spirituals written long before these women were born, proving that our art is interdependent.

We are reminded of the spiritual which states that "We have had to make a way out of no way. We had to take nothing and make everything."

In the lyrical canvas of Lois Mailou Jones, the phrase that explains how we have kept lyricism in our lives is "Over my head, I hear music in the air."

Elizabeth Catlett's vibrant strength in sculpture and drawings can be heard in the divine order to Moses to "Go down, way down in Egypt land and let my people go."

Selma Burke's majestic sculpture brings to mind the heroic line, "I'm a child of the King. I'm a child of the King. With Jesus my Savior, I'm a child of the King."

Great and glorious are the artists gathered here, and great and glorious are their contributions.

If there is no extraterrestrial to question us and start our imaginations to whir, we may be satisfied to say, "Our souls look back and wonder at how we got over."

Some of the answers to that question can be found here in this catalogue.

THE VISUAL EDUCATION OF SPELMAN WOMEN

· · · · · · · · · · · · · · · · ·

M. AKUA McDANIEL

Spelman College Museum of Fine Art

IT IS no mistake that the exhibition, "Bearing Witness: Contemporary Works by African American Women Artists," was conceived at Spelman College, for it is here that creative African American women have been nurtured for 115 years. From the beginning, the visual arts have played a significant role in the intellectual growth of Spelman students. As the institution developed, its educational emphasis shifted from missionary, nursing, and domestic training to teacher training, to industrial arts education (concentrating in home economics), to collegiate liberal arts education. Embedded in each of these paradigmatic shifts, however, were fine art courses designed to enhance these academic frameworks.

First graduating class of Spelman Seminary, 1887. Spelman College archival photograph.

During Spelman's formative years (1881–1892), drawing classes were offered in conjunction with penmanship lessons.[1] Educators believed that the free movement associated with drawing improved gross and fine muscle coordination, thereby greatly enhancing handwriting.[2] After the turn of the century, penmanship-associated drawing was abandoned in favor of an introductory art course, offered by the home economics department, which concentrated on the study of form and color.[3] The academic year of 1899–1900 also witnessed the birth of Spelman's first museum. Reverend J. M. Lewis, an American missionary who worked with several college alumnae in West Africa, donated his collection of stuffed birds from the Americas and Africa, as well as a few art objects to Spelman. These items, along with artifacts from the Holy Land provided by the college's founding president, Sophia B. Packard, were placed in classroom cases across the campus to function as teaching aids.[4] As a result, the practice of using art and artifacts to augment learning became part of the teaching strategy at Spelman.

By 1916, the school's interest in missionary training was overshadowed by a rising interest in industrial arts education. This shift in the curriculum was encouraged by white philanthropic organizations that believed vocational training would best prepare African American women for family life, teaching, and domestic careers.[5] Among the new courses being offered in this industrial arts phase was bench work—a class that taught woodworking skills. In addition to carpentry, the program offered an evening printing course to working women.[6] Although industrial arts education would continue to dominate the curriculum until the early 1930s, Spelman College hired its first professionally trained artist in

1921. Rose Standish, of New York's Cooper Union Art School and the Art Students League, was the Instructor of Fine and Industrial Arts for nearly a decade. During her term at the institution, she offered an art and design course through the home economics department, a mechanical drawing class as a part of the industrial arts program, and a course in "drawing free-hand" for those whose sole concern was the study of art.[7]

The gradual shift to a more fully developed liberal arts curriculum favored fine arts instruction over industrial arts training. However, the school's full commitment to the arts was not realized until 1931 when Hale Aspacio Woodruff (1900–1980), an African American painter, was hired to establish an art department in the Atlanta University Center (AUC).[8] Dr. John Hope, president of Atlanta University, and Florence Reed, president of Spelman College, believed that in order to build a well-rounded liberal arts program, a fine arts component emphasizing painting, sculpture, and architecture had to be included. Woodruff was given the task of providing interested AUC students with the opportunity to study painting on Spelman's campus because of his superior training at the Herron Art School in Indianapolis, Indiana, and his experience abroad. Three years later, Nancy Elizabeth Prophet was hired to teach sculpture, art history, and architecture. As a graduate of the Rhode Island School of Design and the École des Beaux-Arts in Paris, Prophet became the first African American woman to teach art at the college. Her experience as an internationally exhibited artist and her success as the winner of the 1930 Harmon Foundation prize for sculpture made her a role model for Spelman students, especially those interested in becoming artists.[9] In order to provide proper aesthetic training for these women, the Department of Art was established in the mid-thirties, making it easier for students who chose to become artists or art educators to identify with the discipline directly, rather than through education or home economics courses. Courses designed specifically for the artistic education of Spelman women by Woodruff and Prophet during their tenure at the college provided a foundation for faculty who followed.

The museum that was established in 1899 disappeared during the industrial arts phase of the college's history. However, Hale Woodruff continued exhibiting works of art and using them as teaching tools. Through his efforts and the endeavors of others, Spelman College has amassed an internationally recognized collection of paintings, prints, and photographs as well as an impressive body of African sculptures and textiles. With the founding of the new Spelman College Museum of Fine Art, located in the Camille Olivia Hanks Cosby Academic Center, the college has made certain that the arts will continue to play an integral part in the education of African American women well into the next century. As we enter this new phase, Spelman will surely play a pivotal role in providing the nation with future generations of artists/scholars, art historians, critics, and museum professionals.

NOTES

1. *12th Annual Circular & Catalogue of Spelman Seminary for Women and Girls 1892–93* (Atlanta: Spelman Seminary, 1892), p. 12.

2. J. A. Green, *The Educational Ideas of Pestalozzi* (London: W. B. Clive, 1914; reprint, New York: Green Press, 1969), p. 119.

3. *18th Annual Circular & Catalogue of Spelman Seminary for Women and Girls 1899–1900* (Atlanta: Spelman Seminary, 1899), p. 45.

4. *12th Annual Circular & Catalogue*, p. 45.

5. Florence Matilda Read, *The Story of Spelman College* (Princeton, NJ: Princeton University Press, 1961), pp. 191–95.

6. Florence Fleming Corley, "Higher Education for Southern Women: Four Church-related Women's Colleges in Georgia, Agnes Scott, Shorter, Spelman, and Wesleyan, 1900–1920" (Ph.D. diss., Georgia State University, 1985), p. 240.

7. *45th Annual Circular & Catalogue of Spelman Seminary for Women and Girls 1926–27* (Atlanta: Spelman Seminary, 1926), pp. 11, 28, 36.

8. Winifred L. Stoelting, "Hale Woodruff, Artist and Teacher: Through the Atlanta Years" (Ph.D. diss., Emory University, 1978), p. 56. To reach this goal, Hope hired Woodruff to implement a six year arts plan for the Atlanta University Center which included Spelman College, Morehouse College, the Atlanta University graduate school, laboratory high school, and the elementary school.

9. Blossom S. Kirschenbaum, "Nancy Elizabeth Prophet, Sculptor," *Sage: A Scholarly Journal on Black Women*, 4, no. 1 (Spring 1987): 47. Prophet's work was shown in the Salon d'Automne and the Paris August Salon in 1924–27 and in the Salon of the Société des Artistes Français in 1929. She was also befriended by Henry O. Tanner, who personally recommended her for the 1930 Harmon Prize.

Elizabeth Prophet's Former Sculpture Studio, Spelman College. Photography by Harold E. Rhynie.

PASSAGES

A Curatorial Viewpoint

. . . .

JONTYLE THERESA ROBINSON

RECENTLY, I visited Spelman's former Sculpture Building, the old power plant, to determine if any sculpture or relics from the past still remained.[1] In 1939, the brick building had been remodeled into an attractive, well-lighted studio and exhibition space for Professor Nancy Elizabeth Prophet and her students. The 6,375 square foot, slate-roof structure has an open, spacious quality, but there were no sculptures or relics to be found.[2] What I did find was an underground passageway that connects Spelman College to Atlanta University, part of a network of tunnels that spreads throughout the Atlanta University Center and from which all AUC schools receive steam. While standing in front of this tunnel passageway in Prophet's old studio and gallery space, obvious metaphors came to mind. The Underground Railroad and Harriet Tubman came first. More important, however, was the connection between the first exhibition, "Forever Free," in 1981, and this exhibition of contemporary African American women's art at Spelman College. This network of passageways reflects the diversity of ideas, experiences, and paths of the women in the exhibition.

The urgency of "Bearing Witness" cannot be overemphasized. In four years a new century will begin. This exhibition of contemporary African American women artists is not an historical exhibit, nor is it a retrospective. As the century closes, "Bearing Witness" informs us about the present and portends the future.

Explaining the traditional African use of the term "art" may reveal how the works in this exhibition give evidence to, authenticate, and certify the lives of African Americans. The traditional African presupposition is that "art" is not separate from life. It is an integral part of the social structure; it is functional and utilitarian.

Therefore the art in this exhibition combines the two spectacular meanings suggested by the African scholar V. Y. Mudimbe.[3] Although Dr. Mudimbe was speaking about traditional African art, his ideas can be applied to contemporary works. In contributing to the cultural legacy that stretches back thousands of years in Africa, it is critical that African beliefs be used as a reference point for the women and their works in this exhibition. Thus, we acknowledge that these works have a primary utilitarian and functional purpose, but also that ". . . in their materiality . . . all of these objects speak (to those who can really understand) and remind them of the continuity of a tradition and its successive transformations."[4] They are "*memoriae loci*, places of memory."[5] Mudimbe is referring to memory as it relates to the Greek *martyr*, which connotes witness. The works in this exhibition become "windows" through which the artists and onlookers can observe the passing of the old century and the beginning of a new millennium.

Born in 1926, Betye Saar epitomizes the rationale for this exhibit. There is an active witness, a place of memory in her work *Watching* (1995). Sister Saar has created her work on a recycled, decorative furnace grate. Saar, who started creating assemblages after her three daughters were born, rarely searches for anything specific to use in her work, but goes by her intuition and waits for objects to beckon her. She probably acquired this furnace grate at a swap meet, antique shop, or junkyard. Its original purpose was to cover an aperture through which air, hot or cold, was received into a dwelling. In *Watching*, Saar has created a mixed media collage of paper, fabric, and acrylic paint on the flat side of the grate.[6] Peering out from behind the grate's floral latticework—now a window grille—is a "middle aged American woman watching the future—watching and waiting. . . . On the outside is a bird resting on the grid—watching—symbolizing Jim Crow—the bird is tin."[7] She has, as Mudimbe suggested, combined two meanings. The utilitarian function may be observed in the object itself. The artist has then made herself the subject of the work while allowing the recycled or previous life of the grate to certify or bear witness to the hot and the cold temperatures of the present century and the nascent century. It is a complex self-depiction on myriad levels.[8] This work, like this exhibition, is about the role of the contemporary woman.

The exhibition takes place at Spelman College, the oldest and best-known college for black women in the world and the only black woman's college affiliated with a major academic consortium, the Atlanta University Center (AUC). Nineteen ninety-six marks Spelman's 115th anniversary and the 15th anniversary of the college's Women's Research and Resource Center (the first of its kind at a historically black college), as well as the opening of Spelman's Museum of Fine Art and the 1996 Olympic Games in Atlanta. It is also the 15th anniversary of the seminal African American women's art exhibition, "Forever Free."

As curator, I felt that Spelman would be a rallying point for African American women artists. When the invitation for work was extended, the artists responded swiftly. At Spelman these artists could share, teach, promote, inform, celebrate, certify, authenticate, and witness. The exhibition provides passage for the free flow of ideas. The exhibition becomes a creative act of resistance and an act of empowerment for these warriors/women/artists. In *Black Feminist Thought*, Patricia Hill Collins considers places that are "safe" for black women in defining themselves and finding their voices.[9] Spelman, though not perfect, constitutes a "safe place" because ". . . it forms a prime location for resisting objectification as the Other. By advancing Black women's empowerment through self definition the safe spaces housing this culture of resistance help Black women resist the dominant ideology promulgated not only outside Black communities but within African American institutions."[10]

With this gathering of black women artists we have initiated a discourse and now we must look and listen to what these varied voices have to say. We must observe the work critically and self-consciously. As Africans in the Diaspora we must construct our own particular lens through which we can view the modern world in all its complexity. We will not use the lens of others, we will construct our own.

Central to our view are the tangible manifestations of the ideas and experiences of black women artists. As we observe these manifestations, we bear witness to the intersection of a cultural legacy in Africa thousands of years old and a historical context in America that began in the seventeenth century. This emphatically does not mean that to comprehend their work we must use the work of European men or African American men or Euro-American women as a benchmark. Rather, we must center our discourse around black women artists past and present because these warriors/women/artists bear witness to a triple jeopardy. They have been denied male and white skin privilege and have been subjected to art world racism. Despite over three hundred years of racial, sexual, and economic oppression, black women continue to demonstrate that their creative talents will not be suppressed. Multicultural issues, such as race, ethnicity, class, gender, and sexual orientation have engaged the imaginations of artists and writers since the turn of the century, but the particular vision of black women artists has often been ignored. Because of this phenomenon there must be a safe place where black women can be singled out for special consideration and redress. Given this special consideration, how will we come to terms with the work of these women?

I am indebted to Freida High W. Tesfagiorgis for the ideological framework I have used in this catalogue. It springs from her Afrofemcentrist theory whereby the black woman artist depicts and explores the black woman and her realities as subjects. But my specific theoretical framework is distinguished from it in that I have not limited the discussion to images of the African American woman by the African American woman. I have made the African American woman artist the center of my analysis and all references to them are made in relation to their peers and predecessors.[12] Therefore, this ideological framework centers the discussion around black women and uses them and their works as the primary reference points. It suggests that these women and their works are powerful and provocative, capable of standing alone or with each other, and that they, like the exhibition itself, are creative acts of resistance and empowerment.

This exhibition is connected to its predecessor, "Forever Free," in many ways. The historic black women's exhibition "Forever Free: Art by African American Women 1862–1980" was conceived as an historical exhibition and a general survey of Black women artists from the nineteenth century to 1980. The exhibition opened at the Center for the Visual Arts Gallery, Illinois State University, Normal, Illinois. In the catalogue to the show, the essay *African American Art History: The Feminine Dimension* by Arna Alexander Bontemps and Jacqueline Fonvielle-Bontemps, the curator and project director, made a significant start in understanding the art and history of African American women. In "Bearing Witness" it is imperative that we continue the discourse that was initiated with "Forever Free."

In planning for "Forever Free" fifteen years ago, the curator included:

> the art created by black women in America in art history curriculums (sic); [broadened] the public image of black women in America; [gave] the opportunity [for black women to succeed in the art world], [encouraged] interest and participation in the graphic and plastic arts by black women of all ages; [hoped] that it would make a valid and critical standard for the art black women have created in America.[13]

We delude ourselves if we think that the success of a handful of black women artists has addressed the needs that the curator and editor of "Forever Free" detailed. In fact, after that exhibition toured the nation, arts activist Howardena Pindell began gathering data for a seven-year statistical report on museum exhibitions and current gallery representation for the 11,000 Black, Asian, Hispanic, and Native American painters, sculptors, craftspersons, photographers, graphic designers, and architects who live and work in New York State. Released eight years after the opening of "Forever Free," Pindell's report was published in March 1989, in *New Art Examiner*.[14] Pindell's report detailed alarming statistics about representation in museum exhibitions and galleries. Participation by Blacks, Asians, Hispanics, and Native Americans was dismal or non-existent. Though Pindell was examining racism in New York State, her report underscored a national predicament.

According to Lowery Stokes Sims, curator of twentieth-century art at the Metropolitan Museum of Art, museums and galleries cannot discriminate legally, but they can use aesthetic judgment as the basis for exclusion.[15] Racism is insidious and subtle but it can be addressed. There need to be more black administrators, curators, and staff at museums and galleries across the nation. There needs to be more black support for African American museums in this country and African Americans must also become active in mainstream museums. There need to be more exhibitions like "Forever Free" and "Bearing Witness."

Some of the goals outlined in the "Forever Free" catalogue have been tackled, although not nearly enough. Art by black women is now included in some art history curricula and in the past fifteen years at least two anthologies, two monographs, a book of critical essays, and dozens of major art catalogues have been published. *Sage: A Scholarly Journal on Black Women* published an issue called "Artists and Artisans," and a growing number of films and videos about black women artists have been produced. In general, more attention is being paid to black women artists in mainstream publications. With the installation of "Bearing Witness" and the publication of this catalogue, intellectual, credible discussion can occur now that there is a substantive bibliography from which to draw and compare. This catalogue will be an important contribution to the scholarship on American art, African American art, and women's art.

This is the first major exhibition at the Spelman Museum of Fine Art. The number of women included had to be restricted because of limited space. The twenty-five that were chosen represent a highly selective, though very broad range of experience for the black woman artist in the United States and abroad. These artists can reveal where black people have been, where black people are, and where black people are going. They assist us as we negotiate our way. At times they afford us safe passage and at other times they simply direct or point the way—it is up to us to follow the paths they have indicated. Through their work, we can observe art that resonates with the past and anticipates the new millennium. While these artists span the twentieth century, most of the exhibited work is new and much of it has never been exhibited before.

Subject matter and iconography reflect the post–Civil Rights era. There is no angry, confrontational preoccupation with race; nevertheless, some of the statements about race are powerful and chilling. There are also intra-racial commentaries, multicultural expressions, and treatments of the intersection of race and gender. Gender issues loom large, as well they should with twenty-five black women.

These artists live and work in the West, Midwest, South, Northeast, Mexico, and Europe. Some have dual citizenship, some are American citizens living abroad, and some have relinquished their American citizenship. Some have full-time jobs; others are full-time artists. They include professors of art and art department chairpersons, artists-in-residence, visiting artists, and fellowship and research grant recipients. They work in a variety of media and there are performance and film artists, sculptors, painters, quiltmakers, and printmakers. Some deal with African imagery. Some create African American imagery. Some prefer abstract work. Some work strictly from nature, delighting in plant life and landscape. All reject racist and sexist imagery of the black woman.

These are educated artists. All finished college. All have earned graduate degrees, some have more than one graduate degree, and one or two others have or will have advanced degrees. Several of them have doctorates, earned within a university setting, or honorary. Many are also writers and curators. The core of them are baby-boomers, born from the mid-1940s through the 1960s, but two of them have witnessed the twentieth century from its beginning. Their works are in major museum collections and corporate collections. All of the artists have had major commissions in the United States and abroad as well as one-woman exhibitions.

LOIS MAILOU JONES
. . . .

Lois Mailou Jones (b. 1905) has had two long, productive, and inspiring, intermingled careers. As an artist she has been accorded many honors, and in her forty-seven years as a professor of art at Howard University she has taught over 2,500 students. Jones began exhibiting in the 1930s in Washington, D.C., and submitted her work for traveling shows and for exhibitions with the Harmon Foundation, a crucial institution that organized art competitions for black American artists. In 1930 she received an award from the Harmon Foundation for her 1929 charcoal drawing of a *Negro Youth*. Jones started teaching at Howard in 1930 and must have been an impressive professor. It is not happenstance that her students shared her resolve to capture the beauty and spirit of African American people.

It was in these very early years of her career that she began to focus on black subjects and her students were probably very much aware of her critical success with these works. Elizabeth Catlett was a student of Jones during the first years of her career at Howard University. Seeing a woman of Jones's calibre and energy thoroughly involved in her métier made a lasting impression on Catlett. From 1934 to 1937, the year of Catlett's graduation with honors from Howard University, her teacher had a one-woman show every year and also participated in an exhibition with one of her colleagues in the art department at Howard.

In 1987 Jones was an invited guest artist to the National Conference of Artists and the Association of Artists in Brazil. (The National Conference of Artists, founded at Atlanta University in 1959, is one of the oldest organizations of African American art educators and professionals in the United States.) The two works by Jones in this exhibit, *Chanson d' Bahia* and *Simbi, Haiti,* represent Africa in the Diaspora and are related to her travels to Brazil and subsequent travels to Haiti in 1991 and 1993.[16]

In *Chanson d' Bahia*, Jones reveals the rich tapestry of her Bahian sojourn. She remembers the four or five singing maidens dressed in white who met the airplane, the rich patterns of textiles, the feathers and birds, the carnival procession, the distinctive blend of colonial and modern Latin American architecture. Her painting is a souvenir of those moments and visions. In *Simbi, Haiti*, she turns to Simbi, the Haitian goddess of the sea from the Vodun pantheon. Vodun, which is an integral part of the culture of the Haitian people, is an African/Christian/Haitian religion which has an assemblage of rites designed to bring members into harmony with the forces of nature. That Vodun serves as a strong stimulus to artistic expression for Jones can be seen clearly in the Haitian works which she began during her first visits to the Caribbean island nation. In 1953 Jones married the Haitian artist Louis Vergniaud Pierre-Noël. That union and her travels to Haiti beginning in 1954 have had a profound impact on her art. Her palette is intense and vibrant. In *Simbi, Haiti* the artist was inspired by a metal sculpture, a *vèvè* or personification of the sea goddess. The Vodun *loa* or gods are represented by *vèvès*, symbolic drawings of cornmeal, flour, crushed bricks, coffee, and ash made by the mambo (female) or houngan (male) priest around the *poteau-mitan* (central post) in a Vodun ceremony that takes place in an *houmfor* (building for worship). Over the years Jones has returned repeatedly to Vodun themes in her art.

ELIZABETH CATLETT

· · · · · · · · · · · · · · ·

Elizabeth Catlett's *Webbed Woman* asserts an Afrofemcentric consciousness—a black woman artist focusing on the realities and experiences of a black woman as subject. *Webbed Woman* is not an object being acted upon; rather she is the subject of the work and is actively involved in changing her reality. Created in 1995, this full-hipped woman, cast in a rich bronze, draws upon the experiences of black women, yet has universal appeal in that it expresses the sexual, economic, and racial oppression

that many women feel. Catlett has created a nude woman with webs between her legs and arms.[17] Her arms are outstretched as she attempts to remove the webs. Catlett focuses on the solitary struggle of the woman who resists the webs that seek to envelope and subjugate all women. The woman is robust, active, standing firmly with legs set apart. Her response to the symbolic webs continues a decades-long tradition of conveying the black woman's reaction to the realities life holds for her.

"Sexual apartheid characterized most African societies in the precolonial era . . ."[18] While women were prevented from learning the mysteries of blacksmithing, forging, or casting metals, and carving in wood or stone, they did use pliable materials that did not require "men's tools."[19] While an African sculptural tradition in metal, to which Catlett is a direct heir seems remote, she has, nevertheless, over the course of six decades, removed the webs that obscure her connection to that tradition through her writings, her speeches, and her art. In her preface for *Africa Through the Eyes of Women Artists* by Betty LaDuke, Catlett writes:

> In the criticism of my artwork I have had to deal with bias as a black, as a woman, and for social and political reasons . . . these lives . . . [help] me realize . . . that I am not alone. . . . We can feel ourselves a part of this greater international activity that creates art for our people, art that is a part of our lives, art that is a necessity for us.[20]

In a speech entitled "The Role of the Black Artist" given thirty years earlier, Catlett articulated a similar sensibility.[21] Through the years she has remained steadfast in her ideas, her subjects, and her consciousness, and as we shall see, she has greatly affected generations of black women artists.

BETYE SAAR

· · · · · · · · · ·

The same energy and tireless dedication present in the lives and careers of Jones and Catlett is also present in Betye Saar. Let us consider Saar and her career in terms of arts patronage and arts exposure, hard-hitting business issues. For all of the artists in this show, the business aspect of their art is critical, inextricably linked to their survival. Indeed, cross-generationally, we will see that artists of the 1950s and 1960s have viewed women such as Saar, Catlett, and Jones as role models in their quest to control the financial aspect of their lives and careers. Jones, Catlett, and Saar have all enjoyed the prestige and commercial success of their art.

Since 1972, Betye Saar has had approximately forty-five one-woman shows or installations. Some years there have been two or three one-woman projects as well as an equally demanding group show schedule. How does a black woman manage to deftly juggle all the components of daily life and satisfy the rigors of a demanding career and still come out on top? In the 1977 PBS documentary about her *Spirit Catcher*, Saar shares much about her lifestyle and work. During the film the commentator asks: "What is the difference between being a mother and artist?" To which she responds, "There is no difference." Saar has managed to create her art, raise her three children, travel, be a companion to her family, and still take time for herself. She applies great zeal to whatever she does.

FAITH RINGGOLD
· · · · · · · · · · · ·

Our second generation of artists begins with Faith Ringgold. Like Saar and Catlett, Ringgold has had phenomenal success. There are two works by Ringgold in this exhibition. *Freedom of Speech*, commissioned by the Constitution Center in Philadelphia to commemorate the two-hundredth anniversary of the Bill of Rights, was completed in 1990 in Paris.[22] Ringgold asked friends, associates, and people she met to give the names of individuals who exercised their right to free speech. The work is a rich history of the precious right of free speech and Ringgold reminds us that no one should be silenced, that all have the right to speak whether or not we agree with what they say. It is especially poignant that she completed this acrylic-on-paper painting about America while living in a distant land.

The issue of freedom of speech is also inherent in the work *Marlon Riggs: Tongues Untied*.[23] Completed in April 1994, after the gay filmmaker's death, it is a celebration of

his life and career. Ringgold met Marlon in May 1993, when they both received honorary doctorates from the California College of Arts and Crafts in Oakland. Riggs, who was dying of AIDS, explained to the audience that he had almost died a few days earlier and had been afraid that he would not receive his degree. He stood before the audience and sang one of the songs his grandmother, "Big Mama," had taught him: *I Will Not Be Moved (Removed)*.

Ringgold had never met anyone with AIDS, so she asked Marlon if she could do a story quilt about him and he agreed. Ringgold had made her first quilt in 1980 with her mother, Willi Posey. They called it *Echoes of Harlem*. Ringgold's mother wanted to incorporate some freehand cut baskets and triangles of different sizes on the quilt, motifs derived from the African American quilting tradition.[24] Earlier in this mother-daughter collaboration, the two had made *tankas* (quilted cloth-framed paintings) in the 1970s. The first story quilt, *Who's Afraid of Aunt Jemima?* was completed in 1983. This medium was employed because Ringgold wanted to have her unedited words published and accepted as easily as her sculptures and paintings.

Born in 1957, Marlon Riggs was an award-winning filmmaker—the recipient of an Emmy and a Peabody award. His first major work, released in 1987, was *Ethnic Notions*. The 1990 sequel, *Color Adjustment*, extended the study of racial stereotyping initiated with *Ethnic Notions* to African American representation in primetime television. *Black Is . . . Black Ain't* was the third and final statement in Riggs's trilogy. *Tongues Untied*, televised in 1991, was a deeply personal film on the black, gay male experience.

Riggs came to Ringgold's studio only one time. He was so sick that he had to lie down intermittently. During this first sitting, Ringgold captured Marlon's face; photographs enabled her to complete the work. *Marlon Riggs: Tongues Untied* is a whopping 89 inches tall and 59½ inches wide. At the four corners of the work are influential figures in Riggs's life, clockwise are James Baldwin, Audre Lorde, Harriet Tubman, and "Big Mama" (his grandmother). On the quilt, Riggs wears a Miss America tee-shirt, an ironic indication of his black, gay male sexuality. His supportive, faithful, lover/

companion Jack Vincent is symbolized by the white bird sitting atop his shoulder. Ringgold completes this *tour de force* of acrylic on canvas and pieced and quilted fabric with quotes given to her by Marlon: "What Happens to A Dream Deferred? Black Men Loving Black Men; Been In The Storm Too Long; Tongues Untied? Master's Tools Will Never Dismantle Master's House; You Gotta Move; Black Is . . . Black Ain't; Unity Does Not Equal Unanimity."

Every aspect of the multifaceted Ringgold is operative in *Marlon Riggs: Tongues Untied*—writer, historian, painter, mixed media sculptor, performance artist, activist, and teacher—and they combine to bring her point home succinctly.

JEAN LACY
. . . .

Jean Lacy shares with Ringgold and her other contemporaries an artist/activist posture, perhaps because all of them came to maturity amidst the Civil Rights era. Like Ringgold, Lacy participated in demonstrations, sit-ins, boycotts, and other civil disobedience. In her reliquaries, mosaics, banners, and stained glass windows, she combines African American iconography and history.[25] Lacy feels that the time her people have spent worshipping alien imagery in church has done great damage to black children and she has actively endeavored to root out this "brainwashing." For black artists, including Lacy, there is a growing patronage by the African American church. The church commissions some of our most talented artists to create viable images for their edifices and parishioners. In her narrative programs and religious imagery, Lacy, like many other artists, combines myriad sources for her commissions—ancient African costumes, especially Egyptian and sub-Saharan, African myths and tales, African American quilt patterns, and period photographs from the Civil Rights Movement of the 1960s and the 1970s.

In 1970 the United Methodist Church Southern California/Arizona Conference, under the direction of Bishop Charles Golden, determined to address the ineffectiveness of Euro-American iconography for black inner city church school curricula, commissioned Lacy to develop thirty-five Old and New Testament images. Such decisions by Golden—a black bishop, also a rarity—to utilize black Christian imagery for inner city youth and to allow a woman to provide the imagery in the ultra-conservative and still largely male-dominated United Methodist church, reverberated throughout United Methodism. Those who don't approve of the church and feel that it already siphons off much-needed capital in black communities might consider Lacy's work negatively, and object to her using her awesome talent to proselytize or brainwash. However, since millions of black people are already in church, why not present them with positive Afrocentric images and icons to focus on?

Lacy, who joined the Lutheran church, was for many years married to a United Methodist minister. Early in her career she considered a graduate degree in liturgical arts, which would have combined her artistic capabilities with a knowledge of the rites, and the tools and instruments of those rites, prescribed for public worship. Though she did not pursue that degree, her recent commissions are moving her toward the same end. In Lacy's unique vision all denominations of the black church should utilize artisans and artists to create paraphernalia for liturgical use. Our sculptors would work in silver and metal to create communion vessels, crosses, and candelabra. Quiltmakers and textile weavers would create the banners found on chancel walls and the vestments worn by ministers, choirs, ushers, and stewards. For the St. Luke United Methodist Church in Dallas, Texas, an African American quiltmaker will fabricate the banners Lacy designed for the chancel. Lacy also designed a fifty-three stained-glass window program for this church and another multi-window program and renovation for the Trinity United Methodist Church (my maternal grandmother's church) in Houston, Texas.

Two reliquaries (religious objects for holding relics) are Lacy's contribution to this exhibition. The first is a reliquary/music box narrative entitled *Noah (Bert Williams/Bill "Bojangles" Robinson)* and the other is *Prayer for the Resurrection of a Row House in Baltimore*. In *Noah*, Lacy has reworked a music box she acquired, like Betye Saar, at an antique or secondhand shop. She probably paid no more than fifty cents for it. Like Saar, she incorporated its original purpose with her innovative vision to fashion a biting commentary on where we are and where we have come from as African Americans. Originally the music box had a Gene Kelly–type figure on it dancing and singing *I'm Singin' In the Rain*. The ever-incisive Lacy reassembled the box and replaced the original man with a black man dancing a jig and singing *I'm Singin' In the Rain*. The song creates a sense of rejuvenation, a renewal of the spirit, and an awakening. The black man is Noah, in the spirit of the vaudevillian character Bert Willams/Bill "Bojangles" Robinson or "Mr. Bones," which is a sacred as well as a secular interrogation. He performs in a miniature theater dressed in a top hat and cutaway coat. Exactly what is Lacy authenticating and certifying here? She is authenticating that there was and needs to be a great flood to cleanse the earth and end segregation. In front of the stage is a plantation house where the stereotypical figure "Ole Crow," is seen on the steps of the "Great House." The "Ole Crow" figure was lifted from a liquor bottle. In the background of the music box is a chicken coop where a black family and chickens appear, survivors of the flood. Lacy has transformed these mundane images into metaphorical expressions of cultural import. In the drawer of this music box, Lacy has placed a sardine can key, a reference to our slave ship passage.

Her *Prayer for the Resurrection of A Row House in Baltimore* is a two-part tribute to her aunt. There is a reliquary or portable altar in the shape of a row house and a small female figure who can be viewed either inside or outside of the reliquary.[26] The artist envisions this reliquary composite as a work in progress, and suggests that there will be additional parts later on. Lacy's aunt, who lived and died in a row house in Baltimore, worked as a domestic in an exclusive resort home on Gibson Island, Maryland. Though very elegant and educated, she had to survive as a domestic. The artist remembers her washing the glistening, white marble steps of her row house and shows her here with a gold leaf scrub brush, at once a symbol for the duplicity of who she was and what she had to do to survive. The "gutted" row house is made sacred by the use of gold leaf on the roof and parts of the windows and the flame or wing that appears on the right side of the house, symbolizing the house's spirit.

VALERIE MAYNARD

Both Lacy and Valerie Maynard share an interest in improving the conditions of their sistren and brethren throughout the Diaspora. Valerie Maynard's *Get Me Another Heart This One's Broken* and a triptych from her *No Apartheid Anywhere* series are compelling pieces. While living in the Virgin Islands, she heard a radio broadcast detailing the mass destruction of a housing district in a black township in South Africa.[27] The open-ended series was initiated when Maynard realized how expendable people can be all over the world. Maynard, who had never done a series before, began to counter these pernicious, abusive acts for those subjected to them. Because her voice and message are so powerful in this series, both she and her work have also been subjected to censure. There have been patrons who wanted to buy pieces from the series, but she made a decision not to sell any of the works because, ultimately, she wants to show the entire series at one time.

In these two examples she uses templates spray-painted with acrylic. She employs things she finds—chains, screws, saws, ball bearings, hammers, razors, nails, pins, combs, scissors, and graters. They are stenciled and painted, becoming metaphors for debris or "discardable" people. Maynard, along with many other women in this exhibition, has reminded us of the continuity of the most seemingly inconsequential items, past and present. Mundane, insignificant objects take on a vibrant, textural, albeit chilling character in Maynard's hands.

Maynard's self-depiction is explored in the Afrofemcentrist piece *Get Me Another Heart This One's Broken*. Here a socio-cultural, political voice issues a directive. She attends all those people who must endure the sometimes terrifying rigors of daily life—the heart-shattering moments where we refix, retool, and regauge our personal, political, and daily lives. Yes, Maynard has issued the directive, but at the same time she has exclaimed to those parties responsible to cease and desist. She depicts herself as a composite creature, an amalgam of the past/

present, the forebear/offspring, and the predecessor/successor. Maynard simultaneously shows herself in double-profile with her mouth agape, horrified and anguished, and with her mouth closed, detached and reflective, pondering the injustices of past and present. She is the black woman then and now. Her large, creative hand fans out before us, active and involved. The artist paints herself in a muted low-key palette with forms and motifs that recall her ancestral past. She has deep and abiding concern about how the past is connected with the present. Two other artists who share this concern are the sculptor Barbara Chase Riboud and the multifaceted Emma Amos.

EMMA AMOS

. . . .

Emma Amos recalls her early years in Atlanta and rekindles for us the concept of a safe haven—growing up in a completely segregated black environment, going to an all black high school, surrounded by the AUC colleges (Spelman and Morehouse), and being nurtured to prepare her for things to come.[28] As she was maturing, she was totally surrounded by articulate, scholarly, black intellectuals.[29] She did not know that anything was "wrong" with them, but afterwards, when she left that setting, she became more identified with race and gender at Antioch College in Ohio, and in the years beyond.[30] At Antioch she learned difference. The indelible difference made palpable by someone else's objectification of her is examined in the two very large paintings she has in the exhibition—*Tightrope* and *Measuring Measuring*. In *Tightrope* Amos portrays herself as an American female gladiator-type walking across a tightrope while an audience of "fans" watches. It addresses precisely what she has experienced in her life. She depicts herself trying to find balance when others are trying their damndest to make her fall. She is precariously perched on this tightrope with arms outstretched for balance, a paintbrush in one hand and a shirt on its own hanger—as in being clothed in a certain state of consciousness—decorated with a laser-transfer photograph of Mrs. Gauguin's breasts. She is adorned in gladiator boots and a coat, just like the fighters in World Championship Wrestling. Her fighting boxer shorts are fashioned from the American flag and she has placed African fabric around the borders of the painting.

Amos's recollections of her years in New York and her association with Spiral, a black artists' group that consisted of Norman Lewis, Romare Bearden, and Hale Woodruff, among others, are very poignant. She feels that they asked her to join because she was 'only a little girl' and not a threat; she was the youngest member and the only woman.[31] Although Amos has a deep respect for Elizabeth Catlett, when she was a member of Spiral she was not aware of what Catlett was doing in the arts. The members of Spiral only discussed her as an appendage to her former husband, Charles White.[32] At that time she had no female role models to mentor her, to let her know that she could do art, to help her develop a feminist consciousness, and to remain "extraordinarily devoted to the vision of [myself] as an artist."[33] That consciousness is evident in both of the works included in this show. *Measuring Measuring* depicts around its borders, which are made of African fabric, innumerable pairs of legs. In each of the four corners of this work is a hand. The hand is the individual's stamp or distinguishing feature. The three main figures (or photographs of figures) in the painting have no legs. There are, from left to right: a statue of a figure with a black hat, black arms, and white hands holding a photograph of another statue; a photograph of an African woman with tape measuring devices across her body (Amos has drawn in her missing leg); and next to her a Greek statue, *Kritios Boy*, whose lower arms and hands are missing. Amos is dealing with somatological and anthropometric hegemony here. She expresses the need for us to develop our own criteria and standards and not measure ourselves by others. She suggests that the European model may not necessarily be the standard for measurement. She makes a profound statement about the credibility of our own past and our own ethnic types that cannot be filled out, completed, or measured by another past or ethnic type. She bears witness to, authenticates and certifies that certain bodies and physiognomies are not superior to others.

Both Amos and Lorna Simpson touch on the material body as the site of political power, i.e., how we view ourselves and how we believe others view us. Amos is also concerned with the objectification of the black female and how we have been perceived as the other. She reminds black women, as did the writer Audre Lorde, that it is imperative that we love ourselves. Fundamentally, loving ourselves is a political act. No one else can make us whole but ourselves. When there are "parts missing," we must complete the parts. In a culture that despises, devalues, marginalizes, and attempts to erase us or have us balance ourselves on tightropes, we can do no less; anything else is flirting with destruction.

Amos has lived and studied abroad, as have a number of artists in this exhibition including Barbara Chase Riboud, who now lives in France and Italy. Chase Riboud has had a successful career in art and publishing in both America and Europe. Chase Riboud's generational counterpart, Emma Amos, has addressed her career success intra- and inter-generationally as she explains:

> I think I have had to learn that success is not going to come to me the way it came to the blue-chip artists; and that only a small number of artists are really successful in the marketplace, anyway. And it's not going to be me, or, if so it's going to be a late splurge on the order of what happened to Alice Neel, Elizabeth Catlett, or Faith Ringgold. Faith didn't get really well-known until she had been out there for at least thirty years. Hustling that job, that painting—working hard and doing without a lot of responses. I'm doing exactly what I always wanted to do, and that's what keeps me going.[34]

Amos's own piece *Measuring Measuring* validates and confirms a synchronicity in her thinking and visual expression that helps us to understand how she views her accomplishments in the marketplace.

BARBARA CHASE RIBOUD
. . . .

It is not surprising that Mary Edmonia Lewis is Barbara Chase Riboud's favorite African American woman artist.[35] Chase Riboud, who has lived and worked abroad for more than thirty-five years, and Lewis have parallel lives. Both are independent thinkers, not afraid to take risks, not afraid to let others know how they are feeling

or to speak up and be heard in the face of injustice. Both are superb sculptors who have lived and worked in Europe. Both are advocates for equal rights and justice undaunted by racism and sexism; neither retreats at the hint of controversy. In Chase Riboud's *Harrar* or *Monument to the 11 Million Victims of the Middle Passage*, the tragedy and chaos of the Atlantic slave trade, when millions of African people were dispersed in the Americas, is revisited. What Chase Riboud is proposing is the creation of a monument that would symbolize equal rights and justice for black Americans, once victims, but now an integral part of the American experience.

The concept of this sculpture is the result of more than ten years of reflection. It consists of two bronze-cast obelisk-shaped forms between which is suspended a bronze chain wheel consisting of 11 million links, each link representing one Middle Passage victim. The pillars and the suspended chain form an H shape that signifies the ancient African city of Harrar. On the sculpted surface of the obelisks would be engraved the names of every African nation, kingdom, clan, village, city, and river source raped of its fruit by intruders. This project has received wide support and hopefully will commence before century's end. From abroad, Chase Riboud has remained steadfast in her focus on African American culture through all phases of creative expression including her writing, lecturing, and sculptural works.

Tantra is a Hindu word suggesting a circular assembly of signs and symbols. At the center of this circular assembly is the axis from which the expansion of the world takes place. The arrangement of the signs and symbols is purely subjective. Essentially, the Tantric message is that an individual should gather the outer world into a single act of contemplation. This contemplative act can be expressed by any number of things, which can change according to the configuration of the signs and symbols. The overarching meaning of tantric symbolism is that things have no beginning and no end. *Tantra*, the sculpture, is made from silk, gold, and bronze. Chase Riboud is well-known for mixing materials not commonly used together in very dynamic combinations. Silk, fabricated in Lille, France, is dyed to match the bronze used in the sculpture at a workshop in

Paris. All the silk is tied by the artist, who also makes a full-size sculpture in wax as a preliminary step for the final bronze. The finished bronze will be made directly from the full-size wax sculpture. This is how she achieves the detailed undercuts and baroque feel in the bronze—she moves directly from wax to bronze with nothing in between. Sometimes she uses a foundry in Paris, but for the very large sculptural works, she utilizes Pietra Santa, a foundry in Tuscany. Though she occasionally employs an assistant for making the armature and for welding, she does everything else by herself.

BEVERLY BUCHANAN
. . . .

The next group of artists, the generation of the 1940s, includes Beverly Buchanan (b. 1940), Howardena Pindell (b. 1943), Stephanie E. Pogue (b. 1944), Freida High (b. 1946), Rachelle Puryear (b. 1947), Maren Hassinger (b. 1947), Joyce Scott (b. 1948), and Amalia Amaki (b. 1949). Born in Fuquay, North Carolina, Beverly Buchanan's *Shackworks* photographs, paintings, and sculpture are metaphors about life. In addition to reminding us that nothing is permanent, they also remind us that even ramshackled, dilapidated structures have beauty. In *Blue Lightning* and *4 Shacks with Black-eyed Susans*, Buchanan presents two pieces in oil and pastel on paper from her *Shackworks* series. This series evolved out of her *Black Walls* from the 1970s and from the constructions she made from wood and string when she was a young girl growing up on the South Carolina State campus in Orangeburg. Near her residence on the campus was a site for discarded wood pieces and chips used by the students who were in a program in which they had to construct small-scale houses.[36] Buchanan would drag these wood pieces and chips home and make things.[37] There is a relationship between these early assemblages and the cabins and shacks that Buchanan witnessed in South Carolina and in other southern areas. Not only was she influenced by these early constructions, but when she was growing up, "there was a young Black woman in my hometown who wanted to be an architect. I was so impressed with her. When I first started shacks my ideas were really about architecture."[38] Later the

structures had individualized traits or evolved into portraits of people.[39] The manner in which she constructs and assembles these discarded items is reminiscent of the approach of Betye Saar and it should come as no surprise that Saar is one of the artists with whom she feels a strong kinship.[40]

HOWARDENA PINDELL
. . . .

Multi-talented Howardena Pindell has had a distinguished career in art. After a twelve-year involvement with The Museum of Modern Art, rising through the ranks as exhibition assistant, curatorial assistant, assistant curator, and associate curator, this scholar/writer, artist/curator had an extensive understanding of the gallery and museum world in New York City and New York State. In 1989, she sent shock waves through the New York art world with the publication of a statistical report in the *New Art Examiner.* Compiled over a seven-year period, it examined museum exhibitions and current New York State gallery representation for Black, Asian, Hispanic, and Native American artists.[41] Pindell revealed that museums and galleries have practiced a very exclusionary art world racism.[42] Some improvements have occurred since the publication of her report. The report suggested that a new direction would have to be charted—there must be museums and galleries in the United States with black administrators, managers, and curatorial staffs.

Pindell moved from MoMA and the museum world to teaching—from 1979 to 1984 she was associate professor at the State University of New York at Stonybrook and she has been professor of art there since 1984. Pindell has traveled extensively in Africa, Europe, South America, and the United Arab Emirates. Her travels in Africa are the subject of one of the works in this exhibition, *Hathor Temple, Valley of the Kings, Egypt* (1974). The subject of the other work is the New York celebration for South African leader Nelson Mandela, *Mandela's Welcome Parade #1* (1992). Pindell chronicles her sojourn to Egypt in 1972 and highlights the joy and exuberance of Nelson Mandela's tickertape parade in New York City in 1992. Both works are spectacular in that they capture a multi-sensory perception of both the architecture and parade. The three-dimensionality of the photographs—they both have a depth of 3½ inches—enhances the drama of the moment. Both are photographs the artist made from slides. The final photographs are the result of a very lengthy process that she has developed to create the shimmering, mosaic quality in both works.

When the photographs are printed they are made into cibachromes or archival photographs.[43] A cibachrome or archival photograph is printed on acid free paper, which lasts longer and is slower to deteriorate. The photographs are also split and then mounted on museum board. Acrylic and gouache paint are used to unify the split photographs, making it hardly possible to detect what is photograph and what is paint. Pindell started creating split photographs in 1988, an outgrowth of her postcards, which she began to split in 1979.

Hathor is the Egyptian goddess of beauty, love, and motherhood, shown as a cow's head with sun disk and horns. She is often represented with the *ankh* or life symbol. In her *Hathor Temple, Valley of the Kings, Egypt* (1974) Pindell's act of building this three-dimensional surface with acrylic and gouache paint is critical. In this scene the artist has, in the upper reaches of the photograph, created a telescopic/kaleidoscopic jewel-like surface that is dazzling and dynamic. The photograph has the appearance of swerving inward and takes the observer on a tour of the temple by moving her around the gigantic pillars. At the base of one massive pillar in the center of the photograph Pindell captures some *medu neter* (words of God) or hieroglyphs (from the Greek *hieros*, sacred, and *glypheen*, to carve). These sacred writings extol the powers and virtues of Hathor.

Mandela's Welcome Parade #1 (1992) celebrates the visit of Nelson Mandela, leader of the African National Congress, released from a South African prison after a twenty-seven-year incarceration. Pindell captures the pageantry and momentum of this splendid, shimmering spectacle made dynamic and engrossing through her use of a horizontal format. It is a joyous occasion, full of hope and possibility for all who witnessed it then and now.

Like Beverly Buchanan, Carrie Mae Weems, and Lorna Simpson, Pindell uses the medium of photography to interrogate the past, decode the present, and herald the new millennium. With Pindell we witness a certification of Africa in our past and future. Pindell's lens, however, is not idyllic. In both photographs we are reminded of the past chaos and corruption in both Egypt and South Africa.

STEPHANIE POGUE
. . . .

The dynamics of change are embraced in Stephanie Pogue's *Woman on a Pedestal* and *Self-Portrait: Vulnerable*. They are very different from the Pindell works in that they are both autobiographical [44] and both are from a series. Pogue allows us to examine her up-close, and what we find is an intrepid black woman willing to share personal and intimate details. As a black woman in the world of work and as a woman who must interact with other human beings, Pogue reveals painful moments when the triple jeopardy of being black, female, and an artist is overwhelming. In both of these monotypes, she presents herself as a torso—closed, perplexed, and frightened. The torso in both works is seen from the back, slumped over with no legs and arms. The torso is isolated because this is where the heart is, this is where the essence of the body is presented as naked and unshielded; the opaque colors she employs complement this interpretation. In *Self Portrait: Vulnerable* Pogue could, but does not offer a defense for herself. She shows herself being attacked from all sides.

In *Woman on a Pedestal*, Pogue takes charge. She leads the offense and challenges the defense. She feels that this piece has universal appeal. It represents all women. In *Woman on a Pedestal* she reminds us that objectification is a position that few women crave. Others objectify women. Others can present your body in racist and sexist ways. The artist, however, has an edge. The black woman artist can rework, resist, question, and destroy racist and sexual stereotyping. The artist can re-engineer, transform, and confront. Pogue has located us at the center of this exhibition of contemporary black women artists and its ideological framework. These are the reasons an exhibition such as this one is so important—the voices of these black women have spoken *Uhuru* (which means *together* in Swahili): this is the way we see ourselves. We are women who are multi-dimensional—we have many capabilities and can create in a variety of media; we are image makers and abstractionists. We are women of great complexity. We resist European images of us. We resist being placed on pedestals. We resist pedestals. Indeed, Pogue depicts this Ionic Greek pedestal as imperfect in shape. Thus the European standard is imperfect. Pedestal and persona share imperfection. As artist, as image maker, Pogue is able to distinguish herself from the status quo because she created this self-image and she can determine how she is presented, where she is presented, and in what context. Thus the act of creation is self-liberating.

The choice of monotype as a medium reinforces Pogue's message and her persona. This technique has an accidental quality. With monotype, there is no certainty about the final print when it comes through the press. The artist can rework the printed image just as she reworks sexist and racist imagery. She can create a layered effect to demonstrate that she is not superficial and one-dimensional. It also allows Pogue to experiment and expand her expressive range.

FREIDA HIGH

. . . .

As we move from Stephanie Pogue to Freida High, we return to a historical African architectural theme similar to Pindell's *Hathor Temple, Valley of the Kings, Egypt*. But where it may be possible for us as women to feel detached from Pindell's temple in Egypt, that detachment from an island off the coast of Senegal is not possible. With High there is no compromise; each of us is a part of her *Returning to the Door of No Return*. Two years ago when High visited the Isle de Gorée, off the coast of Senegal in West Africa, she took each of us with her. Her African sojourn is made gritty and literal to us through the use of sand in this monumental 8-foot by 5-foot acrylic painting. As she gazed through the "Door of No Return" where millions of African women, men, and children must have passed, she began to remember her ancestors.[45] Her gaze through this ancient, sacred place of hopeful and hopeless memories was at once painful and exhilarating. Through her gaze, I could imagine my own African American state of liminality as we passed through the door, one-by-one, leaving the particular African in us to enter the particular American in us.[46] Like others who have visited this place, we experience Gorée, and the other stages of separation, distance, and irrevocable change, with all our senses. If perchance, we fail to understand the magnitude of these horrific centuries, High impregnates our vision with a testimony so enormous that the screams—silent and audible—can still be heard.

High, who coined the term Afrofemcentrism in 1984, uses her Afrofemcentrist construct to examine the ideas and representative artworks of black women artists and to reveal and clarify the uniqueness of their self-depiction, thereby encouraging greater appreciation of form and technique. In *Returning*, she explains to us exactly what she believes:

> I pay homage, seek comfort, and experience rage . . . in [this] public mourning/reunion place. In [this] "memory place" whether Gorée, Elmina, or elsewhere, [I] touch the trace of the past which remains [my] very present. [I] romanticize, fetishize, cry, embrace, and leave renewed through [my] own experience which stimulates [my] consciousness with memories or others' memories.[47]

RACHELLE PURYEAR

. . . .

Rachelle Puryear also returned to Africa as a part of her quest to learn more about its art and architecture. In 1973 she was awarded an NEA grant and conducted fieldwork on the continent to acquire documentary material. Both she and Freida High have pursued formal training in African art history. In fact, Puryear was contemplating a PhD in African art history, but opted instead to study for a year abroad, which completely changed the course of her life and career. Puryear grew up in Washington D.C.[48] and graduated from Trinity College in 1969. She attended Indiana University, acquiring a master's degree in African art history in 1971. Afterwards, she was employed as Curator of African Art and Assistant Administrator at the Museum of the National Center of Afro-American Artists in Boston. Finally, the time came for her to decide whether to pursue her doctorate in African art history or to spend time developing her art. At this critical point she was accepted as a guest student in the printmaking department at the Royal College of Art in Stockholm in 1974. Now married, she convinced her husband, a Swede, who had lived in the States for six years (they met in Bloomington at Indiana University) that they should try one year in Sweden and then return to America. Puryear worked at the Royal College of Art in Stockholm for two years teaching etching and silkscreen. Finally, the screen department was permanently closed due to health risks involved with screenprinting. Afterwards, Puryear decided to set up a studio with an artist from England whom she had met at the Royal College. In the late 1970s she started teaching at the College of Arts, Crafts, and Design in Stockholm. She was offered a permanent position and subsequently planned and developed a screenprinting workshop there.

In 1988 she was offered the Chair at the Royal College. The entire printmaking department had been renovated to meet Sweden's very strict health and safety standards. Over a seven-year period, Puryear and her colleague Kjell Birath, in conjunction with the company Birath Fargmakeri (screenprinting ink makers), developed a safe water-based screenprinting ink for artists that is now manufactured for use in all Scandinavian art schools. In 1994 Puryear, along with Herbert Gentry, Clifford Jackson, and Ronald Burns, exhibited together at the Terry Dintenfass Gallery in New York City. The exhibition, called "By Their Choice," considered the work of these four African Americans who have decided to live abroad.

Puryear's art and work have been influenced by her decades abroad. While a student at Trinity College she was making art that was basically abstract. In the mid-1970s she began to incorporate abstracted photographic images into her work. This decision was made partly because Puryear enjoys photography, but also because of her move to Sweden. In Sweden, even in the urban environment, there is proximity to nature—to woods, forests, the sea, and rocks scarred by glacial movement during the ice age. Since her move to Sweden her work is based on photographic images combined with hand-manipulated elements as evidenced in *Crevice* and *Bladverket*. She is especially interested in Swedish textile traditions and has learned to weave since moving to Scandinavia. She has also made paper, done collage, and produced mixed media projects in which images are combined with text. Puryear shares with Maren Hassinger an interest in nature and abstract form.

MAREN HASSINGER

Hassinger is a versatile artist of many aspects; she is at home in performance, film, sculpture, and installation. She speaks and writes eloquently about what she does and how it is done. In response to queries about her working methods the artist explained that materials she employs, the tools she utilizes, and the construction methods she engages in are only technical considerations. The actual process is intellectual, emotional, and private.[49] She contributes two maquettes to this exhibition, *Weight of Dreams 1* and *2*. Both pieces are testimony to the desires and dreams we all have and the impact outside forces can have upon them. Hassinger, who was born in Los Angeles, explains: "Pieces get made, like performances, when people ask for them, then all the obsessions are unleashed. When I can understand what I need to see and know then I can make the piece."[50] In a retrospective entitled "Bushes" installed at the Hillwood Art Museum at Long Island University in 1992, the catalogue essayist expressed Hassinger's endeavor to provide ". . . a momentary recovery from [the] loss [of self] . . . in a scientific environment."[51] Her work provides a space where the observer can acknowledge her ". . . painful conflicts and . . . fears while contacting [a] . . . personal . . . liberatory relationship to nature."[52]

Hassinger, who graduated from Bennington College in Bennington, Vermont, and received her MFA from UCLA, has had an illustrious career in teaching and in art. Her work is included in important public and corporate collections throughout the United States. It is distinguished from Joyce Scott's in that it is abstract and largely derived from nature, yet both these women have a delightful sense of humor. This humor, however, does not overshadow the concerns they make visible in and through their art.

JOYCE J. SCOTT
. . . .

Joyce J. Scott creates a dialogue between herself and her audience through her work. *Jar Woman #4* and *P-Melon #1* represent an interactive exchange between artist and observer. Art critic and historian Judith Wilson zeroes in on Scott's work when she writes, "intimate scale and intricately beaded surfaces prompt expectations of preciousness. But, because the dramas they enact are frequently violent and involve central social conflicts—of race and gender—the work exudes a fierce, raw edginess, in spite of the exquisite craft."[53] *Jar Woman* and *P-Melon* are no exceptions. *Jar Woman* eases into our purview, almost timidly, then—WHALLOP—Scott lets us have it. This time it is a mixed media woman carrying lots of paraphernalia. She recalls encrusted *nkisi* figures from the Songye peoples of Zaire or flawless beadwork from the Yoruba of Nigeria. She is an aggregation of divination. She is collected memory. Her stomach is covered with jars filled with special amulets, dolls, cards, previously eaten corn cobs, relics, vessels, plastic embryos, bones, locks, and photos. Scott's mother, artist Elizabeth Scott, saves all these things for her. Macabre and elegant, *Jar Woman* is attended by two *calaveras* or skeletons who cling to her like adornments. The *calavera* is a popular motif that goes back to pre-Columbian times and was united with themes from the Spanish Counter-Reformation. The Aztecs, for example, used the *calavera* and the skull as a motif in their sculpture and painting. The Mexican *calaveras* remind us that Scott did a year of graduate work in Mexico and studied Native American traditional crafts such as weaving and jewelry-making while she was there.

Jar Woman walks with the assistance of a hissing serpent staff that is disarmingly beautiful. The serpent represents knowledge. *Jar Woman* appears to have three eyes—two of her eyes are human and the third is omni-

scient. The *calaveras*, the snake, and the woman all have piercing black circles around their pupils. *Jar Woman* and these creatures are tied up in a web of agreement. They represent Scott's Apostolic/Pentacostal background, where death is not an end but a beginning. A three-dimensional work meant to be viewed from all angles, the standing figure is in *contrapposto*. She is weighed down by everything she carries, including the power of collected memories.

In *P-Melon*, a watermelon is the metonym for the sexual organs of the female body.[54] In fact, Scott serves up a blown glass and beadwork feast of ripe, juicy watermelon and has a beautiful beaded image of a stereotypical male with big red lips enjoying his juicy P-Melon. The melon can also be a cornucopia, a shell-shape, a fertility shape, and a vagina. Scott takes us right to the edge; she is not for the faint-hearted or the timid. To dismiss this work as vulgar is to miss the point. Scott is dealing with the erotic. She says yes to the erotic with the sensual materials she uses and the sensual manner in which parts of the object are made. It is not erotic in the sense of super-sexual, but the materials feel sensual and they glisten. Audre Lorde reminds us that the erotic offers a well of replenishing and provocative force to the woman who does not fear its revelation, nor succumb to the belief that sensation is enough.

Scott is delving into the hard-hitting issues of race stereotyping and the objectification of the black female in *P-Melon*, while at the same time reminding us that to create a miniature blown glass treasure of such beauty and complexity takes skill and knowledge. Scott seeks the unusual in her choice of media—blown glass is not a technique that many African American women utilize. The glass is chosen because it is translucent and because it pushes Scott to the limits of her technical knowledge. To combine blown glass with intricate beadwork coupled with complex imagery and thought is to turn prevalent notions about art and who makes it on their head. As a third-generation artist, the familial route Scott has taken to command such varied techniques has encompassed a maternal grandfather who was a blacksmith and made Afro-Carolinian sweetgrass baskets; a maternal grandfather who carved and decorated canoes; grandmothers who made quilts; and Elizabeth Scott, her renowned quiltmaker mother.[55]

AMALIA AMAKI
. . . .

Amalia Amaki shares with Scott a sensibility toward collected memory and remnants of the past. This sensibility is articulated in *Fan Series: Baby Doll in a Case; Number 1 Fan #2; Souvenir Gaze #2;* and *Fan Series: Overcome Evil With Good.* Amaki pays homage to familial ties in these four works of jeweled fragments, buttons, and old photographs. They are composites of childhood days spent playing with old tins of buttons belonging to a southern mother; ritualistic gatherings of women kin on front porches, in dining rooms, and in kitchens shelling field peas or washing buckets of berries; endless days at church; and unknown backgrounds of insignificant, utilitarian objects.[56] *Fan Series: Baby Doll in a Case* is about implied kinship. The artist combines the photographs of unrelated people and encapsulates the sacred versus the secular with personal herstory. *Number 1 Fan #2* is from a series that combines a blues music theme with hand-held fans. Amaki fuses the public and private and, once again, the sacred and secular. She places an expressive image of blues legend Billie Holiday on the upper portion of this fan and clusters a plethora of white buttons around her and on the bottom half of the fan. In addition to the double entendre reference to black church music and black secular music, she addresses the preciousness and fragility of individuals and groups and recalls decorative hand-held mirrors in vanity sets. The photograph included in *Souvenir Gaze #2* had been abandoned in a dresser drawer with odd pieces of broken jewelry and other objects.

Amaki, Betye Saar, Jean Lacy, and Valerie Maynard remind us that people and objects are not scattered debris. Everything once belonged to someone and although the whole may be unavailable or unobtainable, this does not diminish the fragment's importance. Fragments, debris, and refuse can remind us of past lives and experiences and they can enhance a new life and a new setting as Amalia Amaki elegantly shows us.

In her *Overcome Evil With Good,* the Georgia native reiterates the necessity of preservation. This time she includes photographs of unrelated people, and places them in a family setting, utilizing artistic license. A solitary female dressed in white with a large collar outlined in black and a large black belt in the upper photograph contrasts with the dark-suited circle of male "kin" surrounding her. One of the men in this clan holds a banner that repeats the work's title and reminds us of the endless church sermons and lessons that the artist heard at the Wheat Street Baptist Church during her youth. The lower part of the fan has a calling card that says "Greetings from Prospect, New York." Buttons, zipper fasteners, and other tiny decorative sewing notions enhance the beauty and message of the fan.

VARNETTE P. HONEYWOOD
. . . .

Varnette Honeywood (b. 1950), Philemona Williamson (b. 1951), Stephanie Johnson (b.1952), Carrie Mae Weems (b. 1953), Nanette Carter (b. 1954), Alison Saar (b. 1956), Charnelle Holloway (b. 1957), Lorna Simpson (b. 1960), and Debra Priestly (b. 1961) are the artists who will work into the first half of the new millennium and beyond. We observe what they have to say closely because this group details and treats concepts and ideas that will herald the coming century.

History is the theme of California artist Varnette Honeywood's art: African history, American history, family history, and her own personal history.[57] In 1970, while she was a student at Spelman College, Honeywood changed her major from history to art. Her choice of Spelman was important since at this institution she could meet scores of artists and teachers. Honeywood had strong relationships with her teachers that continued after graduation.

In the 1980s, Black Lifestyles, a fine art and commercial reproduction venture Honeywood started with her sister Stephanie and their family, became a success, and there were important commissions (*Essence* magazine) and one-woman shows (Spelman College). Honeywood traveled abroad (to Senegal, Bahia, São Paulo), and toured black colleges throughout the United States, including Spelman, where she returned several times as a guest of Jenelsie Holloway and the Department of Art.

In 1992 she was artist-in-residence at Spelman and an important retrospective of her work was organized, chronicling the four decades of her life.

A solitary female figure is the subject of Honeywood's *The Caregiver.* The biting social commentary evidenced in the cross-shaped *Preacher's Pet* has been tempered in the very poignant *The Caregiver,* reminding us that there are individuals in Honeywood's immediate family who are ailing and need love and care. A solitary black woman, perhaps Honeywood or her mother, seems engulfed by scissors, syringes, gauze, band aids, capsules, caplets, jars, bottles of medicine, and a pencil and pad to remember when all these medicines need to be administered, as well as a million other details. Three solitary hand motifs remind us that those who are ailing require much attention, and two hands may not be enough. It is a narrative about this family's plight and shows how religious beliefs give support. The wall sign, "God Answers Prayers," is Honeywood's dialogue with her audience. She often uses this technique to send a message. While allowing us to glimpse this personal moment, she uses artistic license to clarify and signify where she stands. Honeywood makes her point amidst African symbols and textiles and in the environment of the home. She says to us: "This is what I am experiencing. This is what I believe. What are you experiencing? What do you believe?" It is a message that she does not want you to overlook or avoid.

PHILEMONA WILLIAMSON

. . . .

Philemona Williamson has equally engaging and important messages, but her pedagogical manner is more subtle. Light comes in through a bevy of windows and bathes Williamson's Manhattan studio.[58] This is the light that helps her see clearly the beautiful colors she painstakingly captures in her exquisite paintings. There are three of these paintings—*Cautious Cold, Field of Water,* and *Curiosity's Path*—in the exhibit. *Curiosity's Path* reflects the depth of meaning in Williamson's art. The painting is about conflict and movement. It helps us break through complex issues relative to the artist, her work, and life. The painting is not autobiographical in the sense that it captures a specific event from the artist's childhood. Williamson is actually creating a metaphor for something far more powerful in *Curiosity's Path.* By choosing a scenario that is not so specific, the artist hopes that the viewer can make up her own story. The artist hopes the observer will recognize something that will pull her into the painting and help her find something there that will allow her to find her own answers.

Curiosity's Path is a narrative painting, but the interpretation of the painting depends on the viewer's mood. Williamson seeks to capture the moment so that the painting has spontaneity. When the viewer looks away and then looks back at the painting, something has changed. It is an ever-shifting panorama—a difficult feat to achieve artistically, yet the talented Williamson pulls it off without a hitch. In addition to the dialogue between the painting and the viewer, a similar dialogue has already occurred between the artist and the painting. The canvas speaks to her and tells her what needs to be changed. Williamson works on different parts of the painting until each is satisfactory. She also likes to work on more than one painting at a time. Something happening in one work will precipitate something in another.

Williamson started *Curiosity's Path* when she was pregnant with her second child. The movement of two separate energies is expressed in the painting, a visual pulling apart. The yellow bus refers to the future, starting school, a new beginning. All of this, says Williamson, could be part of what was happening to her personally. It is a revelation of her quandary about how her life, art, and career will be effected by these events. What will these changes mean? What will happen in the future? The potential danger lurking in the lives of these children within the painting is perhaps, in reality, Williamson pondering her own needs within her own setting. Similar conflicts are seen in the painting *Rolling Distance,* which shows a woman trying to balance herself on two balls. She feels lucky to have both her career and her family, though sometimes it can be difficult to manage it all.

Oil paint is Williamson's primary medium, which she buys already mixed in tubes. She likes to use very small brushes to apply the oil to linen canvas. Linen is a luxury, but she likes the feel of the surface. To apply the paint with such small brushes she must work very slowly, but she has absolute control of the gradations and flecks of color that are so mesmerizing in her work. Despite the slowness of her technique, Williamson likes to work from a live model, preferring to paint from life. She strives to make her colors appear natural, but is especially fond of placing colors where one doesn't expect them.

Cautious Cold examines and questions solitude. A lone figure is anxiously awaiting visitors—it is uncertain whether or not they are friendly. Williamson's message here is that as we approach new situations, we never know the outcome. In *Field of Water*, the girls are juggling parts of their lives, looking for safety. Figures in *Curiosity's Path* are trying to grab hold of the future while still clinging to memories of their past as Time flees. To me, these works present a trilogy in which Williamson makes statements about who she is and what she believes. She also demonstrates, irrefutably, that she connects inter-, intra-, and cross-generationally with the lives of her sister artists. The women in this exhibition are on a mission, all headed in the same direction—the twenty-first century.

CARRIE MAE WEEMS

There is an unmistakable consistency in the work of Carrie Mae Weems. You can detect this consistency even in the title of the series in this exhibition. The title also clarifies what Weems feels her responsibilities are as an artist. In *From Here I Saw What Happened And I Cried*, she reveals how black people have been represented in photographic history, and critiques that representation.[59] The photographic documentation she presents spans two centuries and has pedagogical merit —it was the intent of the original photographers to harm and damage. They documented black people with preconceived notions of inferiority, objectification, and malaise. Weems takes these documents and instructs us using this same bone-chilling technique. She simultaneously looks back and forward through her position as hidden witness. She reminds us that arbiters of evil did not get away with anything then (because she

was there) and that the arbiters of evil will never get away with any such thing in the future (because she, or someone like her, will always be there). She is the soothsayer. She has come to give us the information. She has allayed our fears and told us how to respond. She has provided a "window" through which information can be obtained about race politics, gender, and class.

STEPHANIE JOHNSON

Lighting designer and visual artist Stephanie Johnson also employs photographs to document the history of our progenitors and predecessors, often utilizing multiple and interactive aspects of sound, light, and image in her profoundly moving presentations. Johnson, who lives in Berkeley, California, has created two sculptural works —a freestanding work entitled *Bouquet*, made of light bulbs, steel tubes, and steel boxes, and *When We Say Goodbye, In Memory of Brother Larry*, a memorial piece for her father made of horseshoes and saws.[60]

The steel tubes used in *Bouquet* were retrieved from the junkyard. Here she endeavors to capture the essential nature of children, the fact that they glow. She is not expressing anything about any specific individual. Rather, all children are considered, including those who are differently abled. Recorded sounds of children are a part of the sculpture. Both of Johnson's works have drama and acknowledge her connections (and her mother's) to the theater.

In order to create her father's memorial piece, Johnson had to learn welding. *When We Say Goodbye, In Memory of Brother Larry*, is composed of saws welded to horseshoes. Johnson and her mother attended a memorial service for her father, who was a lifetime member of the Omega Psi Phi fraternity. Her father derived a great deal of pleasure and a sense of camraderie from his association with the Omegas. Generally an isolated and lonely man, he drank heavily. Even so, Johnson remembers her father fondly—he was an educated man with a PhD in child psychology from New York University, and he loved children. The horseshoes represent the Greek letter Q, as in Omega, and the saws represent

Dr. Lawrence J. Johnson, Jr., not as an artisan, but as a man who had to mentally hack and saw his way through life. At the memorial service the Omega brothers left a space for Dr. Johnson in the circle and the artist was so moved by the service that she felt compelled to express her feelings about those poignant moments by creating this piece.

NANETTE CARTER
. . . .

With Nanette Carter, we move cross generationally to consider Elizabeth Catlett, who has been an inspiration to her, just as she was to Emma Amos. When Carter was in graduate school in the 1970s she did not know of any black female artists.[61] She saw Catlett's work only after completing her formal education, so she did not know that she was part of a continuum. Carter had to develop a consciousness of who she was and what she could do on her own. After graduate school she spent nine years teaching, but the response to her art has been so positive that she is now able to devote herself entirely to her work. She finds great joy in the reception her art has received.

She offers three works from her *Window View-Scapeology* series in this exhibition. Carter likes to focus on nature and observe its similarities to human life. There is harmony and discord in nature and it is these contrasts that she puts on canvas and into prints. She shows human attempts to control nature and the powerful manner in which it thwarts their desires. In the *Window View-Scapeology* the artist sees her canvas as a window with compartments that are like window panes. She presents her ideas in these compartments. She utilizes symbols that carry a universal message. They can represent land, or if turned another way, trees or figures. They can also represent a cloudscape, landscape, underwaterscape, or outerspacescape.

Carter primes all of her canvases black. To her, black represents infinity and great space. A black canvas also gives the sense that one is in the presence of a window. For Carter black makes things push out. In this arena Carter captures the rhythms of life and nature. Some appear through repetition, some through color. Carter

wants to create surfaces that have rhythm, fluidity, and tactility. African syncopation is manifest in the work of this very talented woman.

ALISON SAAR
. . . .

Alison Saar, born in Los Angeles in 1956, is the only artist in the exhibition with a dual degree in art history and studio art, which she received from Scripps College in 1978. She received her MFA in 1981 from the Otis Art Institute of the Parsons School of Design. Because of her family and their interests, Saar has observed the situation of the woman artist of color first-hand (via her mother, Betye), and has lived it herself.

Using wood, tin, aluminum paint, and a mirror, Saar creates an 89-inch woman brimming with symbolic references. In *Clean House*, completed in 1993, Saar creates an Amazon with tree branches emanating from her head and upper torso. In some ways the head of the piece recalls an Ikem headcrest fashioned from wood and pigment used by the Ibibio peoples of southwestern Nigeria. Worn during dance ceremonies for young women reaching puberty, the Ikem headcrests usually have three large, elegant protuberances which are curled at the ends. Such a connection seems appropriate for Saar, but far too facile. The woman in *Clean House* conjures up art that is too rich and complex to be looked at only within the context of one African ethnic group. Like the twisting branches extending from this woman's head, Saar takes us through Africa and the Americas, recalling African, Haitian, Afro-Cuban, Afro-Native American, and Afro-U.S. connections. Saar shares a common bond with artists like Lois Mailou Jones, Charnelle Holloway, and Joyce Scott, who, because of their travels, have developed complex visual statements.

CHARNELLE HOLLOWAY
. . . .

Charnelle Holloway comes from a long tradition of artists in a family that includes Henry O. Tanner and her mother, Jenelsie Holloway, also an accomplished artist. In *Fertility Belt for the Career Woman* and *Woman's Ark*, Holloway has created two intensely personal works for the exhibition. *Fertility Belt* is a gift to all passionate women and meant to be worn by those among us who have had to put off childbearing for another love.[62] The face of the *akua ba* (a fertility figure used by the Ashanti of Ghana) is made from repousséed sterling silver, but also includes bronze and other media. Holloway uses African symbolism such as Ashanti *adinkra* (symbols stamped on African textiles) in her work. Two *adinkra* are included on the belt: 1) *nkyinkymiie* (twistings), symbolizing toughness, adaptability, devotion to service, and the ability to withstand hardship; 2) *nyame biribi wo soro*, symbolizing hope and aspiration, "God, if there is something in the heavens, let me reach it." Cowrie shells, symbols of fertility and formerly used as currency in Africa, are also on the belt. Holloway uses them here to keep away the evil eye. Chimes give the belt an interactive quality, they call up energy and are used for meditation. Chimes create a quiescent ambience—serenity and calmness, the aura that is needed for whatever may happen.

In "The Time Before the Men Came: The Past Is Prologue" (from *Mad at Miles*), Pearl Cleage writes a myth about the time when women were Amazons, aware of their own strength and free from any distractions.[63] It was a time when women could do everything. "We were fearless, brave, trustworthy, clean, mentally awake, and morally straight."[64] Holloway, although not familiar with Pearl's myth, has fashioned a woman's ark which could, under some circumstances, replace the strength of collective concentration the author discusses in the myth. "We had integrity, scorning the petty and the vicious, avoiding the obvious, sidestepping the curse of sloppy thinking and obsessive, possessive love."[65] Collective concentration is magic. It is our ability to sit within the magic circle, join hands and collectively focus our minds on one thing and then achieve it. But it took the complete concentration of the entire group and so we worked hard to maintain that concentration; that focus; that power; which is one of the reasons why their lives, why our lives were so peaceful. Superfluous activity is distracting. It weakens you.[66]

The ark that Holloway has created is a secret ark, a woman's ark. There are secret objects and mementoes in the ark, including crystals and a jeweled knife. The ark comes from a time when Amazon women were in power. According to Holloway, there is probably a remnant of this secret society still in existence, from the period when we were Amazons. When sistren come together and support each other, they become Amazons. Of necessity, this group is underground in patriarchal societies. With the creation of the *Woman's Ark*, one of the sacred altars for this exhibition, Holloway and the other women in the show remind us of the importance of our collective concentration.

DEBRA PRIESTLY

Like Holloway, Debra Priestly has also experienced a heightened sense of awareness about who she is and the importance of the art that she creates.[67] This is evidenced in her *Patoka Series*. Patoka refers to the Indiana hometown of her father. Priestly has memories of this place from her childhood, but a heightened sense of awareness of who she is and how she is connected to all that happened to her in ages past did not occur until her sojourn to New Zealand in 1989. It was at that time that the "collected memories" were unleashed. These memories flood through onto her birch plywood surfaces. However, Priestly reminds us that in the *Patoka Series* she is thinking about and expressing things familiar and familial. While these ideas are born out of a storytelling tradition, they are not presented in a literal way. When they appear, they are presented in a "jerky space" on Priestly's surfaces which are sometimes in boxes. Illusion and abstraction are at odds and Priestly instigates a wonderful, almost, playful *tete à tete* with her audience. She works primarily in acrylic on birch plywood, which gives her a richer surface. She paints her ideas inside boxes that project from the wall, making it intriguing for the viewer to determine whether she is looking at the wood surface or inside a box. She also uses intense colors to distance herself from the subject matter. When Priestly's colors are brighter, she is being less realistic.

The Maori in New Zealand brought her closer to herself and those she loved, so that we can now witness a celebration of life, a celebration of her father and the mystical farm where he grew up, a celebration of her early childhood, and a celebration of the connectedness she feels with people in all parts of the world.

LORNA SIMPSON
. . . .

My first response to Lorna Simpson's works is to issue a caveat to all who behold them. This woman is probing into critical issues that confound black people in the Americas relative to their identity, their struggles, their perceptions, their history, and their future. Do not dismiss her brevity and sparsity as shallow and uncomplicated. Sister Simpson like Sister B. Saar combines two spectacular meanings, first, the utilitarian or functional in *Wigs* and *9 Props* (what are wigs and props but functional items?), and second, the continuity of a tradition of *memoriae loci* or places of memory. Sister Simpson is a witness. In her attempts to get her observers involved, she invites them in through her windows using functional items, wigs and props, that appear at face value to be non-inflammatory, comfortable, non-inciteful, even benign. Then she opens the floodgates and unleashes a torrent of information that takes you on a roller coaster ride, with nothing to hold on to as you attempt to steady yourself; Simpson is in charge as she decodes the symbolic and contemporary. A member of the vanguard generation, she prepares us for the new millennium by using strategies that intervene, alter, and even disrupt traditional thinking.

In *Wigs*, Simpson confronts issues of sexual deviance, sexual orientation, self-esteem, self-deception, physical or handicapping conditions, violence, and objectification. And she makes clear the awful consequences to society, including the black community, of not dealing with the differences among us. In the brief commentary she writes to accompany the photographic images, she gives us just enough information to consider. She also uses maxims in her commentary: If the shoe fits, wear it; don't go near the water unless you know how to swim; there are [is] more than one side to every question; nine tailors make a man. She bears witness to the high incidence of cancer in the black community and the need for a wig or prop to cover up the ravages of chemotherapy or radiation. She bears witness to a parent willfully dressing the same child in clothes for a girl one day and then clothes for a boy the next, creating confusion in the child. She returns to the days of slavery in the United States and bears witness to a black male's realization that if his wife wore a wig, then she could, because of her very fair skin, disguise herself as his mistress and he could become her slave, and then, perhaps, they could escape slavery. She bears witness that being black is unacceptable for some and they must cover up their blackness with wigs and props and by so doing measure themselves by someone else's standard.

In both *Wigs* and *9 Props*, she confronts issues of lesbian and gay sexuality and homophobia. Especially in *9 Props*, issues that are too painful, pretentious, patriarchal, powerful, and personal are decoded and interrogated. Entrepreneurship, lesbianism, homosexuality, black female/male relationships, violence, stalking, battering, and the high incidence of AIDS in our community are explored. The passage she took to achieve discourse with these issues is instructive and ritualistic.

After seeing an exhibition of the photographs of James VanDerZee, a Harlem photographer active from the 1920s through the 1980s, Simpson noticed that VanDerZee incorporated the same props or objects in the many hundreds of photographs he took of those who came to his Harlem studio. In response to his work, Simpson recreated in black glass (black as in people, glass as in translucent) nine objects that VanDerZee used repeatedly to 'dress' his Harlem studio. It is very difficult to decipher where Simpson ends and the *9 Props* begin, because they, like she, are witnesses to VanDerZee's sixty years of history. The props are shrewd, cunning, powerful implements in Simpson's hands and represent the intersection of racial and sexual oppression and power. In *9 Props* and *Wigs* she considers, respectively, Beau of the Ball, referring to the Beau as a S/he, and Gladys Bentley. Simpson identifies Bentley outright in *Wigs*. Historically, Bentley's presence in Simpson's work reminds us that although the Harlem Renaissance was a seminal movement in black art, music, and literature, it "was also a significant moment in the history of . . . black lesbians and gay men . . . and the . . . social networks they created—played a crucial role in the[visual arts], in the blues, in the clubs, [in the music] of the Renaissance."[68]

Gladys Bentley was a full-figured black woman with a magnificent growling voice who performed in a white tuxedo and white top hat. She was a talented pianist and she was a lesbian. To deny her is to wholly deny the Harlem Renaissance. Gladys Bentley is our sister. Simpson gives us this information and asks that we consider people and their differences. This is the grammar through which a new millennium is made. We learn to accept people and their differences and to aid and assist when there are people in need.

All of these artists in one way or another have given us a new language for the twenty-first century. They have demonstrated in their own grammar that they understand not only who they are, but what they—and we—must do. Many of them know each other and have been influenced by each other. This catalogue and exhibition reveal an undeniable cohesiveness. These artists may work in isolated pockets, they may say things differently, and they may see things differently, but there is irrefutable unanimity. They are our passage to the twenty-first century. They have acknowledged that they are vigilant, enduring black women who will continue to contribute positively to life in the Americas and abroad on myriad levels, forever free, as they usher in a new century.

NOTES

1. In planning for our new museum, members of the museum committee visited every building on Spelman's campus to inventory the works in our collection.

2. For many years sculpture-related items dating, perhaps, from the Prophet era, were kept by the maintenance division but were eventually discarded after no one claimed them.

3. V. Y. Mudimbe, From "primitive art" to "memoriae loci" *Human Studies* 16 (1993), p. 106.

4. Ibid., p. 107.

5. Ibid., p. 106.

6. Betye Saar, interview by Ariel Brown, Los Angeles, California, October 19, 1995.

7. Ibid.

8. Ibid.

9. Patricia Hill Collins, *Black Feminist Thought: Knowledge, Consciousness, and the Politics of Empowerment* (New York: Routledge, 1990), p. 95.

10. Ibid.

11. Ibid.

12. Freida High Tesfagiorgis, "Afrofemcentrism and Its Fruition in the Art of Elizabeth Catlett and Faith Ringgold," *Sage: A Scholarly Journal on Black Women*, vol. 4, no. 1 (Spring 1987): 25–29. See also "In Search of A Discourse and Critiques That Center the Art of Black Women Artists," in *Theorizing Black Feminisms: The Visionary Pragmatism of Black Women*, ed. Stanlie M. James and Abena P. A. Busia (New York: Routledge, 1993).

13. Arna Alexander Bontemps and Jacqueline Fonvielle-Bontemps, *Forever Free: Art by African American Women 1862–1980*, exh. cat. (Alexandria, VA: Stephenson, 1980), p. ii.

14. Howardena Pindell, "Art World Racism: A Documentation," *New Art Examiner*, vol. 16, no. 7 (March 1989): 32–36.

15. Lowery Stokes Sims quoted in Patricia Failing, "Black Artists Today: A Case of Exclusion," *Art News*, vol. 88, no. 3 (March 1989): 125.

16. Lois Jones, interview with the author, Washington, D.C., October 15, 1995.

17. Elizabeth Catlett, interview by Niambi Sims, New York City, October 23, 1995.

18. Rosalyn A. Walker, "Woman As Artist in Sub-Saharan Africa," in *Forever Free: Art by African American Women 1862–1980*, p. 2.

19. Ibid., p. 6.

20. Elizabeth Catlett, preface in Betty LaDuke, *Africa Through the Eyes of Women Artists* (Trenton, NJ: Africa World Press, 1991), p. v.

21. Elizabeth Catlett, "The Role of the Black Artist," *The Black Scholar*, vol. 6 (June 1975).

22. Faith Ringgold, interview with the author, Englewood, New Jersey, September 1995.

23. Ibid., October 1995.

24. Faith Ringgold, *We Flew Over The Bridge: The Memoirs of Faith Ringgold* (Boston: Little, Brown, 1995), pp. 76, 194.

25. Jean Lacy, interview with the author, Dallas, Texas,October 7, 1995.

26. Jean Lacy, personal communication with the author, October 10, 1995.

27. Valerie Maynard, interview with the author, West Poland, Maine, October 12, 1995.

28. bell hooks, "Straighten Up and Fly Right: Talking Art With Emma Amos," in *Art on My Mind: Visual Politics* (New York: The New Press, 1995), p. 172.

29. Ibid.

30. Ibid.

31. Ibid., p. 178.

32. Ibid., p. 182.

33. Ibid., pp. 182–83.

34. bell hooks, "Straighten Up and Fly Right," p. 193.

35. Barbara Chase Riboud, interview with the author, Paris, France, October 10, 1995.

36. Patricia Phagan, "An Interview with Beverly Buchanan," *Art Papers* (January–February 1984): 17.

37. Ibid.

38. Eleanor Flomenhaft, "An Interview with Beverly Buchanan," in *Beverly Buchanan Shackworks: A 16-Year Survey* (Montclair, NJ: The Montclair Art Museum, 1994), pp. 13, 15.

39. Ibid., p. 13.

40. Ibid., p. 15.

41. Pindell, "Art World Racism: A Documentation."

42. Failing, "Black Artists Today," p. 129.

43. Howardena Pindell, interview with the author, New York City, September 29, 1995.

44. Stephanie Pogue, interview with the author, Hyattsville, Maryland, October 20, 1995.

45. Freida High, personal communication with the author in Wisconsin, August 30, 1995.

46. Ibid.

47. Ibid.

48. Rachelle Puryear, personal communication with the author, Stockholm, Sweden, October 3, 9, 11, and 25, 1995.

49. Maren Hassinger, personal communication with the author, East Hampton, New York, October 17, 1995.

50. Ibid.

51. Maurice Berger, "'The Weeds Smell Like Iron': The Environments of Maren Hassinger," in *Maren Hassinger 1972–1991* (Brookville, NY: Hillwood Art Museum, Long Island University, 1992), pp. 8–9.

52. Ibid.

53. Judith Wilson, "Specific Mysteries The Art of Joyce J. Scott," in *Joyce J. Scott: Images Concealed* (San Francisco: San Francisco Art Institute, 1995), p. 7.

54. Joyce J. Scott, interview with the author, Baltimore, Maryland, September 20, 1995.

55. Judith Wilson, "Specific Mysteries: The Art of Joyce J. Scott," p. 6.

56. Amalia Amaki, interview with the author, Atlanta, Georgia, October 13, 1995.

57. Jontyle Theresa Robinson, *4 Decades: The Art of Varnette P. Honeywood* (Atlanta: The Department of Art, Spelman College, 1992).

58. Philemona Williamson, interview and video by Tony Bingham, New York City, September 29, 1995.

59. Carrie Mae Weems, interview with the author, Boston, Massachusetts, October 3, 1995.

60. Stephanie Johnson, interview with the author, Atlanta, Georgia, September 15, 1995.

61. Nanette Carter, interview and video by Tony Bingham, New York City, September 29, 1995.

62. Charnelle Holloway, interview with the author, Atlanta, Georgia, October 7, 1995.

63. Pearl Cleage, "In the Time Before the Men Came: The Past Is Prologue," in *Mad at Miles* (Southfield, MI: The Cleage Group, 1990), pp. 6–8.

64. Ibid.

65. Ibid.

66. Ibid.

67. Debra Priestly, interview and video by Tony Bingham, New York City, September 29, 1995.

68. Eric Garber, "A Spectacle in Color: The Lesbian and Gay Subculture of Jazz Age Harlem," in *Hidden From History: Reclaiming the Gay and Lesbian Past*, ed. Martin Duberman, Martha Bicinus, and George Ciopsy (New York: Penguin Books, 1987), p. 318.

Figure 1 Elizabeth Catlett, *Sharecropper*, 1970, color linocut, 50/60, 26″ × 22″.
Hampton University Museum, Hampton, Virginia.

WARRIOR WOMEN:

Art as Resistance

. . . .

BEVERLY GUY-SHEFTALL

We ought to stop thinking we have to do the art of other people. We have to create an art for liberation and for life.

Elizabeth Catlett, 1971

After I decided to be an artist, the first thing that I had to believe was that I, a black woman, could penetrate the art scene and that I could do so without sacrificing one iota of my blackness, or my femaleness, or my humanity.

Faith Ringgold, 1985

Every time I think about color it's a political statement. It would be a luxury to be white and never to think about it.

Emma Amos, 1993

TWO OF the most significant events in recent United States history—the civil rights and women's movements—have had a profound impact on contemporary African American women artists. While considerable attention has been paid to the racial politics of the image-making of black women artists and their role in the black arts movement, they have been absent, for the most part, in histories of black feminism and the development of the feminist art movement. In her groundbreaking essays on "Afrofemcentrism" and "Black feminist art-historical discourse," artist and critic Freida High Tesfagiorgis articulates a unique method for analyzing black women artists which simultaneously considers the politics of race, class, gender, and sexuality.[1] This black feminist critique is long overdue, she argues, because "much of what has been written lies within the history of African American art, is secondary to male production, and for the most part is without critiques of class, gender and sexuality . . ."[2]

Sculptor and printmaker Elizabeth Catlett comes to mind most immediately in an analysis of black feminist impulses in the visual art of African American artists. Her pioneering 1946–47 series, *The Negro Woman* (fifteen linocuts, later named *The Black Woman Speaks*), challenged the stereotypical, non-heroic treatment of black women, which characterized Western art for decades, by portraying them as strong, beautiful, political, creative, and intelligent. In fact, women of color, particularly ordinary women such as those portrayed in *Tired* (terracotta, 1946), *The Survivor* (linocut, 1983), *Nina* (linocut, n.d.), and *Sharecropper* (linocut, 1968) (fig. 1) were the primary subjects of her prints and sculptures. She was unapologetic about her focus on women:

> I don't have anything against men, but since I am a woman, I know more about women and I know how they feel. Many artists are always doing men. I think that somebody ought to do women. . . . I think there is a need to express something about the working-class black woman and that's what I do.[3]

A self-defined feminist, she espoused her commitment to the eradication of the oppression of women, particularly black and Latin American women, whose struggles were different from middle-class white women:

> I am interested in women's liberation for the fulfillment of women; not just for jobs and equality with men and so on, but for what they can contribute to enrich the world, humanity. Their contributions have been denied them. It's the same thing that happens to black people. . . . I think that the male is aggressive and he has a male supremacist idea in his head, at least in the United States and Mexico. We need to know more about women.[4]

• 39 •

Homage to My Young Black Sisters (cedarwood, 1968) is perhaps the most stunning example of her commitment to the empowerment of women. In this magnificent sculpture (fig. 2), which was carved to honor brave young women in the civil rights movement, a woman holds her head high and points her clenched fist toward the sky in an unmistakable stance of defiance. Catlett herself also defied conventional gender roles by becoming the first woman to head the sculpture department at the National School of Fine Arts at the National Autonomous University of Mexico in 1959, which angered the male faculty.

Her political stance with respect to black arts was evident in a historic speech delivered in 1961 at the

Figure 2 Elizabeth Catlett, *Homage to My Young Black Sisters*, 1968, red cedar, 68″ × 12″ × 12″. Collection of Mr. Andi Owens. Photo: Becket Logan. Used with permission of Elizabeth Catlett.

National Conference of Artists, an organization of art professors in black colleges. It was the beginning of the civil rights movement in the South and the hundredth anniversary of the end of slavery in the United States. She spoke on "The Negro People and American Art at Mid-Century," during which she asserted the value of all-black exhibitions and of using black history as subject matter. She also articulated her vision of the political function of black art and the necessity for black artists to express their racial identity, communicate with the black community, and participate in struggles for social, political, and economic equality:

> Whether we like it or not, we, Negro artists, are part of a worldwide struggle to change a situation that is unforgiveable. . . . Children can no longer be denied the right to food, to clothing, and to education . . . we must search to find our place, as Negro artists, in the advance toward a richer fulfillment of life on a global basis. Neither the Negro artist nor American art can afford to take an isolated position.[5]

Painter and quilter Faith Ringgold also fought for the rights of black artists who were marginalized or invisible in a predominantly white male art world. In her extraordinary memoir, *We Flew Over the Bridge*, she describes her own struggles as a mother and wife in the 1960s to become an artist and express her female point of view about the historic era of civil rights and black power. In 1963 her attempts to join the mostly black male artists' group Spiral (the only female member was Emma Amos), headed by Romare Bearden, were unsuccessful, though four years later her first solo show of paintings, "The American People," opened at the Spectrum Gallery and was attended by the "old men of black art."[6] In her *Black Light* series, begun in 1967, she would embrace the "black is beautiful" slogan of the era by creating a new palette which would resist the Western preoccupation with white pigment and substitute black.

> In the painting of *Die*, I had depended upon the blood-splattered white clothing of the figures to create the contrast needed to express the movement and energy

of the riot. I felt bound to its use, having been trained to paint in the Western tradition. But I was now committed to "black light" and subtle color nuances and compositions based on my new interest in African rhythm, pattern, and repetition. In 1971 I described these new works as experiments in toning the light to the blacks, browns, and grays that cover my skin and hair; and the shades of blues, greens, and reds that create my forms and textures.[7]

Nineteen seventy would turn out to be a pivotal year for Ringgold and for black women's cultural and literary history, in part because of the publication of Toni Cade's *The Black Woman*, Shirley Chisholm's *Unbossed and Unbought*, Toni Morrison's *The Bluest Eye*, Alice Walker's *The Third Life of Grange Copeland*, and Audre Lorde's *A Cable to Rage*. The second-wave women's movement was also getting underway and Ringgold recalls having been introduced to the movement by lawyer Flo Kennedy in 1967. It was three years later, however, in 1970 that Ringgold became a feminist in order to "help my daughters, other women, and myself aspire to something more than a place behind a good man."[8] She also became seriously involved in the newly emerging women's art movement. In the early 1970s women artists protested their exclusion from museums, mainstream exhibitions, and art history scholarship, and initiated alternative exhibitions and women's galleries for achieving visibility. At the same time black artists were struggling for inclusion at The Museum of Modern Art (MoMA) by establishing a separate wing for their art and demanding Board representation. Ringgold would become an important figure among both protest groups.

In 1970, the group Art Strike was organized by Robert Morris to protest the American invasion of Cambodia. They also objected to American artists' participation in the annual Venice Biennale, and decided to exhibit at the School of Visual Arts in New York instead. Ringgold and her daughter Michele Wallace, outraged by the proposed alternative exhibition in New York because it included only white male artists, formed Women Students and Artists for Black Art Liberation (WSABAL), which eventually was successful in getting black, Puerto Rican,

and women artists exhibited at the "liberated" Biennale, though white women were surprisingly against such a move. During these contentious debates, which now included uncooperative white feminist artists, Ringgold advocated fifty percent women (Michele's mandate) and "open shows," a kind of affirmative action for blacks, especially black women artists who had been discriminated against by the mainstream art world for generations because of a set of criteria for inclusion which favored Euro-American males.

It was also during 1970 that Ringgold joined Ad Hoc, a women's group inspired by feminist art critic Lucy Lippard and Poppy Johnson, which began demonstrations against the Whitney Museum of American Art for its discriminatory practices with respect to women artists; as a result of this agitation, Betye Saar and Barbara Chase Riboud became the first black women to be exhibited at the Whitney Annual (1971). During the same year Ringgold's activism continued with the co-founding (with Kay Brown and others) of Brooklyn-based Where We At, which mounted the first exhibition of black women's artists—"Where We At Black Women Artists."[9] It opened at Acts of Art Gallery in New York and included twelve artists. Ringgold's explicitly feminist art

Figure 3 Faith Ringgold, *For the Women's House*, 1971, oil on canvas, 96″ × 96″. The Women's House of Detention, Rikers Island, New York. Courtesy Faith Ringgold.

also began in 1970 with a mural entitled *For the Women's House* (fig. 3), which was hung at the Women's House of Detention on Rikers Island, New York. The mural contained eight components which depicted women in traditional and non-traditional roles—as a bus driver, drummer, police officer, basketball player for the Knicks, and even the President of the United States. Begun a year later, her *Feminist Landscape* series, acrylic paintings framed in cloth, captured the forgotten history of black women's resistance by embellishing the landscapes with quotations, "words of fire," of historic black feminists such as Harriet Tubman, Sojourner Truth, Maria Stewart, Anna Julia Cooper, Amy Jacques-Garvey, and Shirley Chisholm,[10] the only living woman in the series. Ringgold explains what motivated her feminist landscapes, initially inspired by Chisholm's bid for the Presidency in 1972, and later, her reading of Gerda Lerner's documentary history, *Black Women in White America*, which further kindled her interest.

> Back in the early seventies black women were in denial of their oppression in order to be in support of their men. This made it very important for me to put the words of these valiant black feminists in my art so that people could read them and be as inspired as I had been.[11]

The Slave Rape series, sixteen *tanka* paintings done in collaboration with her mother in 1973, was a manifestation of her feminist impulses and her desire to revise African American history with a strong gender focus. This work links her to a group of black feminist scholars who were challenging the invisibility of black women in mainstream white and black scholarship—Toni Cade, Pauli Murray, Barbara Smith, Michele Wallace (whose controversial feminist polemic *Black Macho and the Myth of the Super Woman* [1979] generated a black sexism debate), Paula Giddings, and others. Angela Davis's landmark essay, "Reflections on the Black Woman's Role in the Community of Slaves," written while she was in a California prison in 1971 on false charges of murder, kidnapping, and conspiracy, unmasked masculine biases in African American political history by calling attention to the erasure or marginalization of women in studies of slave resistance. Davis's radical activism for black liberation also inspired many black women artists including Elizabeth Catlett, whose 1972 serigraph, *Angela Libre*, immortalizes the most well-known African American woman political figure of the contemporary era. Subsequent work by black feminist scholars Darlene Clark Hine, bell hooks, Deborah Gray White, Nell Painter, and Brenda Stevenson underscored the necessity of differentiating between the worlds of enslaved men and women and exploring the intersections of race and gender in the lives of the latter.

The horrendous circumstances that African women endured after being brought in chains to the "New World" in 1619 inspired their yearnings for freedom and made rebellion inevitable. They resisted beatings, breeding, unwanted pregnancies, sexual exploitation by white masters, family separation, and debilitating work schedules. They penned liberation narratives which called attention to their unique situations. In her celebrated antebellum autobiography, *Incidents in the Life of a Slave Girl, Written by Herself* (1861), Harriet Jacobs publicized her sexual vulnerability and stated unequivocally that "slavery is terrible for men; but it is far more terrible for women. Superadded to the burden common to all, they have wrongs, and sufferings, and mortifications peculiarly their own."[12]

Ringgold's first three *tankas* in *The Slave Rape* series, which she describes as some of her most prized pieces because of the work her mother did on them, were *Fear: Will Make You Weak*, *Run: You Might Get Away*, and *Fight: To Save Your Life*. They were described as "large, close-up figures of idealized African women struggling against capture and enslavement."[13] She continued this theme of rape and rebellion in sixteen acrylic paintings, "set against an African landscape of flowers and trees,"[14] in which tiny, nude, fleeing women (which underscores their sexual vulnerability and ostensible dehumanization) are portrayed defending themselves against white slave masters, which Ringgold describes with glee:

> In some of the tankas . . . the tiny figures are armed with hatchets and defend themselves. The captor then retreats and is depicted as a fragment of a man, clothed

in white pants and boots, running from the scene. . . . "Help: Your Sister" shows two women fighting off their captor. "Fight: To Save Your Life" depicts one woman standing alone wielding a ceremonial hatchet in defense of herself. In "Run: You Might Get Away," a lone woman flees in a desperate attempt to avoid capture.[15]

In a remarkable revision of the slave experience, it is women rather than men who are depicted as rebellious, and slave masters who are rendered powerless in the face of warrior women bent on liberation.

Perhaps the most stunning example of the involvement of slave women in dismantling the "peculiar institution" is the work of abolitionist/military strategist Harriet Tubman (nicknamed Moses), probably the most well-known female slave in the United States, and one of the warrior women who appears in the work of black women artists. Catlett's linocut series on black women for the Rosenwald grant of 1946–47 includes an early example of Tubman's impact in a work called *I'm Harriet Tubman. I Helped Hundreds to Freedom.* This was followed by the more well-known 1953 and 1975 linocuts, *Harriet Tubman* and *Harriet* (fig. 4). In addition to being a successful "conductor" on The Underground Railroad, by which she led more than three hundred slaves to freedom, Tubman was a co-conspirator with John Brown on his ill-fated raid on Harper's Ferry (1859), though illness prevented her from joining him. For three years she was also a nurse, spy, and scout for the Union army. During the Civil War, she led the only military campaign (along the Combahee River in South Carolina with Colonel James Montgomery) ever to be waged by a woman. It resulted in 750 slaves being freed in 1863.

Ringgold would also remember our slave foremothers and countless other rebellious women throughout history in her *Women's Liberation Talking Mask* series (fig. 5), which began to appear in 1973. Inspired by African art, these works included intricate beading and raffia for hair. During this period she also turned to story quilts to counter stereotypes of blacks and women and because she needed to tell stories "not with pictures or symbols alone, but with words."[16] Her first quilt, *Echoes of Harlem*, done in collaboration with her artist mother,

Figure 4 Elizabeth Catlett, *Harriet*, 1975, linoleum block print, 12½″ × 10⅛″. Courtesy Sragow Gallery.

Willi Posey, was to be included in "The Artist and the Quilt," a group show of twelve women artists working with twelve quilters.[17] Her narrative quilts, which enabled her to tell the stories of women's lives because they included text as well as painted images, include *Slave Rape Story Quilt* (1985), a bittersweet narrative of a mother and daughter who experience the familiar tragedy of slavery,[18] and *The Purple Quilt* (1986), in memory of the characters in Alice Walker's award-winning novel, *The Color Purple.* The text on the quilt states that the book is a "tribute to all US women (and men) who have survived to tell the story." The quilt contains her "visual conceptions" of the characters (based on her memories of people in the Harlem community) and quotes from the novel, particularly Celie's letters to God. These quilts link her to the black women's literary renaissance of the 1970s and 1980s which has received considerable scholarly attention. As Cheryl Wall indicates, "over the past two decades, Afro-American women have written themselves into the national consciousness. Their work is widely

Figure 5 Faith Ringgold, *Women's Liberation Talking Mask, Witch Series #1*, 1973, mixed media, beads, raffia, cloth, gourds, 42″ high. Courtesy Faith Ringgold.

read, frequently taught, and increasingly the object of critical inquiry."[19]

Ringgold's *Women on the Bridge* series, which she began during the late 1980s, is a continuation of her feminist vision of powerful women who resist narrow gender definitions. In her description of the way in which the painted quilt series evolved, her passion for seeing women differently from men, and her insistence that they be portrayed differently than they had been in Western art, is striking:

> It was going to be about women's courage; comparing women with something as monumental as a bridge. It's always constructed by men who get up there and die making it; and I wanted to pit us against that. I had no idea they would be flying . . . As I drew my pictures . . . I realized the women could not be grounded. But what I ran to my typewriter with was why are you doing women on a bridge? So then I wrote down some things to remember that the bridge idea was significant to me and it would be about women's courage, women doing great, creative, exciting things.[20]

Her feminist activism is also apparent in "The Wild Art Show," an exhibition of over fifty women artists, which she curated for P.S. 1 in 1982.

Ten years earlier, the historic women's gallery A.I.R. (Artists in Residence), had opened in New York, initiated by Barbara Zucker and Susan Williams. This first feminist gallery included among its small group of women artists only one black woman, Howardena Pindell. Eight years later it mounted "Dialectics in Isolation: An Exhibition of Third World Women Artists of the U.S.," which included two African Americans, Beverly Buchanan and Pindell. Like the mainstream feminist movement in general, the feminist art movement was perceived by artists of color to be basically a white middle-class movement. Ana Mendieta made this clear in her introductory essay for the exhibition catalogue, while discussing racism in feminist art circles more broadly. The most extensive treatment of the struggles of artists of color within the feminist art movement appeared in the essay "Social Protest: Racism and Sexism" by Yolanda M. López and Moira Roth. They assert that "despite the many efforts and good intentions of white women in the arena of political art, racial separation and racism existed de facto within the Feminist Art movement from the beginning."[21] For example, in 1973, when Betye Saar curated "Black Mirror," an exhibition about black women artists in the new feminist gallery Womanspace in Los Angeles, she was disappointed at the turnout by her white feminist colleagues and commented, "It was as if we were invisible again. The white women did not support it. I felt the separatism, even within the context of being in Womanspace."[22]

Howardena Pindell, a black woman artist who was active in feminist art circles and was also an associate curator at MoMA, responded to the racism within the women's art movement by creating a twelve-minute video, "Free, White and 21," in which the black narrator (herself) describes the racist experiences she's suffered, all of which are dismissed by a white woman (also portrayed by Pindell) with the response, "but of course, I'm free, white and 21." The video was shown at the "Dialectics of Isolation" exhibition at A.I.R. Pindell also worked tirelessly to expose racism within mainstream art circles[23] and counter the invisibility of women artists of color. This led to her curating "Autobiography: In Her Own Image" in 1988, an important traveling exhibition that showcased and introduced different racial/ethnic women whose work had not been seen before.

A feminist vision is also apparent in the work of painter Emma Amos, who was active in the women's art movement through her association with the feminist art journal *Heresies*, which first appeared in 1977. Though she was a member of Spiral and active in the black arts movement in the sixties, her work on women, black women in particular, was never shown. The male members of the group didn't appreciate Elizabeth Catlett's work, Amos recalls in an interview with bell hooks, and only referred to her as the former wife of artist Charles White.[24] In 1990 Amos would correct this negation of women artists by initiating a series of portraits of women artist friends to present as a legacy to her daughter India on her twentieth birthday. *The Gift* (forty acrylic paintings on paper), inspired by memories of her mother's supportive women friends, is a powerful statement about the creative legacy of women, to which she alludes in an interview with bell hooks:

> They can't X the work out. *The Gift* is not possible to negate. . . . Those women are too powerful to ignore. These friends sat for me as my support, as my mother's friends had supported her. I give them to my daughter India as her support, and I hope anybody who sees them will realize that there's something powerful and strong about women artists, about womanhood.[25]

The Gift includes a dazzling array of artists, critics, and writers including Faith Ringgold, Elizabeth Catlett, Camille Billops, Lucy Lippard, Miriam Schapiro, Kay WalkingStick, Howardena Pindell, Vivian Browne, Moira Roth, and her own daughter, India.

In 1991 she completed the *Women Artists* series, another group of paintings that called attention to women artists and the importance of remembering the history of women. *Giza and Faith* (acrylic on linen canvas, African fabric borders) memorializes Giza Daniels Endesha, a painter and Amos's former student at Rutgers who died of AIDS; it also includes a self-portrait and a portrait of artist Faith Ringgold. Thalia Gouma-Peterson, who curated a major exhibition on Amos in 1993, comments on this series of paintings in which the artist acts as witness:

> Diagonally across from Amos, an image of the well-known African American artist, Faith Ringgold looks at us. This image reproduces one of the portraits Amos did for her series of artist friends, and it too is blown by the wind but, in contrast to the figure of Giza, Ringgold's portrait is anchored to the frame of African cloth. This dignified image is the most reassuring presence in the painting. While the center of the painting, with its allusions to European culture, has collapsed, the two African American artists, Amos and Ringgold, look at each other across the abyss.[26]

Four other paintings in the 1991 series—*Howardena* (intaglio printed silk collagraph, watercolor), *Camille, Remember Me* (silk collagraph) (fig. 6), *Have Faith* (silk collagraph, copper), and *Elizabeth Catlett, India and Emma* (intaglio printed silk collagraph, watercolor) feature black women artists. In *Camille, Remember Me* there are three images—Camille Billops, visual artist and filmmaker; a laser transfer photograph of Amos's mother's friends; and a self-portrait of Amos wearing a tee-shirt with the word "artist." It is not surprising that Amos would bear witness to the creative and political work of Billops. With her husband James Hatch, Billops cofounded the Hatch-Billops Collection: Archives of Black American Cultural History in New York City. Because of its thousands of slides, photographs, and books on black artists it is an important resource and gift to the com-

Figure 6 Emma Amos, *Camille, Remember Me*, 1991, edition 8, silk collagraph with color laser transfer, 31½″ × 41″. Courtesy of the artist.

Figure 7 Emma Amos, *Elizabeth Catlett, India and Emma*, 1991, intaglio-printed silk collagraph, watercolor, 32″ × 41″. Courtesy of the artist.

munity. Her important periodical *Artist and Influence* records the ongoing cultural history of African Americans and includes the voices of black artists who are still marginalized within the mainstream art world. *Elizabeth Catlett, India and Emma* (fig. 7) pays tribute to the sculptor, Catlett, and includes an image of her onyx sculpture, *Recognition*, which shows two women embracing. The importance of mother/daughter relationships is also emphasized here by the image of Amos's daughter clutching a photograph of her artist/mother.

Political commentary in the traditional and avant-garde art of Joyce Scott, who works in jewelry, fiber, beads, quilts, and performance, is most apparent around issues of race and gender. She examines rape, apartheid, sexuality, defiance of racial stereotypes, body image, and genetic engineering. In 1982 she co-founded *Thunder Thigh Revue* (with Kay Lawal), a multi-media performance piece which was described by Lowery Sims as being about "the pain and passion of being the 'other,' an overweight black woman in this society."[27] She describes her *Race Break* series as being inherently oppositional:

> It speaks to inflexibility. To the unyielding state of affairs for a person of color in the world generally and the U.S.A. specifically. To the unjustness, how it hurts. In fact, all the work, whether written, performed, or visual, addresses the constant fight to be balanced in an existence where your skin tone, weight, or ethnicity, validates your impact. Not your kindness, your need to love and give love in return.[28]

These black feminist artists and many others on the contemporary scene—spiritual daughters of Harriet Tubman and Sojourner Truth—are also warrior women, bearing witness to both the joys and turbulence of being black and female in America. When the history of black feminism is written, it must include the work of contemporary black women artists whose ways of seeing and portraying the world have much to tell us about struggle, resistance, and ultimately triumph.

NOTES

1. Stanlie M. James and Abena P. A. Busia, eds., *Theorizing Black Feminisms: The Visionary Pragmatism of Black Women* (New York: Routledge, 1993), p. 240.

2. Ibid., p. 246.

3. Samella S. Lewis, *The Art of Elizabeth Catlett* (Claremont, CA: Hancraft Studios, 1984), p. 102.

4. Ibid., pp. 102–4.

5. Ibid., pp. 97–8.

6. Faith Ringgold, *We Flew Over the Bridge: The Memoirs of Faith Ringgold* (Boston: Little, Brown, 1995), p. 159.

7. Ibid., p. 162.

8. Ibid., p. 175.

9. See Norma Broude and Mary D. Garrard, eds., *The Power of Feminist Art: The American Movement of the 1970s, History and Impact* (New York: Harry N. Abrams, 1994), for a description of the organization, the names of the members, and a photograph, pp. 106–7. This text includes the most extensive coverge of black women in the feminist art movement. Ringgold's *We Flew Over the Bridge* also describes the activities of the organization.

10. See Beverly Guy-Sheftall, ed., *Words of Fire: An Anthology of African American Feminist Thought* (New York: The New Press, 1995).

11. Ringgold, *We Flew Over the Bridge*, p. 196.

12. Jean Fagan Yellin, ed., *Incidents in the Life of a Slave Girl, Written by Herself* (Cambridge, MA: Harvard University Press, 1987), p. 77.

13. Ringgold, *We Flew Over the Bridge*, p. 197.

14. Ibid., p. 198.

15. Ibid., pp. 197–98.

16. Eleanor Flomenhaft, ed., *Faith Ringgold: A 25 Year Survey*, exh. cat. (Hempstead, NY: Fine Arts Museum of Long Island, 1990), p. 23.

17. *Gumbo Ya Ya: Anthology of Contemporary African American Women Artists* (New York: Midmarch Arts), p. 226.

18. See Thalia Gouma-Peterson's insightful analysis of Ringgold's story quilts in Flomenhaft, *Faith Ringgold*, pp. 23–32. See also Gouma-Peterson's "Faith Ringgold's Narrative Quilts," *Arts Magazine*, vol. 61, no. 5 (January 1987): 66–68, for a more extensive discussion of *The Purple Quilt*.

19. Cheryl A. Wall, ed., *Changing Our Own Words: Essays on Criticism, Theory, and Writing by Black Women* (New Brunswick, NJ: Rutgers University Press, 1989), p. 1.

20. Ringgold, *We Flew Over the Bridge*, pp. 11–12.

21. Yolanda M. López and Moira Roth, "Social Protest: Racism and Sexism," in Broude and Carrard, *The Power of Feminist Art*, p. 140.

22. Ibid., p. 152.

23. See her stunning research on institutionalized racism within prestigious New York museums and galleries, which she presented at Hunter College in 1987 and later published as "Art (World) and Racism: Testimony, Documentation, and Statistics," *Third Text*, vol. 3, no. 4 (Spring/Summer 1988): 157–62.

24. See bell hooks, "Straighten Up and Fly Right: Making History Visible," in *Emma Amos: Paintings and Prints, 1982–92*, exh. cat. (Wooster, OH: The College of Wooster Art Museum, 1993), pp. 15–28. The interview is reprinted in hooks's *Art on My Mind: Visual Politics* (New York: The New Press, 1995).

25. Ibid., p. 21.

26. Ibid., p. 13.

27. Lowery Stokes Sims, "Aspects of Performance in the Work of Black American Women Artists," in *Feminist Art Criticism: An Anthology*, eds. Arlene Raven, Cassandra L. Langer, and Joanne Frueh (New York: HarperCollins, 1991), p. 219.

28. Joyce Scott, *En Masse/Fiber* (St. Louis: St. Louis Gallery of Contemporary Art, 1988), n.p.

AUTHOR'S NOTE

I have written here not as an art historian or art critic, but from my vantage point and training as a women's studies scholar who documents the intellectual, cultural, and political history of black women. I am also interested in the participation of black women in both black liberation movements and feminist movements and have analyzed our erasure in scholarly treatments of both struggles. By locating contemporary black women artists within the broader black feminist movement that began in the nineteenth century and continues to the present, this essay complements the point of view in my book *Words of Fire: An Anthology of African American Feminist Thought.*

Figure 2 Harriet Powers, *The Creation of the Animals* (detail), 1895–98. Museum of Fin Arts, Boston, M. and M. Karolik Collection.

TRIUMPHANT DETERMINATION:

The Legacy of African American Women Artists

. . . .

TRITOBIA HAYES BENJAMIN

Did you have a genius of a great-great grandmother who died under some ignorant and depraved white overseer's lash? Or was she required to bake biscuits . . . when she cried out in her soul to paint watercolors of sunsets. . . . Or was her body broken and forced to bear children . . . when her one joy was the thought of modeling heroic figures of rebellion, in stone or clay?

Alice Walker
In Search of Our Mothers' Gardens

AFRICANS FOUND a new and hostile environment in America. The brutality of slavery and the disenfranchisement of free blacks demanded that they recast themselves and their talents, assimilate and adapt in this hemisphere. Black women suffered from subordinated status, perceived "as workers first, women second, and always Black, the three identities locked them into positions of vulnerability. After the abolition of slavery they continued to be exploited as women in the labor market and in the home."[1] Later, the expectations placed upon women in the Victorian Age compelled them to observe a set of prescriptions that defined "true womanhood," i.e., being domestic, submissive, pious, and virtuous.

Women who contemplated a profession outside of the home were viewed as different, strange. By stepping outside of her perceived role in life as childbearer and nurturer, a woman became suspect and her intentions were questioned. Was she too masculine? unhappy? independent thinking? And although society reluctantly approved of white women actively practicing one of the arts, how was the black female viewed in this profession, and, moreover, when did she have time for such activities?

Just as important, however, is the question that Walker begs, "How was the creativity of the black woman kept alive, year after year and century after century?"[2] We have no way of knowing what was lost under the conditions that placed black women at odds with their true desires. But the women who achieved despite the adversities facing them triumphed with a personal resolve and determination that propelled them into a profession reserved for and dominated by the white male.

Against these odds, black women became poets, writers, singers, organizers, conductors of the underground railroad, active in the abolitionist movement, and nurses to black soldiers during the civil war. They also founded orphanages and schools, became business entrepreneurs, photographers, craftswomen, painters, and sculptors. And, very early, they too began to help chart the direction of American art.

TRAILBLAZING: MAPPING
A CULTURAL EXPRESSION

. . . .

SARAH MAPPS DOUGLASS (1806–1882), a schoolteacher in Philadelphia, started her own school in the mid-1820s, teaching the children of many successful African American citizens in that city.[3] Her father, Robert Douglass, Sr., who emigrated from the Caribbean island of St. Christopher, was an officer of the Pennsylvania Augustine Society for the Education of People of Colour; Grace Bustill Douglass, her mother, ran a "Quaker millinery store." As parents of three visual artists, Robert, Jr., William Penn, and Sarah, who were also activists, they provided support and encouragement to each of their children in becoming professional artists.[4]

Given the widespread suppression of African Americans' rights and the low level of educational opportunities afforded to the masses, schoolteachers were viewed as a salvation for the uneducated. W. E. B. Du Bois, scholar, educator, civil rights leader, and intellectual, opined that blacks would be saved by their men and women of genius: "The problem of education, then, among Negroes must first of all deal with the Talented Tenth; it is the problem of developing the Best of this race that they may guide the Mass away from the contamination and death of the Worst, in their own and other races."[5] His view that "from the very first it has been the educated and intelligent of the Negro people that have led and elevated the masses . . ."[6] was applicable in certain parts of the country where schools were founded by individuals who, through privilege or status, were benefited by an education.

Scrapbooks and notebooks were used by women educators as instructional aids in educating female students. As Steven Loring Jones, a Philadelphia-based scholar, explained regarding this phenomenon in nineteenth-century America:

> Notebooks were started by female teachers for adolescent female pupils who, for a decade or more, would have important people in their lives contribute a treasured poem, personal thought or visual paean, sometimes borrowed but occasionally original. These albums appear to be both pedagogical and inspirational in nature, providing the pupils with brief examples of themes and thoughts with which an "educated" person ought to be familiar, as well as tangible examples of African American success within a larger world of conflict and struggle. The scrapbooks give insight into the interconnecting networks of African American professionals throughout the country: these educated activists were not only involved in local community improvement, they were also training the next generation in other regions to continue the struggle.[7]

Sarah Douglass contributed a stunning, signed painting of a rose-dominated bouquet and a prose dedication

Figure 1 Sarah Mapps Douglass, *The Rose*, ca. 1836–37, watercolor, 3¾″ × 2¾″. Elizabeth Smith Papers. Moorland-Spingarn Research Center, Howard University, Washington, D.C.

to an album belonging to Elizabeth Smith in about 1836–37 (fig. 1). Under her painting Sarah Douglass wrote: "Lady, while you are young and beautiful 'Forget not' the slave, so shall 'Heart's Ease' ever attend you."[8] In a March 1, 1833 letter, Douglass sketched a kneeling female slave, the quintessential abolitionist symbol of the time, at the head of her communication.[9] Influenced artistically and politically by her abolitionist mother, Douglass was active throughout her life and continued her artistic work until the end of her years; an 1874 letter discussed her drawing, on an album, of quilt patches that she was doing for the son of a good friend.[10] Other works include a watercolor bouquet of forget-me-nots with a poem, ca. 1843, and an 1846 watercolor, *Fuchsia*, accompanied in a scrapbook by a full-page essay on the flower. These various pieces by Douglass appear to be the earliest documented paintings and drawings by an African American woman anywhere in the United States.[11]

Work done or produced in the home was viewed as "woman's work," and although classified as craft-making, was an important continuum of Africanisms practiced by black women in this country. First devalued because of their functional properties, these products have been re-examined and are now hailed as important sources of women's social, cultural, and art history. The quilt in particular has received considerable attention "as a vehicle through which women . . . express themselves; [and a] utilitarian object [which has been] elevated through enterprise, imagination and love to the status of an original art form."[12] As the hierarchial boundaries between art and craft disappear, the field is being redefined.

The functional and pictorial quilts of Harriet Powers (1837–1911) are works "immersed in symbolism . . . a vision which is expressed through imagery of the Judeo-Christian Bible, but also African symbolism. . . . Powers's quilt is charged by spirituality and the passion of the gods she honors with her work."[13] At the core of Powers's religious symbology are the legends of Biblical heroes such as Noah, Moses, Jonah, and Job, all of whom struggled successfully against overwhelming odds.[14]

Born a slave in Georgia, Powers made her quilts in the appliqué technique which flourished in the South between 1775 and 1875. Her only known quilts are in the Smithsonian Institution and the Boston Museum of Fine Arts (fig. 2). Although narrative quilts are a distinctly American art form, they utilize an appliqué technique traceable to historic Eastern and Middle Eastern civilizations and with discernible roots in African cul-

ture.[15] Gladys-Marie Fry, who has chronicled the life of Powers and other quilters, indicates that:

> Powers' quilts form a link to the tapestries traditionally made by the Fon people of Abomey, the ancient capital of Dahomey in West Africa. These people brought to the South this knowledge of appliqué, which in Dahomey was executed by men but in America was perpetuated by slave women.
>
> In Dahomean tapestries and in Harriet Powers' quilts, stories from oral tradition and oral history are illustrated with appliquéd figures. Many of the Dahomean tapestries contain animals as symbols of kings or as the central figures of proverbs. The Powers quilts include some of the same animals . . . as proverbial characters, and made in a similar style.[16]

The Smithsonian quilt, originally owned by Oneita Virginia Smith (1862–1946) of Georgia, is accompanied by an eighteen-page narrative that describes the events that led to its purchase and examines pictorial symbols, setting the quilt in its artistic and historic context. Smith viewed Powers's symbols "as an exception within the general nineteenth century concept of black inferiority," which described blacks as "musical, but not artistic, religious, but liars and thieves . . . [but she was] . . . artistically expressive and a deeply religious woman of modesty and piety."[17]

Figure 2 Harriet Powers, *The Creation of the Animals*, 1895–98, pieced and appliquéd cotton quilt with plain and metallic yarns, 175 cm × 267 cm, Courtesy of The Museum of Fine Arts, Boston, M. and M. Karolik Collection.

Smith offered to purchase the quilt in 1886, but Powers refused at that time, not selling it until she and her family experienced financial difficulties in 1891. Although she asked ten dollars for it, she accepted five dollars. According to Fry, Smith exhibited it in the Colored Building at the Cotton States and International Exposition in Atlanta in 1895.[18]

Powers and other women who worked in this genre could create in a supportive and familiar environment; those who pursued painting and sculpture often ventured into hostile territory to obtain training in institutions. The policies and curricula in those environments were developed for white men exclusively, and African Americans, male or female, were not looked upon favorably when seeking admittance. As late as the 1890s, the stated policy in art institutions dictated that only men could draw nudes of either sex. Women who were permitted in anatomy classes used casts from antiquity. The rigorous enforcement of this policy permitted no leniency. When Thomas Eakins, premiere American painter and teacher to African American painter Henry O. Tanner (1859–1937), reorganized the antiquated curriculum at the Pennsylvania Academy of the Fine Arts around the study of the nude and anatomy, and displayed a completely "naked" male model in a mixed class, he was dismissed because of his radical methods.[19] At a time when artistic achievement was judged by the artist's ability to respond to classical attitudes and sensibilities, female artists were expected to master academic drawing and anatomy without access to the nude. Locked out and isolated, many women cultivated the 'minor' fields of still life, genre, landscape, or portraiture.[20]

Determined not to be confined to the narrow niche assigned her race and sex in the nineteenth century, Mary Edmonia "Wildfire" Lewis (ca. 1843–after 1911) became an artist by sheer force of personality, exceptional talent, and determination. And, contrary to expectations for her gender, she would choose sculpture as her medium of expression. Born to a Chippewa mother and an African American father, Lewis is the first documented American woman sculptor of African–Native American descent. Along with Robert M. Douglass, Jr., Patrick Reason, and Robert S. Duncanson, she became involved in the abolitionist movement, which in turn became an important source of support for these young artists.

Lewis matriculated at Oberlin College[21] in Oberlin, Ohio, the first interracial and coeducational institution in the United States. Here she joined approximately thirty other black students, including Emma Brown, Fanny Jackson Coppin, and Mary Jane Patterson, all of whom later distinguished themselves as educators.[22] She evinced an interest in the arts, specifically drawing, and later told Boston patrons that "I had always wanted to make the forms of things; and while I was at school I tried to make drawings of people and things."[23]

The *Muse Urania* (1862), her only extant drawing, was probably rendered from an engraving of the Roman sculpture housed in the Vatican Museum. Given as a wedding present to her schoolmate Clara Steele Norton, an ardent suffragist, it shows the muse Urania, a female deity, holding a stylus and a globe in her hands. The subject suggests that Edmonia and her friend may have shared beliefs relating to women's issues of their day.[24]

In January of 1862 Lewis was accused by two housemates of poisoning them. Beaten by outraged citizens, she was left to die in the snow. She survived and was defended in a trial by jury by John Mercer Langston, himself of African–Native American descent, the first black congressman after Reconstruction, and the first dean of the Howard University School of Law. She was released for insufficient evidence. In February of the following year, Lewis was accused of stealing art supplies, and although exonerated, was not allowed to register for the next semester, and was therefore unable to graduate. Certainly these experiences incensed Lewis, but they also strengthened her resolve to overcome the thinly veiled racism she encountered. She left Oberlin to continue her studies in Boston, sometimes called the "American Athens," a center for intellectual and artistic achievement in the nineteenth century.[25] As Lewis proclaimed: "I had heard a great deal about Boston and I thought if I went there I should perhaps find means to learn what I wanted to know. So we came here and my brother hired a little room in the Studio Building for me."[26]

The Studio Building on Tremont Street served as the location for studios of several artists in the 1860s. Lewis and African American painter Edward Mitchell Bannister (1828–1901) maintained studios two doors apart, exhibited at the same abolitionist fairs, and moved in the same circles of patronage.[27] Anne Whitney (1821–1915), a sculptor who abandoned the conventional neoclassic marble of mid-nineteenth century American sculpture for naturalistic bronzes that carried the messages of abolitionism, equality, and feminism, also worked there, and Lewis reportedly asked her for lessons.[28]

Lewis carried a letter of introduction to the abolitionist William Lloyd Garrison, who then introduced her to Edward Brackett, a local portrait sculptor. As tradition dictated, Brackett provided the young sculptor with a plaster foot and other sculpture fragments to copy in clay, and then offered critiques. Later, she completed medallions and portrait busts of individuals associated with the abolition movement such as John Brown, Garrison, Charles Sumner, and Civil War hero Colonel Robert Gould Shaw, leader of the first Massachusetts battalion of black soldiers. Working from photographs, Lewis modeled a reasonably successful bust of Shaw. Shaw's family considered it a good likeness, and neoclassical sculptor Harriet Hosmer described it as "finely moulded."[29] Proceeds from copies of this sculpture and a medallion of John Brown financed her trip to Europe in 1865.

At this time, few women were successful in becoming academic sculptors, but some advances provided a liberating atmosphere for women artists. For example, the first women's college opened at Mount Holyoke, and the first women's suffrage convention was held at Seneca Falls, New York. Women mill workers joined in some of America's early strikes. In their passion for justice, women became antislavery speakers and organizers, playing a huge role in the Civil War. Ultimately they organized on their own behalf.[30] Surely the exhilaration of emancipation added to the hopes and confidence of all.

At mid-century Charlotte Cushman, an actor and activist from Boston who had moved to Rome, urged her friend and protégée, the sculptor Harriet Hosmer, to join her. In Rome she could take advantage of the opportunities usually afforded only to male artists; she could study amid the classical monuments and utilize inexpensive Carrara marble and the skills of marble cutters trained to carve from the artist's plaster model. A coterie of women sculptors followed—Edmonia Lewis, Emma Stebbins, Louisa Lander, Vinnie Ream, Anne Whitney, and Margaret Foly. Henry James called them "that strange sisterhood who at one time settled upon the seven hills in a white marmorean flock."[31]

Lewis's first works were inspired by the Emancipation Proclamation. *The Freed Woman and Her Child* (1866, location unknown) was, as Lewis described, "a humble one, but my first thought was for my poor father's people, how I could do them good in my small way."[32] *Forever Free* (fig. 3) originally called *The Morning of Liberty*, was presented to the Reverend Leonard A. Grimes, a prominent abolitionist, and dedicated at Tremont Temple on October 18, 1869. This ambitious work deviated from the preference for single figure compositions used by neoclassical sculptors and it has been the subject of numerous interpretations. Buick holds that:

> the sculpture presents a reconstructed image of the African American family after slavery and becomes a subtle commentary on the hopes for the newly liberated population. . . . With emancipation, former slaves could marry and live in families. . . . Within this new

Figure 3 Mary Edmonia Lewis, *Forever Free* (detail), 1867, marble. Howard University Gallery of Art.

family that emancipation created, the male also had a role to fill . . . [his] stance and his raised arm, interpreted as either triumphant or aggressive, signify this potential to protect and thus mark his new status as the head of a family. . . . If we read Lewis's work as a unit instead of as a reflection of opposing forces—domination versus subordination, or man versus woman—we see that . . . the male's hand rests 'protectively' on the female's shoulder. Instead, and in terms of nineteenth-century gender ideals, she belongs to the man who has the capacity to protect her. There is no evidence in the work itself that Lewis was critical of their relationship or commenting on female oppression. . . . For them and for Lewis, freedom was seen as a masculinized process. Until the African American man was free to establish a black patriarchy, the woman, they believed, would remain enslaved, as Lewis presented her in *Forever Free.*[33]

Contrary to the usual practice of hiring Italian carvers, Edmonia Lewis did her own carving at first, fearing accusations that others created her work. Honing her skills by copying antique statues such as *Young Octavian* (ca. 1873), and Renaissance masterpieces such as Michelangelos's *Moses* (ca. 1875),[34] she later allowed carvers to transpose her smaller works into large pieces.

Various Lewis compositions embraced race and gender: *Minnehaha* (1867), *Hiawatha* (1868), *The Marriage of Hiawatha* (1871), *The Old Indian Arrow Maker and His Daughter* (1872), *Hagar* (1875), which symbolizes the alienation of black women in white society and expresses Lewis's strong sympathy for all women who have struggled and suffered,[35] and *Cleopatra* (1876).

This last work was exhibited at the Philadelphia Centennial Exposition and was lost shortly after its debut; fortunately, it has recently resurfaced in Forest Park, Illinois, and is currently undergoing restoration by the National Museum of American Art.[36] The work shows the Egyptian queen in the throes of death after being bitten by an asp, and was a *success de scandale*. As one critic has written:

> This was not a beautiful work, but it was very original and . . . striking. . . . The effects of death are represented

with such skill as to be absolutely repellent. Apart from all questions of taste, however, the striking qualities of the work are undeniable, and it could only have been produced by a sculptor of very genuine endowments.[37]

Since Egypt was symbolic of Africa and African people, art historian Charlotte Rubinstein has suggested that "this image may have been a response to the disappointment of the Reconstruction period, with its aborted dreams of equality."[38]

Undaunted by racism and sexism, Edmonia Lewis persevered in her chosen medium although neoclassical ideals and themes began to fade from popularity and the center of artistic endeavor shifted from Italy to France. Little is known of her later life, however, and this mystery must be investigated since her work and her life story are an integral part of the evolving story of American culture.

Portrait painting in America enjoyed great popularity from colonial times through the nineteenth century. American appetites for images of themselves were satisfied by itinerant painters, self-taught artists and others who may have received instruction from European artists traveling in America, or a few who had studied in England. Pioneer African American artists such as Joshua Johnston, William Simpson, Julien Hudson, and David Bustill Bowser had the difficult task of proving to a skeptical world that they could be artists. Notable among African American artists who pursued portraiture is Annie E. Anderson Walker (1855–1929). The youngest of five, Anderson was born in Flatbush, at that time a suburb of Brooklyn, New York. Entering the teaching profession at an early age, she had brief assignments in Jacksonville, Florida, and Orrville and Selma, Alabama. After her marriage in 1875 to Thomas Walker, an energetic attorney in Selma, the couple moved to Washington, D.C. It was there in 1890 that Annie Walker evinced an interest in the visual arts and began taking private lessons in drawing and painting. After a year's study, she showed a marked improvement in drawing and applied to the Corcoran Gallery of Art for classes that offered instruction in elementary and intermediate principles of art and design, work after antique, and life classes. After approval by the admissions committee, Walker was admitted to the elementary class for drawing and given a date to begin classes. When she appeared at the Corcoran, she was told by the admitting instructor that, ". . . the trustees have directed me not to admit colored people. If we had known that you were colored, the committee would not have examined your work."[39]

Humiliated and insulted, Walker solicited the assistance of Frederick Douglass, whose counsel and forthright speeches had earned him respect from blacks and whites alike. Douglass wrote a powerful appeal on her behalf to the committee of the Corcoran, requesting them to ". . . reconsider this exclusion and admit Mrs. Walker to the Corcoran Gallery of Art, and thus remove a hardship and redress a grievous wrong imposed upon a person guilty of no crime and one in every way qualified to compete with others in the refining and ennobling study of art. . . ."[40] Douglass's appeal, however, drew no positive response, and Walker's rejected application was not rescinded.

Within months Walker applied to Cooper Union for the Advancement of Science and Art in New York City and was admitted; she graduated in the class of 1895. Following the tradition of generations of American artists, Walker sought further study in Europe and sailed for Paris in September of that year to enter the prestigious Académie Julian. Her talents and serious search for expression in the visual arts were validated with the selection of her drawing, *La Parisienne*[41] (fig. 4), a sensitive, well-executed pastel portrait of a young woman, for inclusion in the Paris Salon of 1896; a singular mark of achievement. At that same time Henry O. Tanner was awarded an honorable mention for his painting *Daniel in the Lion's Den*. Walker's tireless courage, determination, and persistence in becoming an artist in the face of racism and sexism had been realized with this modicum of success in the Paris art world. After her studies at the Académie Julian, Walker traveled to London, Switzerland, and Italy before returning to Washington, D.C. in December 1896.

For the next two years, Annie Walker worked assiduously at painting and drawing, perfecting her artistry,

Figure 4 Annie E. A. Walker, *La Parisienne*, 1896, pastel on paper, 25½″ × 19¾″. Howard University Gallery of Art, Washington, D.C.

and balancing her responsibilities as the wife of a successful lawyer. Her extant pieces are academic in style and execution, and illustrate an active intuitive ability and spirit, as well as a masterful control of the medium. By 1898, however, due to the strain of her work, societal pressures, and the expectations of "woman's work," Annie Walker suffered a nervous breakdown. This tragic occurrence abbreviated Walker's promising career to only three years of productivity, from 1895 to 1898. She remained an invalid in her home until her death in 1929.[42]

As the suffrage movement gained momentum, "progressive" thinking women were viewed less radically as they entered male dominated fields, especially in wood carving and large-scale public sculpture. The need for large monuments during the Gilded Age, from 1876 to 1905, created opportunities for women artists, particularly sculptors. Moreover, women were now accepted for training at the National Academy of Design, the Pennsylvania Academy of the Fine Arts, the Art Institute of Chicago, the Cincinnati Art Academy, and the Art Students League. Yet, the ultimate art education was still to be obtained in Europe.

Paris attracted many women artists and during the closing years of the nineteenth century they studied at the École des Beaux Arts, the Académies Julian and Colarossi. Although biases and discrimination continued to plague women artists, they gained access to these institutions and, as assistants, to the ateliers of French masters. One such artist was Meta Vaux Warrick Fuller (1877–1968).

Born into a middle-class Philadelphia family, Fuller matriculated at the Pennsylvania Museum and School for Industrial Art (now the Philadelphia College of Art) and, between 1899 and 1902, studied drawing at the École des Beaux-Arts in Paris and sculpture at the Académie Colarossi. In the summer of 1901, at twenty-four years of age, she had an appointment with the French sculptor, Auguste Rodin, the "Michelangelo of his age," to review a portfolio of photographs of her work and a small clay model. She hoped that he would accept her as his student. After leafing through the photographs, Rodin returned them without comment. Completely disheartened, Fuller prepared to leave, but realized that she had not shown him the clay model of *Man Eating His Heart* (also known as *The Secret Sorrow*). As he turned the sculpture, viewing it from every angle and running his hand over it, he proclaimed "Mon enfant, vous étes un sculpteur né, vous avez le sens de la forme!"[43] "My Child, you are a sculptor; you have the sense of form!" was an extraordinary critique for this young artist. Unable to accept additional students, however, Rodin promised to visit her studio often. According to Judith Kerr, historian and Fuller scholar:

> Warrick's creations become more daring in theme and execution. One of her aims had always been to explore the psychology of human emotions, a belief in the function of art that she shared with Rodin. Under his tutelage, she learned to execute such ideas with greater force. She refused to limit herself to subjects that were merely aesthetically pleasing, never avoiding portrayals because they were ugly or abhorrent.[44]

Because of this treatment of such powerful subject matter—"themes of death, war, despair, and human anguish"—her early work has been termed "macabre and gruesome."[45]

After her return to Philadelphia in 1902, Fuller set up a studio and began to frequent art dealers. She soon discovered that local dealers were not interested in her work, and though they offered excuses such as not having an interest in domestic work, they declined her Paris pieces as well. Convinced that she was denied access because of her race, she turned to Philadelphia's black community. As she became involved with the social and intellectual life of Philadelphia blacks, African American themes shared a place with European thematic influences in her sculpture.[46] Several of Fuller's work were exhibited in the Paris Salon of 1903.

Marriage to Solomon C. Fuller in February, 1909, a Liberian who was a director of the pathology lab at Westborough State Hospital and a neurologist at Massachusetts Hospital, did not alter her determination to be an artist, contrary to popular opinion that a woman could not combine marriage and a career. She gave birth to three sons between 1910 and 1916, and although a 1910 fire in a Philadelphia warehouse destroyed sixteen years of work done at home and abroad, Fuller continued to be an important part of the cultural community.

During this period, one of her most important works came when W. E. B. Du Bois invited her to reproduce *Man Eating His Heart*, lost in the fire, for the Emancipation Proclamation's fiftieth anniversary in New York in 1913. Instead of replicating this piece, she created *Spirit of Emancipation*, a three figure group standing eight feet tall. It was ". . . unlike any other of its genre. There were no discarded whips or chains, no grateful freedmen kneeling before a paternalistic Lincoln. Fuller had also not chosen to favor the female figure with Caucasian features, indicating her heightened race consciousness."[47]

This commission began many years of productivity starting with a medallion for Framingham's Equal Suffrage League (1915) and a figure for the infamous Mary Turner Case (*A Silent Protest Against Mob Violence*, 1919), among other works addressing the atrocities of war and violence against blacks.

Most scholars date *The Awakening of Ethiopia* (fig. 5) to 1914 or 1917, but Kerr suggests that the work is a response to James Weldon Johnson's request for a work for the New York City "Making of America" Festival in 1921.[48] As a part of the movement to create a positive and vital culture for the black American, Johnson nurtured young talent. In his *Black Manhattan* (1930), he wrote about the literary production and the visual arts in Harlem during the 1920s, summarizing the African American's position as follows:

> He is impressing upon the national mind the conviction that he is an active and important force in American life; that he is a creator as well as a creature; that he has given as well as received; that his gifts have been not only obvious and material, but also spiritual and aesthetic; that he is a contributor to the nation's common cultural store; in fine, he is helping to form American civilization.[49]

In communication with Johnson, Du Bois, and other intellectuals of the era, Fuller shared this philosophy, as evidenced by the creation of *The Awakening of Ethiopia*. The original version, a 12-inch statuette, displays the left hand open and pointing outward. When later enlarged and cast into bronze, the hand was turned down and placed against the thigh, closing the form and, in my opinion, destroying the interpretation of openness, expectation, and optimism.[50] Hailed as a work that forecasts the Harlem Renaissance, art historian David Driskell proclaimed that:

> the composition reveals a partially wrapped mummy, bound from the waist down but with the hair and shoulders of a beautiful African woman. The suggestion of death is evident in the lower half of the figure while the upper part of the torso is alive and expressive,

Figure 5 Meta Vaux Warrick Fuller, *The Awakening of Ethiopia*, after 1921, bronze, 67″ × 16″ × 20″. Schomburg Center for Research in Black Culture, New York.

Figure 6 Meta Vaux Warrick Fuller, *The Talking Skull*, 1937. Museum of Afro American History, Boston, Massachusetts.

evolving the rebirth of womanhood, and the emergence of nationhood. She wears the headdress of an ancient Egyptian queen . . . but . . . in title and spirit she is unquestionably the image of Ethiopia, mythical symbol of Black Africa.[51]

Fuller wrote that she used the Egyptian motif to symbolize the black American who "was awakening, gradually unwinding the bandages of his past and looking out on life again, expectant, but unafraid."[52]

Fuller's focus on heritage did not abate with this work. Drawing upon an African folktale, *The Talking Skull* (1937) (fig. 6), a powerful Rodinesque sculpture, illustrates a young boy who stumbles upon a skull in the desert, and in a moment of desperation, beseeches it to speak before a group of villagers and the chief.[53]

In 1950, Solomon Fuller's illness required her full attention and she devoted less time to her creativity. After his death in 1953, Fuller contracted tuberculosis and remained in a sanitarium until 1956. Unable to produce sculpture during her confinement, she channeled her artistry into poetry.

During the late 1950s and throughout the 1960s, Fuller received numerous commissions once it was known that she was active again. Her contributions to the Civil Rights movement included donations of sales to various causes. Undaunted by advanced age, her response to the death of three girls in the bombing of the Baptist Church in Birmingham, Alabama, *The Crucifixion*, was as acerbic

as her response forty-five years earlier to the death of Mary Turner (*A Silent Protest Against Mob Violence*).

In a career spanning over seven decades, Fuller embraced portraiture, religion, allegory, and above all, African and African American themes. In her indomitable way, Fuller's insistence on becoming a sculptor kept her focused, and in some regards, able to triumph over race and gender isolation. "At a time when the 'custodians of culture' believed the female artist inferior and the female sculptor an oddity, and when the black artist was burdened with proving the civility of an entire race,"[54] Meta Fuller, conscious of race and gender restrictions, persevered as an artist.

Although both are Philadelphia natives who attended J. Liberty Tadd's art school, there is no documentation of an association between Fuller and May Howard Jackson (1877–1931), and their lives offer sharp contrasts. Unlike Fuller, who left for France in 1899, Jackson "chose to remain completely American in her study . . . never depart[ing] far from the definite and calculated system of modeling that she had been taught at the academy. In fact, this remains the aesthetic basis of her art, prosaic though it may seem."[55] Jackson matriculated on scholarship at the Pennsylvania Academy of the Fine Arts, and some critics, such as Alain Locke, speculated that this decision might have deterred the development of her technical skills, if not her recognition and credibility as an artist.[56] A student in her class during the 1920s, James Porter attests to her abilities as "an expert modeler," yet in his 1943 publication, he felt ". . . there was no great originality in any of the pieces she attempted, and she made no noteworthy departure from the American pictorial tradition in sculpture. . . . She worked largely in a manner chosen by others."[57] Art historian Leslie King-Hammond, however, suggests that ". . . Jackson's isolation, and the absence of direct European influences, actually freed her, both intellectually and artistically, and thus enabled her to develop a distinctly personal style. The corpus of her work centered on Jackson's own ancestry, her fascination with the complex and varied physiognomy of black people as a result of mixing of races in the aftermath of slavery."[58]

Her portrait busts are sensitive character studies

that evoke the sitter's humanity, identity, and personae. Among her many studies are *Paul Laurence Dunbar* (1919), *Rev. Francis J. Grimke* (1920), *W. E. B. Du Bois* and *Kelly Miller* (both 1929), *Jean Toomer* (n.d.), and numerous other individuals who were important pillars of the African American community. In this regard, rendering portraits that were the antithesis of negative, demeaning imagery of black Americans, her "frank and deliberate racialism" was in sharp contrast to the "academic cosmopolitanism" of her peers. Jackson's artistry also includes other ambitious and complex compositions such as *Mulatto Mother and Her Child* (1929), and *Shell-Baby* (1929).

After her marriage to Sherman Jackson, an educator and administrator at the M Street School (later Dunbar High School) in 1902, Jackson moved to Washington, D.C. Two decades later, she joined the newly formed art department at Howard University, organized in 1921 by James V. Herring. Jackson was employed to teach sculpture and modeling from life in 1922. The life class was extended to six hours weekly, and models from the Corcoran Art Gallery posed in the university studio twice weekly.[59]

In the October 1931 issue of *Crisis*, Du Bois gave insight into the life of an artist who was frustrated by race and gender, as he eloquently wrote:

> She was a sculptor with peculiar natural gifts. With her sensitive soul she needed encouragement and contacts and delicate appreciation. Instead of this, she ran into the shadows of the Color Line. Problems of race, class, of poverty and family may affect different persons quite differently. . . . In the case of May Howard Jackson the contradictions and idiotic ramifications of the Color Line tore her soul asunder. It made her at once bitter and fierce with energy, cynical of praise and above all at odds with life and people. She met rebuffs in her attempts to study, and in her attempts at exhibition, in her chosen ideal of portraying the American mulatto type; with her own friends and people she faced continual doubt as to whether it was worth while and what it was all for. Thus the questing, unhappy soul of the Artist beat battered wings at the gates of day and wept

alone. She accomplished enough to make her fame firm in our annals and yet one must with infinite sorrow, think how much more she might have done had her spirit been free![60]

Like Jackson, who focused on the black subject, Laura Wheeler Waring (1887–1948) used "color harmony, delicately brushed into the canvas"[61] for her portraiture. By recognizing a need to examine the African American image, they both imbued their work with certain qualities of class, status, and dignity, a perception sorely lacking in mainstream portraiture of blacks; they achieved the same results. Porter, however, suggests that Waring's "portraits depend more upon atmosphere than practical psychology [and that] she does not allow us to be on intimate terms with her pictures unless we are willing to 'think ourselves into' the life of the subject."[62] Her portrayals of *Anne Washington Derry* (1922), *Mr. Walter E. Waring* (1927), and *Evangeline Hall* (1930) are examples of the reserved objectivity instilled in the sitters' personae. Waring's *oeuvre* also includes still lifes, landscapes, and genre scenes, which have been variously characterized as "Beardsleyesque" and "expressionistic" in tone and execution.

Born in Hartford, Connecticut, Waring studied at the Pennsylvania Academy of the Fine Arts from 1918 to 1924, and at La Grande Chaumiere in 1924 and 1925. As director of the art and music departments at Cheyney State Teacher's College, Pennsylvania, she touched the lives of many young aspiring artists who later distinguished themselves in the arts.

TURN OF THE TWENTIETH CENTURY: TRADITION, IDENTITY, AND REPRESENTATION

. . . .

The twentieth century ushered in a host of technological and scientific discoveries. The mass-production of automobiles, the first successful flight of the airplane, the invention of the telegraph, were among the explosion of inventions and ideas. As the old order changed with philosophical and scientific advancements, so did the art world. A myriad of "isms" replaced each other in rapid succession—fauvism, expressionism, cubism, dadaism, and surrealism—radical styles that reflected the freedom of the artists. Compositions, totally free of the traditional subject, were now predicated on abstract arrangements of color and form. Women painters and sculptors were involved in these radical approaches. And although societal pressures for women to lead home-centered lives still had an impact, more women were able to overcome these obstacles and establish careers as professional artists. Paris, however, remained a source of inspiration for many American artists, especially those of African descent.

Another mecca for African American culture was Harlem in New York City. With the mass migration of thousands of blacks to the north, the employment possibilities during World War I and the promise of prosperity during the 1920s, a sense of community developed there. Moreover, racial pride and an interest in African art during this decade were also factors contributing to the flowering of cultural activities into what is now known as the Harlem Renaissance.

Alain Locke, the first black Rhodes scholar, philosopher, and professor at Howard University, and the self-described "philosophical midwife to a generation of younger Negro poets, writers, artists . . ."[63] wrote the pivotal document, *The New Negro*, in which he comments that though some African American artists had been "notably successful," they had developed no "School of Negro Art."

> We ought and must have a school of Negro Art, a local and a racially representative tradition. And that we have not, explains why the generation of Negro artists succeeding Mr. Tanner had only the inspiration of his great success to fire their ambitions, but not the guidance of a distinctive tradition to focus and direct their talents. The work of W. E. Scott, E. A. Harleston, . . . and Laura Wheeler in painting, and of Meta Warrick Fuller and May Howard Jackson in sculpture, competent as it has been, has nevertheless felt this handicap and has wavered between abstract expression which

was imitative and not highly original, and racial expression which was only experimental.[64]

Locke's criticism was actually an analysis of and a manifesto for African American artists to heed the example of European artists who had explored African art, and to look toward their "ancestral arts" more seriously, developing the "Negro physiognomy" in their work.

About this same time, the Harmon Foundation, begun by the philanthropist and real estate baron William E. Harmon in 1922 "for the stated purpose of encouraging and stimulating individuals to self-help," was "conservative in nature and paternalistic in practice. At the core of its activities was a belief in a well-defined class system ('social order') that enabled wealthy white men such as Harmon to give assistance to those deemed worthy. The standards against which African Americans were measured were clearly those of whites."[65]

By 1926, the Foundation's "Award for Distinguished Achievement Among Negroes" included the visual arts. Judges were selected among well known artists and architects to evaluate the works submitted by twelve applicants in that year; forty-one applied in 1927. The success of the Harmon exhibitions and awards was lauded and continued through 1935, increasing in number each year, indicating that the African American artist flourished in American culture.[66]

The sculptural tradition established by Lewis, Fuller, and Jackson was continued by Nancy Elizabeth Prophet (1890–1960), Augusta Savage (1892–1962), Beulah Ecton Woodard (1895–1955), and Selma Burke (1900–1995). Moreover, these artists used the "Negro physiognomy" mandated by Locke in their work.

Like Edmonia Lewis, Prophet was of African and Native American descent. Born in Warrick, Rhode Island, to a black mother who described herself as "a mixed negro," and a father of the Narragansett ,[67] her parents did not think that art was an acceptable career. They encouraged her to become a housemaid or a schoolteacher. Determined, however, to become a professional artist, she attended classes (the only black student) at the Rhode Island School of Design, graduating in 1918 with a diploma in freehand drawing and painting. Writing in the

Providence Journal of 1930, Nell Occomy, a friend at the school recalled that "Her special forte at that time was portrait painting."[68] No portraits have survived, however, that are attributed to her.

While still a student, Prophet married Francis Ford in 1915; she was twenty-four, he thirty-four.[69] Ford, whose family was from Maryland, had been the only black student to complete the classical course of study at Hope High School in Providence in 1900, and was one of the few blacks admitted to Brown University that same year. Records indicate that he registered again as a freshman in 1904–05, and was photographed with the class of 1907, although records indicate that he did not graduate.[70] According to Blossom Kirschenbaum, an adjunct professor at the RISD, "Prophet and her husband aspired to privileges more typically enjoyed by persons born to higher status than theirs, and they did so without much support."[71]

After graduation, Prophet shunned teaching positions, textile design work, or any employment outside of the discipline. Instead, she sought sponsors to help her financially. She was successful in receiving the support of at least three socially prominent women who provided funds and purchased the work she had created in Providence, enabling her to travel abroad.

Prophet sailed on the *S.S. LaFrance in* 1922 and settled in Paris, where she studied at the École des Beaux Arts. Remaining in France for ten years, she participated in the Salon d'Automne (1924, 1927), the Paris August Salons (1925, 1926), and the Salon des Artistes Français (1929). She received glowing reviews in the French press, with one critic describing her work as "vigorous and energetic, conceived in a nervous, supple, assured style." The same article described her as a loner who did not associate with the bohemian set but worked obsessively by herself.[72]

Prophet maintained contact with Henry O. Tanner, and was befriended by him throughout her residency. It was in Tanner's studio that she met the poet Countee Cullen, who described her persona and sculpture in the July 1930 *Opportunity:* "She swept into the studio with unequalled éclat, wearing a flowing black cape and a broad, black felt hat . . . she seemed to be at peace with herself, content with the direction of her life and her art."[73]

Her small body of work, studies of men and women representing differing moods and expressions, are not portraits of specific individuals. Rather, it reflects her interest in clearly defined modeling techniques and her capabilities in her chosen media—wood and marble—evolving a personal aesthetic. In 1936, Locke observed that "she commands the attention with strong mass modelling and finely restrained surface treatment."[74] King-Hammond concluded in 1978 that "while her work was virile in the confident handling of light, shadow, mass and material, there was a certain coolness that prevailed."[75]

Returning to America in 1932, bolstered in spirit by her participation at the Salons in 1931 and 1932, and confident that she would be competitive, she exhibited at the Boston Society of Independent Artists, the Vose Galleries, Boston, and at the Art Association of Newport, Rhode Island. Sponsored at the Association by Agnes Storer and Maude Howe Elliot, she was voted a member and won the Richard S. Greenough Prize for the polychromed wood head *Discontent* (1930), "a face Dantesque in its tragedy, so powerful in the red polished cowl that envelopes it that it might stand for the very spirit of revolt and rebellion."[76] Prophet, however, said it was "the result of a long emotional experience, of restlessness, of gnawing hunger for the way to attainment [while *Silence* (1930), a marble female head, was] done after months of solitary living in [my] little Paris studio, hearing the voice of no one for days on end," representing, Prophet said "the unifying quality of the body, mind and soul."[77]

Congolaise (1930–31) (fig. 7), with "its intimation of noble conflict,"[78] speaks to the ancestral legacy articulated by Locke and Du Bois during the era; it was exhibited with *Discontent* and *Silence*. Gertrude Vanderbilt Whitney (1875–1942), a co-exhibitor at the Art Association, was very much impressed with *Congolaise;* she purchased the carving for the Whitney Museum and invited Prophet to share her studio that fall.[79]

At the urging of W. E. B. Du Bois, Prophet became an instructor at Atlanta University in 1933. The following year she joined the art department at Spelman, introducing sculpture into the curriculum. She remained there through 1944. It is unclear why she left Atlanta, but Kirschenbaum intimates that "apparently she had

Figure 7 Elizabeth Prophet, *Congolaise*, 1931, wood, 17⅛" × 6¾" × 8 1/16". Whitney Museum of American Art, New York, New York. Photograph © 1996: Whitney Museum of American Art.

suffered some sort of breakdown. For a while she was hospitalized in Rhode Island."[80] Yet, she was able to mount a 1945 solo exhibition at the Providence Public Library.

Prophet never achieved the notoriety that she had hoped for in her home state, and her financial status was always precarious and unsure. Unable to find a teaching position in Providence, she became a live-in maid for the Carley family in 1958, receiving no salary, only room and board. This arrangement lasted about six months.[81] Living in isolation, poor, unable to secure employment, and unable to continue her work, Elizabeth Prophet died in obscurity, barely escaping a pauper's grave, in 1960.

Always troubled by her dual ancestry, and therefore her identity, she insisted near the end of her embittered life that she "had no use for the colored." Proclaiming her Native American heritage exclusively, she refused to be included in Cedric Dover's 1960 publication *American Negro Art*, stating that she "was not a negro,"[82] and rejecting the limitations it imposed, although she had cooperated with Porter for his previous book *Modern Negro Art* (1943).

Although Prophet was befriended by some of the leading white women sculptors of the day (Whitney, Janet Scudder, and Olive Bigelow) she had neither their connections, marriage to money as a form of support, or well-connected patrons. Unfortunately, her career is more typical than exceptional, more poignant than successful.

Similar experiences followed the career of Augusta Christine Savage. Although she enjoyed a notoriety that exceeded Prophet's, her sculptural pursuits were not greatly appreciated during her lifetime. Her commitment to black Americans and their treatment in American society was more intense, and her perceptions more politically astute than those of her sister artist. The seventh of fourteen children, she was born in Green Cove Springs, Florida, to a carpenter, farmer, house painter, and Methodist minister, and a housewife. Her parents discouraged her from creating clay objects. In a 1935 interview, she recalled that her father referred to her figures as "graven images," and that "[he] licked me five or six times a week and almost whipped all the art out of me."[83] Savage began to contemplate nursing as a profession instead.

Married at the tender age of fifteen, she gave birth to a daughter, her only child, in 1908; she was widowed a few years later. By 1915, Savage's father relocated the family to West Palm Beach. Due to the lack of local clay and a disgruntled father who discouraged her artistic expressions, she discontinued sculpting for several years.

While still in school, she met a local potter and persuaded him to give her twenty-five pounds of clay. She sculpted several works that impressed the principal of the school she attended. Recognizing her talent, he convinced her father to allow her to teach a clay modeling class at the high school for six months, earning one dollar a day.

At the Palm Beach County Fair, Savage ran a booth where she sold clay ducks and chickens she had made to wealthy tourists. She received a special prize of $25, an honor ribbon, and encouragement to pursue her interests in New York City. The fair superintendent gave her a letter of recommendation to sculptor Solon Borglum, founder of the School of American Sculpture, and advised her to seek admittance there.

Arriving in New York in 1921 at age 29 with $4.60, she announced her plan to become a successful artist in six months.[84] Because of high tuition costs, Borglum referred her to Cooper Union, a tuition-free art school, for instruction. Admitted a few days after a review of her work by the school's principal, she was advanced to the second-year class after only two weeks. After a month she was advanced again.[85] However, unable to find employment to support herself, she contemplated leaving school in the fourth-year class. The principal, recognizing her talent, found her temporary employment, and persuaded the advisory committee to award additional funds for her living expenses. Friends of the Schomburg Library, also hearing of her difficulties, commissioned a bust of W. E. B. Du Bois. As he sat for this portrait, Savage came under the influence of the philosophy and personality of this leader.

Receiving a scholarship from the French government in 1923 for summer school in Fontainebleau, France, she was prepared to excel in her profession. Unfortunately, she encountered racism of major proportions. When two recipients from Alabama were informed that an African American would be on the same boat, the girls complained that they could not be expected to travel or room with a "colored girl," and Savage's scholarship was withdrawn. Publicly airing the incident to prevent "other and better colored students" from being subjected to the same treatment, the newspapers ran the story for several weeks. Distinguished leaders came to her support, many of them asking President Harding and the French government to intercede, but the admissions committee would not rescind their decision. Hermon MacNeil, president of the National Sculpture Society, and a sculptor of Native Americans, invited Savage to study privately with him in his Long Island studio. She received much sympathetic public attention and press coverage as a result of her rejection by the French.[86]

Two years later, she received a working scholarship to the Royal Academy of Fine Arts in Rome but a series of family problems depleted her funds for travel and living expenses. She relocated her parents from Florida and cared for her paralyzed father. His death and subsequent funeral and burial costs and the moving of the remainder of her family to New York due to a Florida hurricane resulted in the delay and finally the cancellation of the Italy trip.

Savage's work was brought to the attention of the Julius Rosenwald Fund president. Based on the display of several works, but specifically the sculpture of her nephew Ellis Ford, entitled *Gamin* (1929), "a head in clay that caught the vitality, the humanity, the tenderness and the wisdom of a boy child who has lived in the streets,"[87] she received her first Rosenwald Fellowship to study in France.

Augusta Savage arrived in Paris in 1930 to study at La Grande Chaumiere. Two works were accepted for the Salon d'Automne that year, and at the Grande-Palais and Salon Printemps. Receiving a second Rosenwald Fellowship to extend study through 1932, she simultaneously received a Carnegie Foundation grant to travel in France, Belgium, and Germany for eight months.

Upon her return to New York, she established the Savage Studio of Arts and Crafts at 163 West 143rd Street. Some of the brightest aspiring young artists, such as Ernest Crichlow, Gwendolyn Knight, Jacob Lawrence, Morgan and Marvin Jones, William Artis, and Norman Lewis, to cite a few, came under her tutelage.

As the Great Depression swooped across the country every worker, businessman, and artist was affected. The most important consequence of the New Deal was a series of government programs that provided jobs for thousands of artists, black and white, men and women. It has been recognized by scholars of American art as the "seedbed for the great blossoming of American talent that led to America's leadership in world art in the 1940s."[88] And, since government programs were supposed to be free of discrimination, women artists, for the first time in history, donned overalls, climbed ladders, and worked in public spaces in large numbers, side by side with their male colleagues.[89] From the upper echelons to the bottom ranks, women played leading roles. As the WPA got under way, Savage fought for the right of African Americans to work under its auspices. Badgering politicians, conducting press conferences, and organizing black artists to have their voices heard, she was successful in creating the Harlem Community Art Center, a national showcase where more than fifteen hundred residents took classes. Eleanor Roosevelt attended the ceremonies that marked the opening of the Center; Savage became the first director.

In 1938, Savage received a commission for a work representing the African American's contribution to American music. It was to be included in the World's Fair of 1939. She created *The Harp* (fig. 8), inspired by the lyrics of J. Rosamond and James Weldon Johnson's "Lift Every Voice and Sing," also called the Black National Anthem. Placed in a prominent position at the entrance to the Contemporary Arts Building on the Fair Grounds, the sixteen-foot-high sculpture was modeled in the form of a large musical instrument, with the figures of singing men and women emerging out of the hand of the Creator. A kneeling youth in front of the cylindrical figures extends a bar of musical notations to the audience. Savage was the only black artist, except for the composer William Grant Still, represented in the Fair. The work received wide publicity and became known throughout black communities. Awarded a silver medal by the Women's Service League of Brooklyn for pioneering women featured at the Fair (she was one of four women artists), Savage was now positioned more securely in the arts community and her voice as an art educator, administrator, and artist was clearly heard. She had gained respect and recognition in her community as a teacher and professional artist.

Funds from the New York Commission of the World's Fair were not available, and, regrettably, sufficient private revenue was not generated to cast the large plaster sculpture into bronze. *The Harp*, like many other works, was bulldozed at the end of the Fair. Only a few small souvenirs cast in iron from the original maquette, called *Lift Every Voice and Sing*, and photographs remain as testimony to its greatness.

Figure 8 Augusta Savage, *The Harp* (also known as *Lift Every Voice and Sing*), 1939, plaster with black finish, 16′ high. Photo: Carl Van Vechten, Yale University Library.

A pivotal figure in the development of African American art, Savage worked with other prominent artists such as Charles Alston, Aaron Douglas, Henry Bannarn, and James Wells to raise the consciousness of the community to recognize the need of a structured arts education program for young students and adults. With the Savage Studio of Arts and Crafts, The Harlem Artists Guild, The Uptown Art Laboratory, and the renowned Harlem Community Art Center, Savage triumphed administratively, wielding tremendous political, social, and artistic influence during the fifteen years that she lived and worked in Harlem. As an artist, she consistently employed the black subject, imbuing it with dignity and humanity, power and sensitivity. As a teacher, her devotion and dedication to educating young artists is elegantly summarized in her own words, "If I can inspire one of these youngsters to develop the talent I know they possess, then my monument will be in their work. No one could ask more than that."[90]

After 1945, she left Harlem for Saugerties, New York, to reestablish a relationship with her daughter. She continued to teach children in local summer camps and to do portraits of tourists in the area. On frequent visits to New York City during this period she only performed minor repairs to works owned by friends. By 1962, in relative obscurity, Augusta Savage died of cancer at the age of 70.

After meeting an African at the age of twelve, Beulah Ecton resolved to "promote a better understanding of the African with his rich historical background and to preserve some of the folklore, religious, and social customs of the various [ethnic groups] which were fast disappearing . . . on the African continent."[91] Born in rural Ohio near the town of Frankfort, Ecton and her parents migrated to California when she was an infant. Although born a slave, her father, William P. Ecton, fought in the Civil War, and later achieved success in both Ohio and California as a businessman. Her grandmother, also a slave, was, as Ecton noted "an expert weaver, making her own dyes and designs," while her uncle "carved ivory, wood, and created many designs in metal."[92]

After graduation from the Polytechnic High School, Ecton cultivated her interest in sculpture with studies at the Otis Art Institute, the Los Angeles Art School, and the University of Southern California. An opportunity to study abroad was lost when she complied with the wishes of her family to remain at home. Her early marriage to Brady E. Woodard delayed her artistic career as the duties of a homemaker and wife took precedence over her creative work. Eventually, the young artist was able to set up an improvised studio at the rear of her home where she was able to continue her interest in sculpture.

When several of Woodard's works were displayed in the window of the *California News* newspaper office, accompanied by illustrations of her work printed in the daily editions, invitations from the L.A. Public Library and important commissions through the Urban League

followed. Her long-standing interest in things African, however, developed into an intricate collection of African masks and studies of ethnic images. In the fall of 1935, Woodard was given a one-woman exhibition at the Los Angeles County Museum displaying these visually distinctive sculptures. On view for two months, Woodard's work attracted widespread commentary, and thousands of visitors during its exhibition. Woodard stated that:

> I have created these masks in an effort to preserve some of the early types of Africans, and not to caricature them. In no instance have there been exaggerations. Each mask is based upon historical research and in some instances, actual contact with natives. Papier mache, beads, and feathers have been used to carry out the realistic qualities of these masks . . . enabling me to preserve the subject in all of its life-like effect."[93]

With titles such as *Bapotos Chief*, *Ubangi Woman*, and *Medicine Man*, they represent Woodard's anthropological and aesthetic interest in African peoples. Later, her sculpture, which ranged in material from wood and bronze to clay and stone, revealed her interest in the African American as evidenced in works such as *Sharecropper*, *Bad Boy* (fig. 9) and *She*, a representation of womankind, symbolic of universal suffering but sustaining pride and quiet dignity.

Like Augusta Savage, her desire to mobilize and promote the work of black artists led Woodard to organize the Los Angeles Negro Art Association in 1937, and in 1950, the Eleven Associated Artists Gallery, for the purpose of "encouraging young artists with talent and developing public appreciation of the work of Negro artists."[94]

Woodard's commissions to create busts of many prominent Los Angelenos, and her exciting African sculptures captured the attention of international museums. Regrettably, her death at the age of fifty-nine ended what might have been her greatest triumph—an exhibition of her work scheduled for several German museums.[95]

Savage's origins were similar to those of Selma Hortense Burke in that they were children of Methodist ministers, and Burke also dug up clay to model small figures. Born in Mooresville, North Carolina, Burke was

Figure 9 Beulah Ecton Woodard, *Bad Boy*, 1936, terra-cotta, 8″ × 6¾″ × 5″. Collection of the California Afro-American Museum Foundation, Los Angeles, California.

one of ten children. Her father, unlike Savage's, encouraged her to develop an appreciation for the arts early in her life. Her mother, an educator and homemaker (who lived to be 103), did not discourage her from pursuing the arts (her maternal grandmother was a painter). In addition to his ministry, Neal Burke was a chef on several sea lines. His globe-trotting landed him in South America, the Caribbean, Africa, and Europe, and he collected artifacts and fine art objects made in those countries. Moreover, two paternal uncles who had graduated from Hood Theological Seminary traveled to Africa as missionaries during the late nineteenth century. As part of their mandate to teach Christianity to the Africans, they took the indigenous religious figures and masks and placed them in trunks rather than disposing of them. Upon their deaths, these artifacts and other personal belongings were returned to the Mooresville home. African sculpture, therefore, became one of Burke's first references to art and the first objects that she duplicated. "I have known African art all of my life," she explained. "At a time when this sculpture was misunderstood and laughed at, my family had the attitude that these were beautiful objects."[96]

Since Mooresville had only an elementary school for black children, Burke was sent to the Nannie Burroughs School for Girls in Washington, D.C. Her attendance there, however, was brief because "at Burroughs there was no encouragement for the arts. If you wore your silk-ribbed stockings, patent leather Mary Janes, and gloves, you were a lady. I wanted to be a lady and an artist."[97]

When Burke was fourteen, William Arial, a white educator and superintendent of schools, took her into his home for tutoring. Constantly battling some of the townspeople over befriending a black child, Arial became the first of Burke's patrons. The young aspiring artist had to travel to Winston-Salem (nearly fifty miles away) to obtain a high school education. She attended the Slater Normal and Industrial School (now Winston-Salem University), where she studied with France and Jack Atkins and Lester Granger. Her mother also insisted that Selma get a practical education to sustain her livelihood. Burke, therefore, pursued a nursing career at the St. Agnes School of Nursing, under the auspices of St. Augustine College, Raleigh, North Carolina, becoming a registered nurse in 1924.

In 1925, Burke moved to Philadelphia, where relatives resided. To earn a living, the young artist practiced nursing in the area for two years. After the stock market crashed in 1929, the 1930s presented problems of epidemic proportions for most Americans. Employed through these turbulent years, Burke, however, was unscathed by the Great Depression. Writing in the Winston-Salem *Sentinel*, Tom Sieg characterized those years as follows:

> [Selma Burke] ended up working for a charmingly crazy white woman, a Cooper, of the family for which Cooperstown, New York, was named. The woman turned out to be affectionate, generous, and very rich. By the time her employer died four years later, Miss Burke had a fantastic wardrobe, had become a regular at the Metropolitan Opera and Carnegie Hall, and had an acquaintance with royalty—and a nest egg.[98]

Nursing sustained her financially, but it was not the profession she desired for life. Seeking professional instruction in sculpture, Burke went to New York City in 1935. To earn money when she first arrived, she took a job modeling at Sarah Lawrence College, while continuing her work in sculpture. She soon met Claude McKay (1890–1948), writer, author, major figure in the Harlem Renaissance, and coeditor of the nation's outstanding avant-garde literary and political publication, *The Liberator*. Burke respected his accomplishments and his knowledge of European and African arts. Their relationship, though stormy, widened her circle of friends. She came to know Eugene O'Neill, Langston Hughes, Max Eastman, Sinclair Lewis, James Weldon and Rosamond Johnson, and Ethel Waters, among others.

Burke immersed herself in work. Winning a scholarship to Columbia University and a Rosenwald Award for a paper on sculpting materials in 1936, she gained further recognition that same year with a Boehler Foundation Award.

In 1938, Burke went to Europe and spent nearly a year in France, Germany, and Austria gathering fresh material and experiences while improving her craftsmanship. In Vienna she studied ceramics with Povolney, and in Paris she studied the human figure with Aristide Maillol, a major influence in early twentieth-century sculpture.

Feeling confident of her abilities, Burke resolved to obtain a professional degree in sculpture. She returned to Columbia University to work as an assistant to Oronzio Maldarelli, a well-known sculptor. Burke's quasi-classical leanings gave way to experimentation. "It is very inspiring to release a figure from a piece of stone or wood," Burke declared. "Very often I look at a piece of stone or wood for a year or longer. Sometimes I will have completed the piece mentally before attacking the material."[99]

During the years at Columbia Burke nurtured many meaningful relationships. Margo Einstein, daughter of Albert, was one of her classmates and a lifelong friend. Her visits to their home through the years, and the Einsteins' quiet support, encouraged Burke in her aspirations as a sculptor. She graduated with a masters degree in 1941. In November of that year Burke exhibited at the McMillen Galleries in New York City with representational compositions.

When World War II broke out, Burke joined the Navy and drove a truck at the Brooklyn Navy Yard, because as she said, "I felt that during the war artists should get out of their studios," but she injured her back and was hospitalized. It was during her hospitalization that she heard of the national competition sponsored by the Fine Arts Commission in Washington, D.C. to create a profile portrait of Franklin Delano Roosevelt. Burke entered the competition and was awarded the commission in 1943. Expected to create the profile from photographs, Burke researched newspapers and library records for such an image. Finding no photographs in profile, she wrote to the president requesting a sitting to make sketches from life. He gave her an appointment for February 22, 1944, just before his death on April 12.

The 3′6″ by 2′6″ bronze plaque depicting Roosevelt's profile listed the four freedoms: freedom from want, freedom from fear, freedom of worship, and freedom of speech. It was installed September 24, 1945, at the then-new Recorder of Deeds Building in Washington, D.C., with ceremonies to honor the occasion.

Much controversy has surfaced in recent years as to whether Burke's profile of Roosevelt on the plaque was used directly by the Bureau of the Mint of the U.S. Treasury for the Roosevelt dime. Few artists had had the opportunity of a private sitting with Roosevelt during his lifetime, and Burke's profile had been evaluated as a good likeness of him. John R. Sinnock, chief engraver at the Mint in 1945, who is credited with the design of the Roosevelt dime, according to the National Archives and Records Administration of the Franklin D. Roosevelt Library in Hyde Park, confirms that the source of the Roosevelt image on the coin was the "sculpture of FDR done by Selma Burke."[100] Because Burke's image was the most recent rendering created from life, Sinnock, in consulting the relief, made only minor alterations. Burke's head of FDR expresses a kind of hauteur that suggests, as she stated, "the going forwardness that we needed at that time. I wanted to inject the feeling of pride and a positive direction."[101] Sinnock, on the other hand, lowered Roosevelt's head for the design, and made a few changes in the arrangement of his hair.

Burke joined Savage at the WPA-sponsored Harlem Community Art Center, teaching sculpture workshops, and she conducted art clinics under the auspices of the Friends Council on Education. She shared Savage's dedication to youth and strongly believed that young minds should not be discouraged for lack of training or an outlet for expression.

Marriage to Herman Kobbe, famed architect and former candidate for lieutenant governor of New York, in 1949 meant a more public life for the artist. In the 1950s, the couple moved to New Hope, Pennsylvania, long recognized as an artist's colony, home to writers, musicians, and visual artists. Burke became an intricate part of the Bucks County community, holding many civic and arts related positions. In 1968 she opened the Selma Burke Art Center in Pittsburgh, where classes were offered in drawing, painting, ceramics, sculpture, visual communication, television production, and puppetry. A full range of activities included exhibitions by professional artists (group and one-person), concerts, lectures, demonstrations, and films. The theme of the center, "a place to grow and a place to show," was implemented and sustained until its closing in 1981.

Grounded in the modern aesthetic, Selma Burke's work has remained primarily figurative (fig. 10). Rejecting nonobjective, formalist trends, she has described herself as "a people's sculptor, one who deliberately creates a work that anyone can, in some way, relate to."[102]

The prolific artist Lois Mailou Jones has produced work of a consistently high quality for over sixty years. Called the "Grande Dame of African American Art,"[103] Jones has continued to evolve stylistically and professionally since 1930. A professor of art for five decades, Jones has touched the lives and influenced the careers of many African American artists who have gone on to make valuable contributions to American art.

Born in 1905 in Boston, her parents, Thomas and Carolyn Jones, encouraged her interest in the arts. As a young child, she constantly drew the environment in which she lived. Recognizing Jones's talent, her parents supplied the young artist with crayons, colored pencils, and paints. At age seven, she received her first set of watercolors, a "pet medium" that she continues to enjoy today. The High School of Practical Arts provided the educational foundation needed to nurture a young talent, and the curriculum reinforced her abilities and skills. Jones became an honor student and won

Figure 10 Selma H. Burke, *Temptation*, n.d., stone, 15½″ high. Howard University Gallery of Art, Washington, D.C.

four consecutive scholarships to the vocational drawing classes at the Museum of Fine Arts, Boston, between 1919 and 1923. In addition to a full day at the high school, Jones studied at the Museum in the afternoons and on Saturdays. After graduation, she matriculated at the School of the Boston Museum of Fine Arts on four successive scholarships between 1923 and 1927, graduating with honors in design.

Jones sought employment in her field, and with a challenge from Charlotte Hawkins Brown "to go south," she established the art department at the Palmer Memorial Institute in Sedalia, North Carolina (1928–30). When James V. Herring invited her to Howard University as instructor of design and watercolor painting, she joined James A. Porter (1905–1970) and James L. Wells (1902–1992). Together they forged a curriculum unique among historically black colleges and universities. For forty-seven years (1930–77), she touched the lives and influenced the aesthetic foundations of artists such as Delilah Pierce, Elizabeth Catlett, David Driskell, Malkia Roberts, Earl Hooks, Mildred Thompson, Mary Lovelace O'Neal, Lou Stovall, Sylvia Snowden, and legions of others.

As a young woman, she expressed her interest in the arts to sculptor Meta Warrick Fuller and composer Harry T. Burleigh during a summer on Martha's Vineyard where her family had vacationed since the mid-nineteenth century. They advised her to travel to Paris for recognition if she wanted to find a niche in the art world. For her first sabbatical Jones chose the Académie Julian in Paris, and with the aid of a General Education Board Fellowship, she sailed for France on the *S.S. Normandie Le Havre* on September 1, 1937. Her sojourn there marked a shift in her career from that of designer, illustrator, and teacher to that of painter. The experience, Jones said, "allowed me to be shackle free, to create and to be myself."[104]

Although her work during this period reveals a commitment to the organizing principles and preferred palette of the impressionists and post-impressionists, her paintings are clearly personal interpretations. As Porter noted: "Thus far her painting has been in the tradition of, but not in the imitation of Cézanne. . . . Miss Jones wishes to confirm Cézanne but at the same time to add an original note of her own. . . . Sensuous color delicately adjusted to the mood indicates the artistic perceptiveness of this young woman."[105] Works such as *Rue Norvins, Montmartre, Paris, La Mère, Déjeuner, Place du Tertre, Montmartre*, all done during her maiden journey (1937–38), are examples of this emergence into the competitive arena of painting. Jones was determined to chart a career as a painter, and a solo exhibition in February 1939 at the Robert C. Vose Galleries in Boston confirmed that she was on the right path. Hailed by one reviewer as having "the right to be called [the] leading Negro artist,"[106] the art critic for *The Christian Science*

Monitor declared, "While in Paris, she was imbued with the qualities the Impressionists sought to achieve through painting with broad brush work, in summary patches of color which catch the effect of sunlight upon surfaces. Miss Jones is an Impressionist without the strict methods of divided color."[107]

Although her work was included in numerous exhibitions over the next few years, because of racial bias it was not always a certainty that her paintings would be accepted for consideration in major exhibitions. To avoid rejection and humiliation, Jones often shipped her work directly to museums and galleries. Knowing of the Corcoran Gallery of Art's policy which forbade participation by African American artists, Jones's friend Céline Tabary, whom she had met in France, submitted *Indian Shops, Gay Head, Massachusetts* (1940) (fig. 11) for the 1941 exhibition. A scene from Martha's Vineyard, it won the prestigious Robert Woods Bliss Prize for Landscape from The Society of Washington Artists. With this award, Jones broke the color barrier. Fearing that if she claimed her award in person the honor would be rescinded, she allowed the certificate to be forwarded through the mail. Jones's success at the Corcoran bolstered her confidence as an artist. As her work began to

Figure 11 Lois Mailou Jones, *Indian Shops, Gay Head, Massachusetts*, 1940, oil on canvas, 28½″ × 33½″. Collection of the artist.

receive positive critical opinion, her reputation grew, and she continued to exhibit throughout the United States during the 1940s.

Marriage to Haitian graphic artist and designer Louis Vergniaud Pierre-Noël in 1953 and travel to the island nation in 1954 was the beginning of a new way of seeing for Jones. Her early Haitian paintings explored the picturesque elements of the marketplace and its people. Although the essence of Europe was still very much apparent at the beginning of her visits, the palette and the formal organization of her paintings gradually evolved into a brilliantly spirited style—fresh, energetically fluid, and highly individual. This new style, evidenced in works such as *Les Vendeuses de Tissus* and *Bazar du Quai, Haiti*, both of 1961, deftly illustrates the confluence of Jones's early years as a textile designer and the ensuing decades as a painter.[108] These works signaled clearly that Europe did not yield the exuberance so vital to expressing the vigor of an African-based culture.

In the 1960s, Jones drew more upon her knowledge of design and her passion for color while synthesizing the diverse religious and ritualistic elements of Haitian

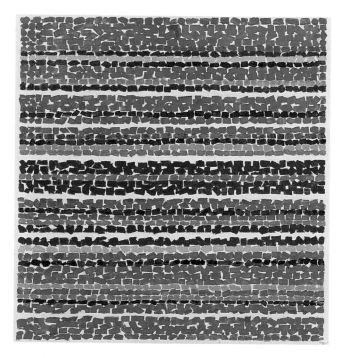

Figure 12 Alma W. Thomas, *Light Blue Nursery*, 1968, oil on canvas, acrylic, 50″ × 48″. National Museum of American Art, Smithsonian Institute, Washington D.C.

life and culture. This period showed a more expressive, colorful, hard-edged style that fused abstraction with decorative patterns and naturalism. These characteristics asserted themselves more powerfully in the 1970s and 1980s after a trip to Africa, where she conducted research on contemporary African artists.[109] The impact of her trip was seen immediately in works such as *Magic of Nigeria* (1971), *Ubi Girl from the Tai Region* (1972), and later in *Damballah* (1980), *Symbols d'Afrique I* (1982), and *Mère du Senegal* (1985).

Returning to France in the summer of 1989, Jones completed a body of work that brought her career full circle, recalling an earlier era. Reminiscent of the Impressionist/Post-Impressionist style she had abandoned more than thirty years earlier, they illustrate her continued fascination with nature and her desire to capture the fleeting beauty of place and time. A major retrospective, organized by the Meridian International Center of Washington, D.C., highlighting seventy years of an illustrious career is now in its fifth year.[110] At ninety years of age, the "Grande Dame of African American Art" continues to be active as a painter and lecturer, traveling for both professional responsibilities and to recharge her creative spirit. While teaching and demonstrating a commitment and dedication to generations of students, Jones has also created a body of work characterized by technical virtuosity, consummate skill, versatility, structure, design, and clarion color.

It was the love of color and its "life giving properties"[111] that captured the interest of Alma Woodsey Thomas (1896–1978) (fig. 12). A colleague and fellow Washington-based artist who painted with Jones in her Little Paris Studio,[112] Thomas described her own work as "Geometric abstractions composed of mosaic-like patterns of vivid colors rhythmically arranged in concentric circles or parallel lines."[113] The first graduate of the art department at Howard University in 1924, Thomas devoted her career to teaching in the public schools of Washington, D.C., while nurturing her own art and organizing exhibitions of African American artists.

After retirement in 1960, she devoted herself to painting full time. Lowery Sims, curator at the Metropolitan Museum of Art, has said that Thomas's "work of the 1960s is characterized by a shortening and regimentation of strokes, as well as a restriction of the palette (individual colors are nonetheless brilliant and translucent), which is well suited to the more discrete surfaces and the objectification of the creative process that marked the artistic phenomena of the decade, Minimalism and Color Field Painting."[114]

The first African American woman to achieve critical acclaim within an abstract medium, she was accorded a one-woman exhibition at the Whitney Museum of American Art in New York, and at the Corcoran Gallery of Art in Washington, D.C., in 1972. "Alma Thomas shattered many stifling attitudes about being black and a woman, about old age, about color, about starting late, about teaching. . . . Color offered her a way to grow."[115]

Other colleagues of Thomas and Jones, whose works reflect the prevailing "isms" of the period (Impressionism, Precisionism) while responding to nature and the environment, were Hilda Wilkinson Brown (1894–1981) (fig. 13), Delilah W. Pierce (1904–1992) and Vivian Schuyler Key (1905–1989). Brown, a graduate of Minor Normal School (now the University of the District of Columbia), received a BS degree from Howard University and an MA from Columbia. She was described as a "traditional woman, an idealist in the manner and mores of the then current womanhood. What stood Hilda Brown apart in her times was that she also fervently pursued her own individuality."[116] She pursued her education at Miner Normal School and the Cooper Union in New York. Later she received a BS at Howard University, attended the Art Students League, and received a masters degree at Columbia University. It is her influence as a teacher, however, that is her contribution to the Washington community, where in 1923, she designed the two-year art curriculum for the Minor Normal School in art history, design, and the studio arts. As chair of the department, she also integrated the fine and industrial arts into the teacher training program in 1929. By 1933,

Figure 13 Hilda Wilkinson Brown, *3rd and Rhode Island, LeDroit Park*, oil on canvas, 23″ × 28″. Collection of Lilian Thomas Burwell, Washington, D.C.

she had introduced the 'modern' approach to art education in the Elementary Schools, encouraging the replacement of imitative art by individual creativity.[117]

In many ways, the career of Delilah Pierce parallels that of Brown in that her educational training was similar (Minor Normal School; BS degree from Howard University; MA from Columbia University, with postgraduate and studio work at other institutions). Her travels to Africa greatly influenced the direction of her work, as did the themes of marine life and nature from her visits to Martha's Vineyard in Massachusetts. And, like Brown, she was greatly involved in the teaching of young aspiring artists in the Washington, D.C. public school system, and in higher education as a visiting professor at Howard University and, until her retirement, at the D.C. Teacher's College (University of the District of Columbia). Like Jones and Thomas, Brown and Pierce planted and nurtured the seeds of creativity in many of our artists.

While Vivian Schuyler Key shares birth date and year with Lois Mailou Jones (3 November 1905), her career has not been as productive or as long-lived. Born in

Hempstead, New York, Key, like Jones, expressed an interest in the arts in elementary school with drawings that were posted on the bulletin boards and in the hallways of her school. After completing high school, where she followed a curriculum of three years of art classes, she entered the Pratt Institute School of Fine and Applied Art, graduating with a certificate in General Art in 1926. Unable to find employment after graduation, she worked as a decorative artist at a production factory painting designs of flowers, figures, animals, and geometric design patterns on silk fabric and giftware. She worked in and out of these factories throughout her career. A chance meeting with W. E. B. Du Bois, in 1926, however, shifted Key's creative focus. As a free-lance artist, she designed large maps and charts of Africa for his use in Pan African Congress meetings. Subsequently, her drawings and watercolors were also purchased and featured on the cover of *The Crisis* magazine, reaching a wide readership in the black community.[118]

Between 1930 and 1936, Key had three children and experienced economic reversals and family problems due to the Great Depression, yet her work was selected for exhibition in the 1930, 1931, and 1932 Harmon Foundation's local and traveling exhibitions. And, as one critic noted:

> Interestingly, the 1931 catalogue of the Harmon Foundation exhibition describes Vivian as 'working against many discouragements in her serious art work.' And while this is certainly true given her race, gender, inability to find work beyond that available in production factories, and little income, her self-portrait "Study in Yellow" accepted into the 1931 exhibition presents a confident woman projecting a daring arrogance that's confirmed by the slightly turned head whose raised chin and pulled back shoulders belie the depth of her difficulties."[119]

Key worked for the WPA as a Senior Arts and Crafts and Music Leader in the Queen's Public School system, and although her desire had been to work on an easel project, she resigned her WPA assignment after two years and returned full-time to production painting.[120]

Key's career of decorative, portrait, and oil painting, book and magazine illustrations, and sculpture spans seven decades. Her drive, determination, and creative fervor propelled her against the odds that perpetually faced her.

Elizabeth Catlett has often said that "Art should come from the people and be for the people."[121] Choosing subjects that embrace socio-political issues concerning women, African Americans, and Mexicans, her compositions combine strength of form, polished craftsmanship, and employ the human figure; Afrocentric, they always seem familiar. Her works are female-centered and like Prophet and Savage, Catlett evokes a reverence for the black image. Whether in wood, stone, marble, terra-cotta, or graphic media, her works are compelling and engaging.

Born in 1915 in Washington, D.C., Catlett studied at the Howard University Department of Art with James A. Porter, Lois Mailou Jones, James V. Herring, and James L. Wells between 1932 and 1937, graduating *cum laude* with a BS in art. Later that year, she accepted a position as instructor and supervisor at a high school in Durham, North Carolina, where she participated in the struggle for equal salaries for black teachers.

In 1938, Catlett enrolled in the graduate program at the University of Iowa, where she studied with Regionalist painter Grant Wood. It was Wood who directed her to "work from what we know best and [she] started then working with black subject matter and with the subject matter of women."[122] Wood was also a master carpenter and he encouraged his students to use wood. It was his knowledge of form and content she took with her when she switched media.[123]

In 1940, Catlett was awarded an MFA in sculpture, the first MFA degree that the university had ever bestowed, and the highest degree attainable for studio artists at that time. Her thesis project was a marble sculpture of the mother and child, a theme that she continues to explore today; it won the first prize in sculpture at the 1940 American Negro Exposition in Chicago.[124] *Mother and Child* evokes the simplified mass, unified conception, clarification of form, technical and aesthetic elements still present in her oeuvre five decades later.

After graduate work, Catlett traveled south, returning to teach at Prairie View College in Texas in the summer of 1940. She then served as chairman of the art department at Dillard University in New Orleans from fall 1940 to 1942. In Chicago during the summer of 1941, she studied ceramics at the Art Institute of Chicago. There she met African American painter and printmaker Charles White (1918–1979). They married, and returned to New Orleans where she continued teaching at Dillard.

Between 1942 and 1943, Catlett, now in New York, studied with Ossip Zadkine, a French sculptor. Like Wood, Zadkine was noted for a disciplined approach to his work, but he espoused a system of cubist abstractions and of interchanged positive and negative shapes.[125] Catlett found his academic rigor useful for technical purposes, but disagreed that abstraction could be readily understood by all. In 1944, while taking a course at the Art Students League, she discovered the medium that allowed her to convey social, political, and cultural statements through her art—lithography.

Receiving a Julius Rosenwald Fellowship to do a series of works on black women in 1945, Catlett produced *The Negro Woman* (1946–47), a linocut series which delineated working class women in images of the ordinary and the heroic, women of the blues, women of intellect, women of servitude, and women of revolution, revealing Catlett's commitment and sensitivity to their struggles.[126] Freida High Tesfagiorgis, professor of African and Afro-American Art at the University of Wisconsin concluded that:

> This series . . . was indeed a landmark in the pictorial representation of Black women for it liberated them from their objectified status in the backgrounds and shadows of white subjects in the works of white artists, and from the roles of mother, wife, sister, [and] other in the works of Black male artists.[127]

Now fortified with a two-dimensional and a three-dimensional approach to "create an art for liberation and for life," Catlett took up residence in Mexico, first studying at the Taller de Grafica Popular, where she fully grasped the social function of art and the need to put art to the service of working people in their constant struggle against exploitation. She later studied at the Escuela de Pintura Y Escultura, where she learned how to make the traditional, hollow, ceramic sculpture of the pre-Columbian period. At the Taller, Catlett met painter and printmaker Francisco Mora, whom she married in 1947 after her divorce from Charles White.

In 1958, Catlett was hired at the National University of Mexico's School of Fine Arts as a professor of sculpture for the upper division, and within a year, was appointed director of the department. She continued to serve in that position until her retirement in 1976.

Heir apparent to the legacy of sculptors before her and trailblazer for those who follow, Elizabeth Catlett has "successfully bridged the gap between traditionalists and experimentalists, and between a philosophy of social engagement and the aesthetics of 'art for arts sake'"[128] which overlaps her expressions in graphics and in three-dimensional forms.

Historian Elton Fax has noted that "Her sculptures of women are awesomely strong and, like her terse conversation, they are bereft of all non-essentials. Their heads tilt upwards at defiant angles, and their feet are planted squarely under them."[129] Regarding her prints, the art historian Richard Powell proclaims that, "Apart from the exceptionally narrational . . . much of Catlett's graphic work is divided between explicit, title/image narratives and implicit, visual narratives (or rather, message pictures)."[130]

While sociopolitical commentary and a strong sense of empathy lie at the core of Catlett's work, other women artists who emerged during the Great Depression as painters, sculptors, and printmakers also embraced the trend of social realism and the impact of the Mexican muralists during the 1930s and 1940s. Artists who worked on murals in public places, including hospitals, were Charles Alston, Aaron Douglas, Georgette Seabrooke Powell, Elba Lightfoot, Selma Day, Vertis Hayes, and Sara Murrell. Their work at the Harlem Hospital incorporated historical perspectives on medicine, African Americans, and African folklore. Although little is known of the lives and activities of the women cited above after the Depression, Powell has remained intricately involved in the arts as activist, educator, and artist.

The recent subject of a retrospective at the Anacostia Museum in Washington, D.C. (March–May 1995), Georgette Powell (b. 1916) was born in Charleston, South Carolina, but lived in New York City from 1920 to 1959. A graduate of Cooper Union, she was an active member in the Harlem Artist's Workshop and a participant in the WPA mural division. She designed and painted murals for the Harlem Hospital and the Queens General Hospital from 1936 to 1939. *Recreation in Harlem* (1936), a large, ambitious work, was "at once symbolic and realistic, show[ing] real people who lived in the community, occupied with daily activities, but only in fragments. . . . Although the people and their actions are believable, the painting does not attempt to reproduce reality."[131] The murals ignited a controversy, pitting the African American artist's right to represent positive black images against the hospital's objection to the depiction of "Negro subject matter."[132] At the end of a two year battle fought mostly on paper, the Harlem Hospital mural artists emerged victorious. However, this was a victory won at great personal cost to Powell—because of the delay, she was unable to continue her schooling and she lost her internship credit, and thus her Cooper Union certification.[133]

Relocating to Washington, D.C. in 1959, Powell continued her career in the arts through exhibitions and by 1966, established the Powell Art Studio, the forerunner to Operation Heritage Art Center (1969), known today as Tomorrow's World Art Center. As its founder and director, Powell's arts and education organization has served the youth, senior citizens, and other special constituencies in the District of Columbia and metropolitan area for over two decades. Although her artistic productivity has not been consistent or continuous, her involvement with the community as activist and promoter has, in a manner similar to Augusta Savage, invested in the aspiring young artists of tomorrow.

In a similar manner, Margaret Taylor Burroughs (b. 1917), has used a variety of media to "describe, teach, preserve, and enhance humane values in general and the Black experience in particular"[134] throughout her life. Like Savage, she was a key figure in the establishment of the South Side Community Art Center (1940) during the WPA era. The founder and former director of the Ebony Museum of African American History and Art (now the DuSable Museum of African American History) in Chicago, and the National Conference of Artists (NCA, 1959), Burroughs was born in Saint Rose, Louisiana. When she was very young, her family migrated to Chicago, where she availed herself of many of the educational opportunities, including study at the Chicago Teachers College (now Chicago State University), and later at the Art Institute of Chicago where she received both a BFA (1944) and an MFA (1948) degree.

Productive as a writer of children's books and poetry and as a visual artist, her range of media includes painting, sculpture, and the graphic arts. Burroughs states that: "The whole motivation of my work, be it a portrait, a vase of flowers, or people on a picket line or in a demonstration, is in the final essence, for the liberation of my people in particular and for the end of imperialist oppression of all the underprivileged people of the earth of all races, creeds and colors."[135] Still active as a civic and cultural leader, she continues to oversee the nurturing of future artists.

CONTINUING THE LEGACY: 1960s AND BEYOND

• • • • • • • • • • • • • •

The Brown vs. Board of Education ruling of May 1954 signaled the beginning of the Civil Rights era, a period of social upheaval and protests that reverberated throughout the United States. Desegregation "with all deliberate speed" was to become the sound byte of the 1960s, as America became a cauldron stewing from centuries of racism and inequality. In December 1955, Rosa Parks boarded a bus in Montgomery, Alabama, and for more than a year, Montgomery became the scene of a non-violent battleground for human rights. By December 21, 1956, when the buses were fully integrated, the civil rights movement had produced an important leader in Martin Luther King, Jr., and honed the most effective weapon of protest—non-violence—ever devised.

Sit-ins, marches, freedom rides, and pickets were intense throughout the decade. The March on Washington of 1963 galvanized all segments of society—young and old, black and white, leaders and followers, sharecroppers and Congressmen all gathered before the Lincoln Memorial in the nation's capital for America's largest protest rally. The Civil Rights Law of 1964 and the Voting Rights Bill of 1965 were two gains during this era.

The intensity of confrontation grew as the constitutionality of America's racist beliefs and practices was challenged in the courts and in the streets. As cities burned and social discord escalated, every facet of America, from college campuses to the nation's capital, was politicized. The assassinations of John F. Kennedy and Martin Luther King, resistance to the Vietnam War, the civil rights movement, and a questioning of values and beliefs among young Americans who began to view society as materialistic, callous, and unfeeling ushered in a new mood and attitude. By the end of the 1960s "this national phenomenon had transformed the student movement, the women's movement, the church, and other segments of American society."[136] A new mood seized the country and the changes were tremendous. Just as art reflects its time, these changes were soon to be seen in the artworks produced during this era.

One major shift was in the relocation of the art product from the hallowed halls of museums and galleries. "Happenings," earthworks, environmental pieces, street murals, conceptual art, laser lights, minimalism, the "dematerializing" of the object, all became a part of the lexicon of American art. But as one writer noted, "Multicultural ethnics, women, and most especially Blacks were excluded from mainstream recognition. On the one hand, the Black artist was viewed as a social anomaly and on the other as a European replica in blackface."[137]

As never before, there was an urgent need for black artists to organize themselves and to examine the issues of politics and aesthetics in response to the crises of the times. The questions that begged to be answered by artists were: "What is our role and responsibility in these turbulent years?" "What are our attitudes and commitments in relation to the struggle for Civil Rights?"

"How can we use our art to reach the masses of the people?" Individual artists and organized groups responded with overwhelming results.

The groups called themselves Spiral (1963, New York); Weusi (1965, New York); Organization of Black American Culture (OBAC) (1967, Chicago); AfriCobra (1968, Chicago); the Black Emergency Cultural Coalition (1968, New York); Women, Students and Artists for Black Art Liberation (WSABAL), (1970, New York); Where We At: Black Women Artists (1971, New York), among others. Black artists began to forge a new aesthetic, defining a visual language that not only addressed the social and political fervor of the times, but embraced their African heritage, and depicted their unique American experiences. The range of expressions are as varied as there are artists to express them.

Geraldine McCullough (b. 1922) has explored a variety of media including welded sheet copper, polyester resin, and bronze casting. Her figures and abstract forms possess a life-like vitality, from the powerful abstract-expressionist paintings, to monumental forms of African sculpture. The textured surfaces often give energy to the compositions as they twist and extend in space (fig. 14).

Through her travels to Africa and other parts of the Third World, Malkia Roberts (b. 1923), has averred to "affirm the identity, dignity and beauty of black people"[138] in her works of expressionistic paintings (fig. 15). From the late 1960s to the present, she has continued in the tradition of Thomas, Brown, Jones, and Pierce, as educator and artist. She is one of the matriarchs of this legacy.

Known today for her "Afrofemcentrism,"[139] the art of Faith Ringgold (b. 1930) has undergone several metamorphoses: from grassroots experiences in Harlem as an activist, where her paintings such as *The Flag Is Bleeding* and *Die*, both 1967, reflected the strong social and political unrest of the 1960s; followed by her *Family of Woman* masks and *Slave Rape* painting series in the 1970s, to her soft sculpture creations of the same decade. Today, her quilts tell stories, using the traditional feminine craft to make statements about the lives of women—coming full circle from Harriet Powers and her symbolic quilts of the nineteenth century.

Figure 14 Geraldine McCullough, *Ancestral Parade*, 1994, bronze, 46″ × 37″. Courtesy of the artist.

Figure 15 Malkia Roberts, *Out of the Blues*, 1983, oil and acrylic on canvas. Spelman College Museum of Fine Arts Collection, Atlanta, Georgia.

The cloth, fabric, and fiber employed by Powers and Ringgold have also been used by artists such as Senga Nengudi (b. 1943), Viola Burley Leak (b. 1944), Januwa Moja (b. 1946), Joyce Scott (b. 1948), Xenobia Bailey (b. 1958), and Julee Dickerson-Thompson (b. 1956), among others, as they draw upon the craftsmanship of the past to create wearable art, and to respond to the socio-political issues of today. They effectively blur the lines between craft and fine art, forcing new definitions and reassessments.

Aesthetic choices and personal approaches to creative expression can be observed in the artists' response to color, texture, shapes, biomorphic forms, nature, or the experimental. Although sculpture was not considered the medium for women to conquer in the nineteenth century, today's artists have expanded the use of this genre and the concept of the third dimension into new visions. In addition to wood, stone, and metals, we see a marriage with high-tech materials of the postmodern era, and with non-traditional materials. Artists such as Inge Hardison (b. 1914), Marie Johnson-Calloway (b. 1920), Artis Lane (b. 1927), Shirley Stark (b. 1927), Bessie Harvey (1928–1994), Mildred Thompson (b. 1936), Valerie Maynard (b. 1937), Barbara Chase-Riboud (b. 1939), Beverly Buchanan (b. 1940), Catti (b. 1940), Helen Evans Ramsaran (b. 1943), Maren Hassinger (b. 1947), Bisa Washington (b. 1951), Rene Townsend (b. 1952), Denise Ward-Brown (b. 1953), Alison Saar (b. 1956), Kabuya Bowens (b. 1957), and Renee Stout (b. 1958) are but a few who blend the traditional with the modern, the found with the high-tech, the socio-political with the historical, and the present with the past in their three-dimensional works.

The ceramic sculpture of such artists as Persis Jennings (b. 1920), Camille Billops (b. 1933), Yvonne Edwards Tucker (b. 1941), Viola Wood (b. 1949), Winnie Owens Hart (b. 1949), Martha Jackson Jarvis (b. 1952), Sana Musasama (b. 1953) expand our perception of this material and its limitless applications from the traditional to the innovative. And, in the arena of installations and performances, our knowledge of the spiritual, the magical, the occult, while changing the meaning of an object in a specific context, is heightened in the works of Betye Saar (b. 1926), Yvonne Pickering Carter (b. 1939), Sandra Rowe (b. 1940), Carole Byard (b. 1941), Howardena Pindell (b. 1943), Mildred Howard (b. 1945), Patricia Ravarra (b. 1947), Adrian Piper (b. 1948), and Lorraine O'Grady (b. 1961).

Painting, prints, and mixed media works all offer challenges that are as old as the profession itself, yet contemporary African American women artists continue to respond to the changing art world and contribute to the varied "isms" as we move into the twenty-first century. From representationalism to minimalism, from expressionism to abstract expressionism, from surrealism to constructivism, from precisionism to conceptualism, from modernism to post modernism, et al., we observe a sense of commitment and dedication to the process and to the medium. Many of these artists are multi-talented—as painters, printmakers, mixed-mediaists, collagists, textile designers—and their work is an important factor in the American equation. Artists such as Ruth Waddy (b. 1909), Jewel Woodward Simon (b. 1911), Eva Hamlin Miller (b. 1911–1992), Gwendolyn Knight (b. 1913), Corinne Mitchell (1914–1993), Juette Johnson Day (b. 1919), Georgia Mills Jessup (b. 1926), Norma Morgan (b. 1928), Vivian Browne (1929–1993), Lilian Burwell (b. 1927), Ann Tanksley (b. 1934), Yvonne Parks Catchings (b. 1935), Betty Blayton (b. 1937), Emma Amos (b. 1938), Kay Brown (b. 1932), Margo Humphrey (b. 1942), Mary Lovelace O'Neal (b. 1942), Sylvia Snowden (b. 1942), Stephanie Pogue (b. 1944), Suzanne Jackson (b. 1944), Rose Powhatan (b. 1946), Dindga McCannon (b. 1947), Adrienne Hoard (1949), and Varnette Honeywood (b. 1950) provide diversity in trends and directions reflecting their personal and aesthetic choices.

Equally important in continuing the legacy established by these visual artists is the documentation of their work in American art history. Black women, as scholars, critics, and art historians, also continue the legacy established by Porter, Locke, Murray, and Brawley[140] and have made significant contributions to the discourse in their research and writing. Committed to scrupulously researching, documenting, and correcting the egregious imbalance in the history of American art, there has been an appreciable increase in African American scholars who fill the lacunae of America's art history. Prominent among these scholars and critics are Samella Lewis, Regina Perry, Mary Schmidt Campbell, Lowery Sims, Leslie King Hammond, Rosalind Jeffries, Sharon Patton, Freida High Tesfagiorgis, Jacqueline Fonvielle Bontemps, Judith Wilson, Lizzetta Lefalle Collins, Tina Dunkley, Kinshasha Conwill, Jontyle Theresa Robinson, Alvia Wardlaw, Juanita Marie Holland, to cite a few who have served in various roles—as professors, curators, gallery owners and directors, exhibition organizers, and administrators—shaping opinion and attitudes about African American art and artists.

From the tradition of "respective preserves," our artistic foremothers adopted new ways of channeling their creative urges in eighteenth- and nineteenth-century America. This transfusive quality, adapting to and mastering materials that had not been their forte, is indicative of the triumphant spirit and determination of these artists who persevered in the face of adversity, struggled against familial ambivalence, and were at variance with American society's restrictions based on race and gender. But the lives and careers of these African American women artists provide substantive evidence of a multi-faceted range of disciplines filled with a variety, scope, and profundity that cannot be denied. By adopting a tenacious philosophy and remaining focused on the perpetuation of our ethos, these artists will continue to proclaim important news in their art, bearing witness to the past as well as heralding the twenty-first century and beyond.

NOTES

1. Gloria Wade-Gayles, "No Crystal Stair, Visions of Race and Sex," in *Black Women's Fiction* (New York: Pilgrim Press, 1984), p. 6.

2. Quoted in Beverly Guy-Sheftall and Patricia Bell-Scott, "The Creative Spirit," *Sage: A Scholarly Journal on Black Women*, vol. 4, no. 1 (Spring 1987): 2.

3. See Steven Loring Jones's well-documented and informative article, "A Keen Sense of the Artistic African American Material Culture in 19th Century Philadelphia," *The International Review of African American Art*, vol. 12, no. 12 (Summer 1995), pp. 9–10. Jones indicates that there were sixteen schoolteachers in the 1856 statistics in Philadelphia, Pennsylvania. The scrapbooks, located in the Moorland Spingarn Research Center at Howard University and The Library Company of Philadelphia, yielded the sketches and poems noted. Douglass's colleague, Ada H. Hinton (active 1840s –1900+) also contributed work to these albums. She too combined literary and artistic skill in the albums of young women students. Two works, *Untitled Floral Bud*, 1840?, watercolor, and *Untitled Floral Piece*, 1840?, oil and ink, are illustrated. To my knowledge, the illustrations of Douglass and Hinton are published here for the first time.

4. Robert Douglass, Jr. (1809–1887) was a painter, printmaker, and photographer. He studied with the leading portrait painter of the day, Thomas Sully of the Pennsylvania Academy of the Fine Arts. He spent eighteen months in Haiti, 1837–39, and by 1840, he was in London studying at the National Gallery. When he returned to Philadelphia in early 1841, he scheduled illustrated slide lectures on his travels in Haiti. William Penn Douglass (n.d.) began his career as a sign painter. He was also chairman of the Colored Young Men of Philadelphia.

5. Quoted in Sterling Stuckey, *Slave Culture* (New York: Oxford University Press, 1987), p. 268.

6. Ibid.

7. Jones, "A Keen Sense of the Artistic," p. 10.

8. Ibid.

9. Ibid.

10. Ibid.

11. Ibid.

12. Elaine Hedges, "The Nineteenth Century Diarist and Her Quilts," *Feminist Studies*, vol. 8 (Summer 1982): 295–97, cited in Crystal A. Britton "Conditions for Black Women Artists: An Overview," in Vivian Schuyler Key, *One of Many Voices 1926–1980*, exh. cat. (Brooklyn, NY: The Society for the Preservation of Weeksville and Bedford-Stuyvesant History, 1990), p. 12.

13. Crystal Britton, "Conditions for Black Women Artists," p. 12.

14. Gladys-Marie Fry, "Harriet Powers: Portrait of a Black Quilter," in *Sage: A Scholarly Journal on Black Women*, vol. 4, no. 1 (Spring 1987): 11.

15. Ibid.

16. Ibid.

17. Ibid.

18. Ibid., p. 12. According to Fry, Jennie Smith offered to buy the quilt at the 1886 fair, but Powers refused to sell it for any price. Around 1890, experiencing difficult financial pressures, Powers sent word to Smith that the quilt was now for sale. Smith was herself unable to purchase it in 1890, but in 1891 she reopened negotiations. Her own words are very interesting and shed light on Powers's attachment to this quilt: "Last year I sent her word that I would buy it if she still wanted to dispose of it. She arrived one afternoon in front of my door in an ox-cart with the precious burden in her lap encased in a clean flour sack, which was still enveloped in a crocus sack. She offered it for ten dollars, but I told her I only had five to give. After going out consulting with her husband she returned and said, 'Owin' to de hardness of de times, my old man lows I'd better teck hit.' Not being a new woman she obeyed.

After giving me a full description of each scene with great earnestness, she departed but has been back several times to visit the darling offspring of her brain. She was only in a measure consoled for its loss when I promised to save her all my scraps. . . . " That black women were expected to defer to their husbands rings loudly in Smith's observation that Powers "Not being a new woman obeyed." Furthermore, her returns to see the quilt indicate that this product was viewed as more than a utilitarian object in the household.

19. Milton W. Brown et al., *American Art* (New York: Harry N. Abrams, 1979), p. 278.

20. Britton, "Conditions for Black Women Artists," p. 12.

21. Oberlin College had promoted coeducation since its founding in 1832 and began admitting African Americans in 1835.

22. Lynda Roscoe Hartigan, *Sharing Traditions: Five Black Artists in Nineteenth Century America*, exh. cat. (Washington, DC: National Museum of American Art, Smithsonian Institution, 1985), p. 87.

23. Ibid.

24. Charlotte Streiffer Rubinstein, *American Women Sculptors* (Boston: G.K. Hall, 1990), p. 52, and Arna Alexander Bontemps and Jacqueline Fonvielle-Bontemps, "African American Women Artists: An Historical Perspective," *Sage: A Scholarly Journal on Black Women*, vol. 4, no. 1 (Spring 1987): 17.

25. Theodore J. Stebbins, *The Boston Tradition: American Paintings from the Museum of Fine Arts*, exh. cat. (Boston: Museum of Fine Arts, 1980), p. i.

26. Rubinstein, *American Women Sculptors*, p. 52.

27. Juanita Marie Holland, "Reaching Through the Veil: African American Artist Edward Mitchell Bannister," in *Edward Mitchell Bannister 1828–1901*, exh. cat. (New York: Kenkeleba House, 1992), p. 22.

28. Rubinstein, *American Women Sculptors*, pp. 45, 52.

29. Hartigan, *Sharing Traditions*, p. 89.

30. Rubinstein, *American Women Sculptors*, p. 25.

31. Henry James, *William Wetmore Story and His Friends* (Boston: Houghton Mifflin, 1903; reprint, New York: Grove Press, 1957), p. 57.

32. Hartigan, *Sharing Traditions*, p. 93.

33. Kirsten P. Buick, "The Ideal Works of Edmonia Lewis: Invoking and Inverting Autobiography," *American Art*, vol. 9, no. 2 (Summer 1995): 6–7, 9.

34. This work is in the National Museum of American Art, Washington, D.C.

35. Rubinstein, *American Women Sculptors*, p. 54; Hartigan, *Sharing Traditions*, p. 94.

36. Long considered lost, the life-size, two-ton statue was identified in a Chicago suburb in 1988. The asp in Cleopatra's hand has been broken off. It is currently in the National Museum of American Art, Washington, D.C. See Romare Bearden and Harry Henderson, *A History of*

African American Artists from 1792 to the Present (New York: Pantheon Books, 1993), pp. 73–75; see also Marilyn Richardson, "Edmonia Lewis' The Death of Cleopatra: Myth and Identity," *The International Review of African American Art*, vol. 12, no. 2 (Summer 1995): 36–52.

37. Rubinstein, *American Women Sculptors*, p. 54.

38. Ibid.

39. E. L. Thornton, "The Cancer of Prejudice—Eating Deep Into American Character," *The New York Age*, May 23, 1891, p. 1.

40. Letter to Messrs S. H. Kaufman, Edward Clark, F. D. McGuire, from Frederick Douglass, November 3, 1891. (Photocopy from the Butcher Collection, Butler Library, Columbia University, New York. Photocopies provided by Dr. Philip and Mrs. Ruth Butcher of Maryland.)

41. *La Parisienne* is in the Howard University Gallery of Art Collection, Washington, D.C.

42. "Wife of Thomas Walker, Dead—Achieved Fame as Artist, Had Picture Accepted by French Salon," *Washington Tribune*, June 14, 1929, p. 1.

43. William Francis O'Donnell, "Meta Vaux Warrick, Sculptor of Horrors: The Negro Girl Whose Products Are Being Compared to Rodin's," *The World Today*, November 1907, p. 1139.

44. Judith Nina Kerr, "Meta Vaux Warrick Fuller (1877–1968)," in *Black Women in America, An Historical Encyclopedia*, Darlene Clark Hine, ed. (Brooklyn, NY: Carlson Publishing, Inc., 1993): p. 471.

45. Arna Alexander Bontemps and Jacqueline Fonvielle-Bontemps, *Forever Free: Art by African American Women, 1862–1980* (Alexandria, VA: Stephenson, 1980), p. 9.

46. Kerr, "Meta Vaux Warrick Fuller," p. 471.

47. Ibid., p. 472.

48. James A. Porter, *Modern Negro Art* (New York: Dryden Press, 1943, reprint 1969), p. 218, dates this work as 1917, bronze, although the work appears to be plaster and has the hand pointing out. All other sources that include it in discussions use the date 1914: Elsa Honig Fine, *The Afro-American Artist: A Search for Identity* (New York: Holt, Rinehart and Winston, 1973), p. 76, illustrates the bronze work as plaster; Mary Schmidt Campbell, "Introduction" in David Driskell et al., *Harlem Renaissance Art of Black America* (New York: The Studio Museum in Harlem and Harry N. Abrams, 1987), p. 27. At the time of submission of this essay for publication, the author had been unable to obtain additional information regarding the date from The Schomburg Center for Research in Black Culture, New York, where the work is housed.

Judith Nina Kerr "God-given Work: The Life and Times of Sculptor Meta Warrick Fuller, 1877–1968" (PhD diss., University of Massachusetts, 1986, has provided an in-depth discussion of this work with communications between Fuller and the committee beginning in 1921. As she states: "Meta gave the name *The Awakening of Ethiopia* to the foot-high statuette that she sent to the America's Making Festival. She had toyed with the idea of doing a piece on the theme of "The Rise of Ethiopia" since her brief collaboration with Freeman Murray. But during the intervening years, her concept of it had evolved from a tribute to the modern African state to a celebration of the new intellectual vitality she sensed in black America. . . . The cultural "renaissance" that Meta sensed unfolding reminded her of another brilliant period in black history—that of the Negro kings of Egypt. Thus, she used an Egyptian motif in *The Awakening of Ethiopia* to symbolize the American of African descent who, in her words, "was awakening, gradually unwinding the bandages of his past and looking out on life again, expectant, but unafraid." (pp. 260–261). This statement was, according to Kerr, written by Fuller to Mrs. W. P. Hedden, October 5, 1921, as she was conceptualizing the completion of the work for the America's Making Festival (p. 405).

49. James Weldon Johnson, *Black Manhattan*, with a preface by Allan H. Spear (New York: Atheneum, 1969), pp. 283–84.

50. The writer has been unable to determine when the second bronze life-size work was created and why the hand, in the original statuette pointing out, is now closed and placed against the thigh. Research is ongoing to determine the change of its position and when it was re-created.

51. David Driskell in *Harlem Renaissance Art of Black America*, p. 108.

52. Kerr, "God-given Work," p. 261.

53. "The Talking Skull" was a story that Meta Fuller told to her children about a young tribesman who wanders out upon the desert waste. Stumbling upon what at first seems to be a large stone, he discovers it to be a human skull and speaking aloud, he exclaims, "I wonder how you came here." To his amazement, the skull answers, "Tongue brought me here and if you are not careful, Tongue will bring you here." The young tribesman runs back to his village, and eager to astonish everyone, including the chief, tells of his adventure. The villagers go with the boy to see this 'talking skull', but hating liars, warn him that if it does not talk, he will lose his head. No matter how the boy pleads, not one word will the skull utter. Angered at the thought of having been deceived, the chief beheads the boy with a single stroke of his blade. Finally, when everyone is gone, the skull cries out in a loud voice: "Tongue brought me here and I told you if you were not careful, Tongue would bring you here." Kerr, "God-given Work," p. 308.

54. Nathan Huggins, *Harlem Renaissance* (New York: Oxford University Press, 1973), p. 195, cited in Kerr, p. 4. She notes that Huggins uses Lewis Mumford's term "custodians of culture" to define the white art establishment in relation to the black artist's role in the early twentieth century, in "God-given Work," notes, p. 363.

55. Porter, *Modern Negro Art*, p. 92.

56. Leslie King-Hammond, "May Howard Jackson," *Black Women In America: An Historical Encyclopedia*, p. 624.

57. Porter, *Modern Negro Art*, pp. 92–93.

58. King-Hammond, "May Howard Jackson," p. 624.

59. Walter Dyson, *Howard University, The Capstone of Negro Education, A History: 1867–1940* (Washington, DC: The Graduate School, 1941), pp. 141–142.

60. *The Crisis* (October, 1931), vol. 4, no. 10, p. 351.

61. Porter, *Modern Negro Art*, p. 109.

62. Ibid.

63. Richard Barksdale and Keneth Kinnamon, *Black Writers of America, A Comprehensive Anthology* (New York: Macmillan Publishing Co., 1972), p. 573.

64. Alain Locke, "The Legacy of the Ancestral Arts," in *The New Negro*, ed. Alain Locke (New York: Albert and Charles Boni, 1925; reprint, New York: Atheneum, 1969), pp. 264, 266.

65. Gary A. Reynolds, "An Experiment in Inductive Service," in *Against the Odds: African American Artists and the Harmon Foundation* (Newark, NJ: The Newark Museum, 1989), pp. 27–29.

66. In 1927 forty-one black artists applied for the awards in fine arts; the 1928 awards were selected from among 102 applicants; in 1929 eighty-seven artists applied; seventy-three works were seen in sixteen cities across the country during the 1930 and early 1931 traveling exhibitions. See Gary A. Reynolds and Beryl J. Wright, *Against the Odds: African American Artists and the Harmon Foundation*, pp. 27–43.

67. Lynn Miller and Sally Swenson, *Lives and Works: Talks with Women Artists* (Metuchen, NJ: The Scarecrow Press, 1981), p. 165.

68. Blossom S. Kirschenbaum, "Nancy Elizabeth Prophet, Sculptor," *Sage: A Scholarly Journal on Black Women*, vol. 4, no. 1 (Spring 1987): 47.

69. Ibid., p. 46.

70. Ibid.

71. Ibid.

72. Rubinstein, *American Women Sculptors*, p. 244.

73. Countee Cullen, "Elizabeth Prophet: Sculptress," *Opportunity*, July 1930, p. 205.

74. Cited in Bontemps, *Forever Free*, p. 28.

75. Ibid., from Leslie King-Hammond, "Prophet," *Four from Providence*, ed. Lawrence F. Sykes, ed. Four From Providence (Providence: Rhode Island College and Rhode Island Black Heritage Society, 1978), p. 9.

76. Cullen, "Elizabeth Prophet: Sculptress," p. 205.

77. Cited in Rubinstein, *American Women Sculptors*, p. 245, from "Nancy Prophet Wins Success as Sculptress," unidentified news item from library, Rhode Island School of Design, July 8, 1932, p. 10.

78. Porter, *Modern Negro Art*, p. 139.

79. Rubinstein, *American Women Sculptors*, p. 245.

80. Kirschenbaum, "Nancy Elizabeth Prophet, Sculptor," p. 49.

81. According to Kirschenbaum, Edward Carley had first met Prophet when she came to see the Commissioner of Education looking for a teaching position. He dates this acquaintance before 1958. Not available for an appointment, Carley spoke with Prophet about her recent breakdown, and he determined that she was a somewhat dislocated person. When his wife was pregnant with their fourth child, Carley brought Prophet to dinner at their large house. He could not afford to hire her, but she took a room on the second floor and stayed with the family to help out. Weekends she went back to the Benedict Street house she had inherited from her father. Carley also stated that she washed the floors about every day. She could cook all sorts of dishes and cakes, and decorate them. She made a plaster-of-Paris mask of one of the children. Finally, his wife had to ask Prophet to leave. But she would still drop in at Carley's office once in a while to talk, or she would call on the telephone. See Kirschenbaum, "Nancy Elizabeth Prophet, Sculptor," p. 49.

82. Cedric Dover, writing in 1960, indicated the following: "those who took pride in Nancy Elizabeth Prophet's successes will have to reconcile themselves to her loss. She writes that 'an anthropologist must certainly know' she is 'not a negro.' Perhaps he does—and a little more as well." *American Negro Art* (New York: New York Graphic Society, 1960), p. 56.

83. Deidre L. Bibby, *Augusta Savage and the Art Schools of Harlem*, exh. cat. (New York: The Schomburg Center for Research in Black Culture, 1988), p. 12, and Rubinstein, *American Women Sculptors*, p. 283.

84. Bibby, *Augusta Savage*, p. 12.

85. Ibid.

86. See *The New York World*, May 10, May 12, and May 20, 1923, and Romare Bearden and Harry Henderson, *Six Black Masters of American Art* (New York: Doubleday, 1973) pp. 85–88, 95.

87. Rubinstein, *American Women Sculptors*, p. 285.

88. Ibid., p. 260.

89. Ibid.

90. DeWitt S. Dykes, Jr., "Savage, Augusta Christine," in *Notable American Women: The Modern Period, A Biographical Dictionary*, ed. Barbara Sherman et al. (Cambridge, MA: The Belknap Press of Harvard University Press, 1980), p. 629.

91. Photocopy of article provided by Miriam Matthews to the author, December 30, 1976, from Golden State Mutual Insurance Company Files, Los Angeles, California. Also see Miriam Matthews, "Beulah Ecton Woodard, (1895–1955)," *Black Women In America Encyclopedia*, p. 1281.

92. Harmon Foundation Files, Personal information submitted by Beulah Woodard, dated July 25, 1938. Collection of the Manuscript Division, Library of Congress, Washington, D.C.

93. Ibid.

94. Matthews, "Beulah Ecton Woodard," p. 1282.

95. Ibid.

96. Selma Burke, interview with the author, March 1970; *Black Women in America Encyclopedia*, Tritobia Hayes Benjamin, "Selma Hortense Burke," p. 191.

97. Jacqueline Trescott, "Sculptor Selma Burke: A Life of Art for Art," *The Washington Post*, March 17, 1975, pp. B-1, 2.

98. Cited in James G. Spady, "Three to the Universe: Selma Burke, Roy DeCarava, Tom Feelings," in *Nine to the Universe: Black Artists* (Philadelphia: Black History Museum Publishers, 1983), p. 17.

99. Selma Burke, interview with the author, March 1970.

100. Benjamin, p. 193.

101. Jones credits Jeff Donaldson, artist, art historian, and dean of the College of Fine Arts, Howard University, with the appellation of "Grande Dame of African American Art" during the retrospective exhibition held at the Howard University Gallery of Art in 1972. Jones reminded him that Laura Wheeler Waring had preceded her as a painter. To this comment Donaldson responded that Waring's body of work was primarily portraiture, but that Jones's oeuvre included portraits, landscapes, cityscapes, seascapes, street scenes, etc. And, when looking at the lineage of women in the arts, our first women artists, save Annie Walker, were all sculptors. From a series of interviews with the artists in 1986, and subsequent discussions throughout the years. All direct quotes are from those sessions.

102. Tritobia Benjamin, "Selma Burke," *Black Women in America Encyclopedia*, p. 193.

103. Rubinstein, *American Women Sculptors*, p. 297.

104. Lois Mailou Jones, interview with the author, 1986.

105. James A. Porter, Introduction, *Lois Mailou Jones: Peintures 1937–1951* (Tourcoing, France: Presses Georges Frere, 1952), n.p.

106. A. J. Philpot, *Boston Globe*, February 3, 1939.

107. *The Christian Science Monitor*, February 2, 1939.

108. Tritobia Hayes Benjamin, *The Life and Art of Lois Mailou Jones* (San Francisco: Pomegranate Artbooks, 1994), p. 79.

109. Jones received a total of five grants under the title "The Black Visual Arts" between 1968 and 1976. She conducted research in Haiti, America, and eleven countries in Africa. The second grant, for interviewing contemporary African artists, took her to Sudan, Kenya, Ethiopia, Zaire, Nigeria, Ghana, Ivory Coast, Liberia, Sierra Leone, Senegal, and Dahomey between April and July of 1970.

110. The venues for "The World of Lois Mailou Jones" exhibition included The Meridian International Center, Washington, D.C.; Peachtree Gallery and Hammonds House Galleries, Atlanta; The Huber Arts Center, Shippensburg, Pennsylvania; Delta Arts Center, Winston-Salem, North Carolina; California Museum of African American Art, Los Angeles; Hampton University Museum, Hampton, Virginia; The Schomburg Center for Research in Black Culture, New York; Wichita Museum of Art, Wichita, Kansas; J.C. Penney Headquarters Gallery, Dallas, Texas; Swarthmore College, Swarthmore, Pennsylvania; Terra Museum of American Art, Chicago; Louisiana Arts & Science Center, Baton Rouge, Louisiana; The Corcoran Gallery of Art, Washington, D.C.; The University Art Gallery, University of Pittsburgh; The Walt Whitman Cultural Art Center, Camden, New Jersey.

111. Bontemps, *Forever Free*, p. 36.

112. In 1948 Lois Jones and her lifelong friend Céline Tabary, whom she met in France in 1937, organized The Little Paris Studio. Composed of art teachers in the public school system and in higher education, the participants met weekly in a group for criticism and encouragement. Each artist completed six compositions within an academic season, forming the basis of an exhibition in the spring. These annual shows, anticipated by the Washington art community, included Lois Jones, Alma Thomas, Delilah Pierce, Richard Dempsey, and other Washington artists.

113. Bontemps, *Forever Free*, p. 37.

114. Lowery Stokes Sims, "Alma Thomas," *Black Women in America Encyclopedia*, p. 1166.

115. Bearden and Henderson, *A History of African American Artists*, p. 453.

116. Lilian Burwell, *Hilda Wilkinson Brown, A Washington Artist Rediscovered*, exh. cat. (Washington, DC: Howard University, 1983), p. 1.

117. Ibid., p. 2.

118. Key's drawings were featured on the cover of *The Crisis* magazine's November and December 1927, and June 1928 issues. The drawing *Lift Every Voice and Sing* won *The Crisis* magazine Krigwa Cover Contest's first-prize Amy Spingarn Award of $150. Two other illustrations were featured in the February 1928 issue. Her last four drawings were sold to *The Crisis* in 1929; three were featured as cover illustrations for the January, February, and October issues; the fourth was used as an illustration for a short story. See Britton, "Conditions for Black Women Artists," pp. 37, 49, 50.

119. Ibid., pp. 38–39.

120. Ibid., p. 40.

121. Bontemps, *Forever Free*, p. 68.

122. Freida High Tesfagiorgis, "Afrofemcentrism and Its Fruition in the Art of Elizabeth Catlett and Faith Ringgold," *Sage: A Scholarly Journal on Black Women*, vol. 4, no. 1 (Spring 1987), p. 28.

123. Samella S. Lewis, *The Art of Elizabeth Catlett* (Claremont, CA: Hancraft Studios, 1984), p. 14.

124. Ibid.

125. Ibid., p. 17.

126. Tesfagiorgis, "Afrofemcentrism," p. 28.

127. Ibid.

128. Ibid.

129. Elton Fax, "Four Rebels in Art," *Freedom Ways*, vol. 4 (Spring 1964), p. 217.

130. Richard J. Powell, "Face to Face: Elizabeth Catlett's Graphic Work," in *Elizabeth Catlett, Works on Paper, 1944–1992*, exh. cat. (Hampton, VA: Hampton University Museum, 1993), p. 52.

131. Bontemps, *Forever Free*, pp. 31–32.

132. "Art Changes Things: The Art and Activism of Georgette Seabrooke Powell," exh. brochure (Washington, DC: Anacostia Museum, 1995), n.p.

133. "The Harlem Hospital Correspondence," photocopy of material circulated by the Anacostia Museum during this exhibition which also provided transcriptions of selected correspondence related to the mural project. For further information on the files and the communications, see the Louis Block Papers, Collection of the Archives of American Art, Washington, D.C.

134. Rosemary Stevenson, "Margaret Taylor Goss Burroughs," *Black Women In America Encyclopedia*, p. 198.

135. Bontemps, *Forever Free*, p. 64.

136. Leronne Bennett, Introduction, *Images of a Turbulent Decade 1963–1973* (New York: The Studio Museum in Harlem, 1985), p. 9.

137. Leslie King-Hammond, "Search for an Aesthetic Identity: The Art and Politics of the Black Artist in the 1960s," in *Selected Essays: Art and Artists from the Harlem Renaissance to the 1980s* (Atlanta: National Black Arts Festival, 1988), p. 53.

138. Bontemps, *Forever Free*, p. 39.

139. This term was coined by Freida High Tesfagiorgis in 1984 to designate what she saw as a "unique assertiveness-consciousness in African American women—Black feminism appearing much too incomplete." For an extended discussion of Faith Ringgold in this context, see Tesfagiorgis, "Afrofemcentrism," pp. 25–32.

140. Early African American scholars who researched and published information on African American art and artists are: Freeman H. M. Murray, *Emancipation and the Freed in American Sculpture: A Study in Interpretation* (Washington, DC: Published by author, 1916); Benjamin G. Brawley, *The Negro in Literature and Art in the United States* (New York: Dodd, Mead, 1934); Alain L. Locke, *The Negro in Art: A Pictorial Record of the Negro Artist and of the Negro Theme in Art and Negro Art, Past and Present* (Washington, DC: Associates in Negro Folk Education, 1940); James A. Porter, *Modern Negro Art* (New York: Dryden Press, 1943).

Debra Priestly, *Patoka #10 Dried Apples*, 1994, acrylic pastel on birch, 32½″ × 24½″.

AFRICAN AMERICAN WOMEN ARTISTS
Into the Twenty-First Century

· · · · · · · · · · · · · · · · · · ·

LOWERY STOKES SIMS

*I am an artist who is African American. My work is
universal and specific, drawn from my personal experiences,
as well as from a collective spirit. It acknowledges and
expresses the human condition as an African American
woman expresses it. It is how I see my family, my culture,
my world, and how I fit into those contexts.*[1]

Pat Ward Williams

THERE IS no question that African American women
artists have come into their own over the last three decades. In the context of the civil rights and women's movements, they have been afforded a wider variety of
opportunities to showcase and market their work, and
have begun to receive the critical attention they have
long deserved. But despite these advances, the perception of African American women artists remains vague
and unfocused. In her discussion of a theoretical approach to African American women's literature, Valerie
Smith notes that the experiences of African American
women have not been fully recognized as distinct from
those currently defined as exclusively racial (and therefore dominated by African American men) or gendered
(and therefore dominated by Caucasian women). This,
she concludes, has thwarted the development of a more
"totalizing" comprehension of African American women
within American society.[2]

From the first moment that African American artists
appeared on the American art scene, they were prepared to
compete. They were trained in standard European-based
art curricula—and even excelled within those precepts.
They also sought to imprint their unique experience and
heritage on their artmaking. This essay will survey the
artistic enterprise of African American women visual artists over the last three decades, and identify some of the
recurring issues and themes that have been manifest in
their work. This is meant to be a preliminary discussion
towards a "totalizing" comprehension of this group of
artists that would help demonstrate their integral position within American culture, and indicate their unique
potential for assuming leadership at the forefront of
American arts and letters in the next century.

While literary, cultural, and social history fields have
generated important studies of African American women,
there have been relatively few projects that have sur-
veyed the creativity of African American women artists.[3]
The 1980 exhibition, "Forever Free: Art by African
American Women 1862–1980," organized by Jacqueline
Fonvielle-Bontemps, was a groundbreaking effort in its
presentation of a more "global" and conceptual approach
to African American women artists.[4] In addition to providing the most complete survey of African American
women's art to date, essays by Roslyn A. Walker, Jacqueline Fonvielle-Bontemps, and Arna Alexander Bontemps
located the historical precedents of black women's creativity in Africa. This illuminated issues of gender and
women's role in society, and the history and reception of
African American women artists in this country. The essays also covered issues of identity and images of African
Americans in American art, and manifestations of cultural continuity in the use of materials and techniques.

In 1987 *Sage: A Scholarly Journal on Black Women*
published an issue called "Artists and Artisans," the first
special issue on black women artists ever to appear in a
scholarly journal. For over a decade, *Sage* has been the
source of important original research on African American women, including visual artists.

In 1988 I published a study of African American
women artists involved in performance art, which

revealed additional questions and issues: the question of artistic purpose, and what forms would best serve their creative outlets and at the same time enliven and broaden the audience for their artistic expression.[5] This project led to the 1988 exhibition, "Art as A Verb: The Evolving Continuum," which I curated with Leslie King Hammond, in which the work of African American artists working in performance, video, and installation was explored.[6]

That same year, the exhibition "Autobiography: In Her Own Image"—organized by Howardena Pindell at INTAR Latin American Gallery in New York City—dealt with the challenges faced by women of color in defining themselves against racist and sexist roles and images imposed from the outside.[7] Although this project included a diverse group of women—among them Emma Amos, Margo Machida, Kay WalkingStick, Alison Saar, Young Soon Min, and Ana Mendieta—it demonstrated how women of color in this society, despite many differences, face a similar lack of a "totalizing" definition because of the erasures that exist when race (or non-Caucasian ethnicity) and gender were examined in the usual way.

The most recent survey of African American women artists is the 1995 compilation *Gumbo Ya Ya: Anthology of Contemporary African American Women Artists.* Initiated and published by Midmarch Arts Press, it is a survey of over two hundred African American women artists currently living and working in various mediums. The individual essays on each artist were written by a varied group of writers, critics, and art historians, and provided an overview of the world and work of African American women artists. In the words of Leslie King Hammond, it is "a collective of voices, which, through their commingling synergy, vibrantly explore, challenge, invent, remember, reconfigure, innovate, improvise, act out, act up, cut up, piece, and perform their responses to the American experience in a complex 'exchange and re-exchange of ideas between groups.'"[8]

These are only a few of the art projects over the last three decades that have focused on African American women. We can also count innumerable exhibitions, monographs on individual artists, catalogue essays and entries, encyclopedia projects, and journal articles. Together this material provides the basis for a more complete study of African American women's presence within the art world. In this context the exhibition project, "Bearing Witness: Contemporary Works by African American Women Artists," organized by Spelman College, is an important rung in the development of the study of African American women artists. That Spelman College has played a key role in the education of African American women artists and scholars is demonstrated by the inclusion of several Spelman students, alumnae, and faculty who have been included in many of the projects discussed above: Mary Elizabeth Prophet, Yvonne Parks Catchings, Jenelsie Walden Holloway, Varnette Honeywood, Charnelle Holloway, Lynn Marshall Linnemeier, Tina Dunkley, Pearl Cleage, Akua McDaniel, and Jontyle Theresa Robinson.

> When I was child, I hid these strange things I'd see and feel and now I'm puttin' them in wood . . . and just about everything I touch is Africa . . . I must claim some of that spirit and soul.[9]
>
> Bessie Harvey

In the 1980s and 1990s the receptivity afforded African American women artists and their work was determined by two distinct, but complementary, critical modes. The first was multiculturalism, which recognized the co-existence of African American, Asian American, Latina American and Native American cultural identities with that of Europe; the second was deconstructivism, which postulated a dismantling of dominant Eurocentric, male values, and world views, through the presentation of female and non-white value systems. These analytic frameworks provided a context within which to examine the specific issues raised in and by African American women's art: the continuity with traditional African practices and innovation; the role of the artist within the community; the creation of images to counteract the particularly pernicious tradition of negative African American stereotypes in this society; and the examination of their identities as women, which would affirm their own art historical genealogy, and pave the way to the future.

The uniqueness of black women's creativity in America is demonstrated when we consider the role of the arts in traditional African societies. Roslyn Walker comments upon their functionality:

> Art is the visual expression of very profound beliefs held by the society in which it was created and *used*. In African society art is used in the exercise of religions, socialization, education, political leadership and for entertainment.[10]

While men tended to do the carving and smithing, women made pottery for domestic use.[11] On this side of the Atlantic, however, not only did African American women artists work in the medium of easel painting (Annie Walker being one of the first to do so), but they were also a dominant force in carved sculpture among African American artists in the nineteenth century. From Edmonia Lewis to Meta Warrick Fuller, Elizabeth Prophet, Elizabeth Catlett, Geraldine McCullough, Barbara Chase Riboud, and Alison Saar, African American women continue to be prominent practitioners in this medium.

Where women did make sculpture in traditional African societies (for example in the ancient Kuba/ Bushongo kingdom in Zaire), it was modeled rather than carved. This pattern connects sculpture with the more utilitarian legacy of domestic pottery, which was executed by African women. Similar work is still carried out in the clay sculptures of Jackson Jarvis, Winnie Owens Hart, and Arlene Burke Morgan, whose work mediates the notions of ceramics as vessels and sculpture. These clay sculptures by contemporary women demonstrate the legacy of textural sense and formal adroitness that marked a continuity of African American female creativity from the first diaspora.

This seeming inversion of mediums on the part of African American women can also be seen as a disruption of tradition. Certainly in terms of patterns of patronage and the place of art in the community, there is a shift to a more isolated museological context for art that is distinct from the way art is more integrated into daily life in Africa. Arna Bontemps, however, suggests that these developments may actually not be a break with tradition, but another form of continuity. He has postulated that:

> the functional significance in art in African societies was as likely, or more likely, to survive the trauma of enslavement than clearly observable aspects of the art itself. Thus, it is not illogical to assume that black women in America continued to manifest a strong aesthetic affinity for tactile perception and sculptural form.[12]

This notion of tactility as a transmitter of cultural values can also be demonstrated in the work of African American women in other mediums. Howardena Pindell, for example, began to incorporate sewing into her paintings—at times actually cutting the canvases into stripes and reassembling the strips by interweaving them and stitching them—because she was attracted to "the internal geometry" and "terrain quality" it gave the surface.[13] Even in the work of women known primarily as painters—Emma Amos, Varnette Honeywood, Philemona Williamson, Nanette Carter, Mary Lovelace O'Neal, and Debra Priestly—we can observe an approach to the surface that is definitely textural either in its presentation of added elements or in the patternistic design elements in the composition.

The introduction of elements associated with "women's work"—appliqué, stitching, beading, quilting—effects an inversion or perversion of easel painting, which has historically been considered the province of white males. As Faith Ringgold has observed:

> I thought about the association of painting with the Western tradition. As long as you're painting, you're going to be influenced by European traditions. So I moved into fabric and the soft sculpture to get away from that altogether. A second reason was that I wanted to draw on the strength of my own heritage in sculpture and in cloth.[14]

The explicit intentions of these artists indicate an artistic strategy similar to that of African American women artists who work in performance art and installation.

These modes of expression were found to serve not only as a bridge between the seclusion of the artist's studio, the museum and gallery, and the realities of the world at large, but also as a means through which they could express and define themselves in a particularly compatible context.

Such transgressive strategies allow African American women artists (like many Euro-American women) to side-step expectations of specialization and notions of "high" art, and to combine and incorporate mediums and modes not necessarily or readily embraced by "high" art circles.[15] That such activities involve a combination of art forms, and insinuated aspects of "body arts" definitely suggests a connection with African antecedents, where the arts are often seen in concert, not just as isolated phenomena. The early work of Joyce Scott, for example, comes to mind, in which the artist not only created jewelry and apparel, but organized "performances" of their display within environments she also created.

An important aspect of this rupture of art world hierarchies and categorizations has been the working relationship between trained African American artists and their self-taught counterparts in the African American community. The most prevalent aspect of that relationship has been mentoring—in which parents, relatives, and neighbors, using personal means of creative expression, served as role models to artists without access to or contact with the art establishment. Sculptor Beverly Buchanan has specifically remarked on the impact of observing her father's woodworking when she was younger. Buchanan now constructs shack sculptures as memorials to the structures that have been the site of so much of African American rural life. She also incorporates decorative elements with found objects that mimic the ornamentation of the space around the home.[16]

Most interesting about these interactions are the special relationships between mothers and daughters, which resulted in particularly rich artistic collaborations. In the early 1970s Faith Ringgold worked with her mother Willi Posey on a series of works inspired by traditional Asian wall hangings called tongas. Posey stitched the fabric frames within which Ringgold painted images and words of poems or thoughts arranged vertically to mimic Japanese or Chinese calligraphy. Later Ringgold adapted the technique of quilting in her painting, combining sewn and appliqué work with painting on canvas. Joyce Scott has also worked collaboratively with her mother Elizabeth Scott, an inventive and expressionistic quilter. Mother and daughter are the third and fourth generation of quilters in the Scott family and combine traditional forms with innovative and personal statements. Joyce Scott also incorporates a wide range of folk craft traditions (which she has studied all over the world) into her beaded sculpture and art-wear.

Betye Saar and her daughter, sculptor Alison Saar, are academically-trained artists who work separately and together on various art projects. Like Ringgold and Scott, they too have found a path for their work that mediates the boundaries between "folk art" and "high art." The elder Saar's particular skill in manipulating found objects has sustained her creativity for over thirty years. In the 1960s and 1970s she created assemblages in boxes filled with vintage photographs, greeting cards, and black memorabilia, which transformed heirlooms from the community into elements in her potent political statements. Alison Saar's sculptural works proclaim a folk inspiration more directly both in subject matter and in technique. What the younger Saar particularly admires about self-taught artists is that they continue to work "even though no one is out there saying 'So go ahead, make art and you can be a famous artist.' They're just doing it for reasons that are internal and they really have a message."[17]

Martha Jackson Jarvis's work demonstrates how continuity with Africa is expressed not only in technical matters, but also in conceptual ones. The basis of her sculpture and installation work is the recycling of pottery shards, which recall burial practices where broken crockery (symbolizing a rupture with this world) is placed on African American grave sites to provide for the soul in the afterlife.[18] She indicates that her works are "reconstructed vehicles of communication, conduits through which forces flow" and these forces emanate from the "powers that affected life in its broadest aspects in society."[19]

A similar relationship with African traditions can be seen in the work of Renée Stout, who brings African American traditions of charms and divinations to her work. Stout draws on a rich well of folklore and wisdom from the Caribbean, the southern United States (especially Louisiana), and even the urban areas of the north to create sculptural works that are both fetishistic and evocative. Michael Harris has discussed at length the affinity of Stout's work with African medicinal and prophylactic practices, specifically as manifest in the *nkisi* figures of the Kongo people of Zaire.[20] Stout's work, like that of Jackson Jarvis and Betye and Alison Saar, signifies what Harris describes as the African American woman artist reclaiming her place in her community as "magician, a root worker, and a revivalist, recharging particular cultural sensitivities."[21] Particularly in the making of objects and in installation work, this predilection is a strong current in contemporary African American women's art.

Whether we like it or not, we, Negro artists, are part of a world wide struggle to change a situation that is unforgivable and untenable [today]. Children can no longer be denied the right to food, to clothing and to education . . . we must search to find our place as Negro artists, in the advance toward a richer fulfillment of life on a global basis. Neither the Negro artists nor American art can afford to take an isolated position.[22]

Elizabeth Catlett

In the context of African American art history, the social relevance of the art of African American artists has often been adjudicated on the basis of its stylistic characteristics. An indication that figuration is more prevalent than abstraction among African American artists as a whole is evidenced by the fact that the majority of the artists in this exhibition work representationally. African American artists such as sculptors Geraldine McCullough and Barbara Chase Riboud, and painter/printmaker Nanette Carter, who work in abstract styles, continue, therefore, to struggle for recognition, facing resistance from certain camps of black self-image-making, which perceive abstraction as being outside an authentic black identity. Although an extensive analysis of the abstract work of these artists is not possible here, it should be pointed out that such assumptions should be reconsidered in light of the fact that abstraction is an integral component of African art, both in the consideration of figuration and in the decorative appointments of traditional forms.

During the 1960s and 1970s, African American artists began to ally themselves with their communities as part of the attempt to define a new, assertive African American identity. African American women artist's groups—Women Students and Artists for Black Art Liberation (WSABAL) and Where We At Black Women Artists, in particular—attempted to make the visual arts more relevant to the realities of the African American experience and re-establish a more direct relationship with the community. Arna Bontemps has reaffirmed the key role that African American women artists have played in sustaining their communities:

Black women, by virtue of their statistical presence and economic importance . . . were undeniably essential to the ultimate survival of the black community. It follows, therefore, that black women—through the intellectual aesthetic choices they made and the traditions they helped preserve—played a vital role in developing those meaningful forms of self-expression by which black people in America have managed to survive two and a half centuries of chattel slavery and nearly half a millennium of racial oppression.[23]

The modes of representation brought to bear on the political situation of African American artists is particularly seen in the work of Faith Ringgold. While her work has covered a wide range of political subject matter—from mapping the destructiveness of racial strife in this country, to the paradoxes of racism in the context of technological achievement, to the exclusion of African Americans from mainstream art history—her message has been rendered more accessible by her adoption of a strong, direct figuration and poster-like organization of images and text. Ringgold would later use performance art in a similar way to make work that "the community could relate to easily."[24]

Ringgold also devised an approach to color she called "black light" to convey racial values in her work. She noted:

> When you do a lot with white . . . you may lose your sensitivity to other colors. The white gathers the light. . . . Black art must use its own color to create its own light since that color is the most immediate black truth. . . . [B]lack art must not depend on light or light contrast in order to express its blackness, either in principle or fact.[25]

What Ringgold alludes to here is an aesthetic sensibility analyzed by Freida High Tesfagiorgis in her study of Afrofemcentrism: colors, rhythms, and textures having an "Afro-American cultural base."[26] This concern demonstrates how the presentation of positive African and African American images has been integral to the African American woman artist's perception of her role within society. No mere polemicist, she is also an affirmer, a reclaimer of images that will counteract the negative ones of African Americans in this society, which in the words of Albert Boime have been used to "shape ideas, define social attitudes and fix stereotypes."[27]

In their endeavors to create positive images, African American artists have had a pervasive concern for the liberation of the minds and hearts of African American people. In the particular case of African American women, the issue of image is inevitably caught up in questions raised by the fabled dichotomy about the comeliness of Sheba (black *but* comely versus black *and* comely). Art historian Judith Wilson has noted that as a bi-racial African American woman, she has had to mediate conflicting messages from the outside world about who and what she is.[28] This has involved a consideration of "the complexity of the ties between . . . who we think we are . . . who society tells us we are . . . how we see ourselves."[29] Women are often the purveyors of a culture's notion of beauty and desirability; however, in this country, African American women were set apart from that sphere in relation to women of European descent. That such a fate was also shared by Asians, Latinos, and Native Americans is a marker of the economic, social, and political history of this country that need not be detailed here. But the question has to arise: What kind of images would be made by women whose very physical existence was, until very recently, considered an anathema in the halls of fine artistic creation?

Certainly the creation of self-affirming images that celebrate the beauty of black women has been an overriding concern and has informed the work of artists such as Lois Mailou Jones, Elizabeth Catlett, and Varnette Honeywood. Another strategy has been the rehabilitation of stereotypical imagery. Betye Saar's rescue of the image of Aunt Jemima from the fringes of African American consciousness is a prime example. By placing this image of shame and degradation at the center of the discourse, Saar also reclaimed the sexualized body and persona of the African American woman, defying European standards of beauty, and providing a vehicle for discussion of body politics among African American women. This discourse had already been anticipated in the work of Elizabeth Catlett, who in the 1940s and 1950s carved voluptuous women drawn from African and ancient Mexican prototypes, which celebrated an affirmative and fertile female prototype.[30]

Joyce Scott used her performance series, *The Thunder Thigh Revue*, to celebrate black women's bodies as signifiers of an alternative bodily aesthetic, bringing issues of identity and body politics from the arena of the personal to the public. Such conceptualizations mine the subversive potential of seemingly passive stances and challenge hegemonic notions of female beauty and desirability. Scott also mined nineteenth-century history to find the story of Sarah Braatman, the steatopygous Hottentot woman, who was paraded around Europe and exhibited like a side-show attraction. Scott's strategies are even more powerful when seen within the totality of her work, which examines political issues such as apartheid, cultural imperialism, lynchings, and violence toward black women and children.

Lorna Simpson's work has presented the black female body in a number of situations: clothed, unclothed, in its entirety, or in component parts. While the focus of her work is memory, absence and obsession, Simpson's close attention to the black female body has also served to fetishize or celebrate aspects of it that have been denigrated, for example, hair texture. Simpson's purpose is not mere prurient display, but, as Amalia Mesa-Bains has noted, a co-option of the eroticized black female body in order to reclaim it and own it again.[31]

Simpson's use of photography is also a reminder of the role of that medium in the creation of positive black images over the last century and a half. In comparison to our knowledge of black images in paintings and sculpture produced by both white and African American artists in the nineteenth century, the awareness of photographic images that reveal the richness and depth and variety of the African American experience—especially that of women—is still lacking. Issues of market and demand determine the distribution and preservation of the photographic images of African Americans. The need to explore this history has been expressed by Deborah Willis.[32] We are fortunate to live in an era in which there is a growing awareness of this work because of artists such as Willis, Simpson, Carrie Mae Weems, and Pat Ward Williams. Williams reminds us that photography has proven to be a medium of intensely personal expressive potential for African American women artists, one that can be stretched, blown up, mounted, and installed in a variety of contexts.[33] The use of photography lends a particular graphic quality to their work, and demonstrates the degree to which such a medium—like performance—is imminently suited to the work of African American women artists.

> Like any politically disenfranchised group, Black women could not exist consciously until we began to name ourselves.[34]
>
> Gloria T. Hull and Barbara Smith

Over the last three decades African American women have had to balance the needs of the black liberation movement with issues raised in the context of the women's movement. Although the perception may be that African American women have been pressured to give priority to the politics of race to the exclusion of their own concerns as women, the political dynamics of American society with regard to race are perhaps more stark for African American women. Black women artists face unique burdens. The dilemma of the African American woman artist has been eloquently described by Howardena Pindell, who recalled her experiences when she first arrived in New York city and attempted to find her place in the art world:

> I was first told that my work wasn't black because it wasn't showing a certain kind of imagery, and then I was put down a bit for being a woman. . . . That meant I had to show in a white context, and that was a problem. . . . The only other approach was the women's movement. This was in the late 60s and early 70s. . . . I entered the "arena," so to speak, at this point.[35]

Adrian Piper has expressed similar views of what she calls the "the triple negation of colored women artists":

> A CWA [Colored Women Artist] who expresses political anger or who protests political injustice in her work may be represented as hostile or aggressive; or a CWA who deals with gender and sexuality in her work may be represented as seductive or manipulative; or a CWA who chooses to do her work rather than cultivate political connections within the art world may be seen as exotic or enigmatic. These are all familiar ways of stereotyping the African American "other." . . . CWAs . . . have to battle gender and race stereotypes simultaneously.[36]

Although a viable African American feminist literature has blossomed over the last twenty years, feminist issues are still perceived by African American men to be at odds with considerations of racial politics. Within the visual arts, furthermore, black feminist theorizing has lagged behind the fields of literature, cultural, and social studies. bell hook's book, *Art on My Mind: Visual Politics*, includes monographic essays and interviews with various black women artists. The focus of her collection, however, is more identity politics in general than African American feminist theory specifically.[37] The premier theory for African American woman artists is still Freida High Tesfagiorgis's philosophy of Afrofemcentrism, which suggests that African American women can accommodate both racial and feminist concerns in their work. In her 1987 article, "Afrofemcentrism and Its Fruition in the Art of Elizabeth Catlett and Faith Ringgold," Tesfagiorgis describes an "Afro-female-centered . . . consciousness in the visual arts," noting that this consciousness focuses on the black woman subject as depicted by the black woman artist.[38] Tesfagiorgis seeks to provide an alternative to mainstream conceptualizations of feminism, grounded as it is in Euro-American values, and, as Valerie Smith has noted, in classist presumptions.[39]

> Conceptually, Afrofemcentrism gives primacy to Black-female consciousness-assertiveness by centralizing and enlarging intrinsic values, inadvertently liberating 'Black feminism' from the blackenized periphery of feminism.[40]

The perspective of the Afrofemcentrist artist is to be:

> shaped by traditions of core Black culture and distinctive Afro-American female experience, both within and outside of that culture. Embracing African principles of natural harmony Afrofemcentrism affirms holistic existence while particularizing an assertive female stance.[41]

Tesfagiorgis alludes to a perspective on male/female relationships that speaks to a balance of dualities rather than a conflict of opposites. In her affirmation of a "holistic existence while particularizing an assertive female stance," Tesfagiorgis echoes Alice Walker's definition of a "womanist" position in the early 1980s:

> A black feminist or feminist of color. From the black folk expression of mothers to female children, "you acting womanish," i.e. like a woman. Usually referring to outrageous audacious courageous or willful behavior. Wanting to know more and in greater depth than is considered "good" for one. Being grown up . . . Responsible. In charge. Serious.[42]

Tesfagiorgis and Walker provide contexts for the philosophical approaches of many younger African American women who entered the art world in the 1980s. Lorna

Simpson, Carrie Mae Weems, Joyce Scott, Alison Saar, and Martha Jackson Jarvis embody this assertive womanhood as they strive to act as cultural conduits exploring mechanisms of memory, reclamation, and celebration. They draw on the strengths of the rich subject matter and conceptual themes from African American folk traditions and rituals that have managed to survive in the Americas. Their work, which examines issues that have determined the positioning of black women in this society as well as their imaging, seems to exemplify what Gwendolyn Knight Lawrence defines as feminist: "something to do with the intellectual, with philosophy, you're pulling into visual language what you should have and what's happened to you . . . it's more protest . . . [having] to do with the psyche . . . and being a woman."[43]

Tesfagiorgis also touches on the notion of culturally specific approaches to materials, and as noted earlier in this essay, a special tactile and multiple media sensibility seems to be a dominant factor in the work of African American women artists as a group.[44] She delineates guidelines for positive representations of African American women: as "subject as opposed to object," as "primary," as "active rather than passive," as being "imbued with aesthetics of the African continuum." Such representation should also convey "the sensitivity of Afro-American women's self-recorded realities."[45]

> The factors that distinguish Afrofemcentrism in Black art is the Black female perspective which insightfully enlarges and activates images of Black women, celebrating heroines and documenting herstory while integrally addressing political, social and personal issues.[46]

This task of creating an African American woman's artistic genealogy has been addressed by painter Vivian Browne who, in the late 1980s, created several paintings that featured depictions of single trees or forest areas. Close scrutiny of these works revealed that amid the brushstrokes that defined the branches and leaves, she had interjected quotations from African American women writers. Browne literally used the form of the tree to create a family tree that encompassed not only her visual arts heritage as an African American woman, but also her literary heritage. Such a motif also informs the art work of S. Diane Bogus, who establishes arboreal landscapes as arenas for African American female creativity. Valerie Maynard also turned to a tree motif for her collaborative installation and performance with Judith Jackson for the Atlanta Arts Festival in 1992.[47] Within this context we can also place the work of Maren Hassinger, who utilizes branches to create ceiling installations that evoke woodland groves, and unfurls great coils of wire to approximate trees and bushes.

Hassinger's secluded groves reflect a parallel interest on the part of African American women artists to create spaces that affirm their value system. Beverly Buchanan's shack sculptures, for example, celebrate the resiliency and endurance of African Americans in rural situations. Several of those sculptures and a series of photographs focus on the shack built by Mary Lou Furcron, a woman who also became known for the garden she planted around her home.[48] Betye and Alison Saar's collaborative spirit house, and Freida High Tesfagiorgis's ritual structures celebrate African American womanist spaces. Tesfagiorgis, like Buchanan, also extends the sphere of influence from the structure itself to the immediate surroundings as ritual spaces and gardens.

In her demand that African American women's art display "the sensitivity of Afro-American women's self-recorded realities," Tesfagiorgis touches on the subject of self-representation, which recent art criticism has questioned with regard to African American women. At issue is whether it may be assumed that the identity of the artist necessarily dictates the character of the work. Do race and gender automatically predetermine the subject and nature of the work of African American women? In her recent article on Edmonia Lewis, Kirsten Buick tackles the problem of autobiographical readings of African American women's art.[49] More than deciding any historical fact definitively, Buick raises issues about self-image and representation.

Autobiography has certainly been a potent source for the creativity of African American women as a whole. Philemona Williamson, for example, draws on her own childhood experiences for compositions whose almost playful subjects belie an underlying, haunting disequilibrium. Emma Amos, however, tackles the questions raised by Buick's inquiry more directly. If Edmonia Lewis engaged the strategies of representation in which the self was suppressed—which Buick asserts was a way for her to transcend gender and race and avoid stereotyping—then Emma Amos sets up a disjunction in her self-portraits, in which, fully recognizable, she resorts to strategies of transgendering and cross-dressing to assert her position in the art world on a par with great masters such as Matisse and Picasso. In the text of her 1993 exhibition at Art in General, Amos disputes the notion that artist and subject matter are synonymous in the work of African American artists, and points to the absence of such suppositions about white artists who can co-opt black subject matter without any assumptions about their identity being raised.[50]

If, as noted in the previous section, women are the purveyors of community values, then African American women have not only been the creators, but also the guardians of positive images and values in their work. As sculptor Renée Townsend observes, African American women artists:

> have always been able to capture humanness, thereby displaying their ability to communicate a feeling, an attitude, and a spirit within the work which bridges the gap between the real world (the spiritual world) and the physical world by activating that spirit in the works of art.[51]

But in order to do so effectively they have also had to reinvent their own images, long denigrated and devalued in this society. African American women stand at the threshold of the twenty-first century confident and assured, ready to fulfill promise and potential that has been garnered over the last four hundred years.

> Dialogue is something artists are continuously entering into. . . . For the artists, it's a never-ending quest for information and knowledge, for new ways of seeing and perceiving the environment in which we live. And through dialogue, we bridge the gaps between the past and the present, and project ourselves, our culture and all of humanity into the future.[52]
>
> Martha Jackson Jarvis

From Ringgold's and Amos's sewn and painted canvases, to Pindell's encrusted paint surfaces and Betye Saar's collage and assemblage boxes, the use of sewing and other additive techniques illustrates "the concept that object and materials possess certain energies."[53] This sensibility has marked the work of Pindell, Saar, and Renée Stout, all of whom profess to have been intrigued by processes in African art that involve the accumulation and display as manifestations of power.[54] This indicates the distinguishing element of African American creativity over the last thirty years: an increasing embrace of notions of ritual.

Certainly, African American women have created a niche for themselves between the traditional and innovative, which places them at the forefront of this development. Their "holistic" approach to art—from painting, sculpture, drawing, and watercolor, to photography and installation—indicates additionally a will to break boundaries and create new parameters for art making. This spirit was eminently encompassed in the 1987 multimedia installation, *Mojo Tech*, conceived by Betye Saar at the Massachusetts Institute of Technology. The elements in this installation focused "on technology as an element of magic and on art as ritual."[55] Such a notion of the fusion of tradition and cyberspace would seem to be the theoretical focus of African and other Americans as a whole as we move towards the twenty-first century.

The need to ground art-making in an integral cultural site becomes more urgent as African American artists, women and men, come to grips with issues beyond race and gender that have dominated our attention over the last century. They have had to grapple with how those issues play out in concerns about quality of life, the environment (as in Mary Lovelace O'Neal's painting series on the plight of the whale), and other lifestyle signifiers such as sexual preference and aging. Since the 1980s, they have also had to consider issues such as appropriation, whereby control over their own culture and ancestral legacy has been increasingly co-opted by a new global communications network.

The biggest challenge facing African American artists is their mainstreaming within the cultural ethos of this country. Writer and Nobel Prize laureate Toni Morrison demonstrates the centrality of the black presence in the American sensibility not only as subject, but also as an integral aesthetic modality in American art. For Morrison, blackness in Euro-American literature serves as a metaphorical catalyst for self-discovery and resolution on the part of various characters—invariably white. Morrison clarifies "the taken-for-granted assumptions that lie in their usages, and finally . . . the source of these images and the effect they have on the literary imagination and its product."[56]

In the visual arts the codification of African American artists at the periphery of American culture contradicts the growing recognition that, as Christopher Read asserts, identity is the central aspect of postmodern culture.[57] bell hooks notes that those very notions of "otherness and difference" that mark postmodernism "indicate that there is a growing body of work that can provide and promote critical dialogue and debate across boundaries of class, race and gender."[58] It is in such modalities that the work of African Americans as a whole, and African American women artists in particular will be seen as we move into the twenty-first century. Whether or not their work engages new mediums or subject matter, what is clear is that there is a new-found assertiveness and self-assurance on the part of African American women artists, determined to make their mark in their communities, on their history, and on the world in general.

NOTES

1. Pat Ward Williams, artist's statement, January, 1993.

2. Valerie Smith, "Black Feminist Theory," in *Changing Our Own Words: Essays on Criticism, Theory and Writing by Black Women*, ed. Cheryl A. Wall (New Brunswick and London: Rutgers University Press, 1989), pp. 38–57.

3. See for example Smith, *Changing Our Own Words;* bell hooks, *Ain't I a Woman: Black Women and Feminism* (Boston: South End Press, 1981).

4. Arna Alexander Bontemps and Jacqueline Fonvielle-Bontemps, *Forever Free: Art by African American Women 1862–1980*, exh. cat., (Alexandria, VA: Stephenson, 1980).

5. Lowery Stokes Sims, "Aspects of Performance in the Work of Black American Women Artists," in *Feminist Art Criticism: An Anthology*, ed. Arlene Raven, Cassandra L. Langer, and Joanne Frueh (Ann Arbor and London: U.M.I. Research Press, 1988), pp. 207–25.

6. *Art as a Verb: The Evolving Continuum, Installations, Performances and Videos by 13 African American Artists*, exh. cat., essays by Leslie King Hammond and Lowery Stokes Sims (Baltimore: Maryland Institute College of Art, 1988).

7. *Autobiography: In her Own Image*, exh. cat., essays by Howardena Pindell, Judith Wilson, and Moira Roth. (New York: INTAR Latin American Gallery, 1988).

8. *Gumbo Ya Ya: Anthology of Contemporary African American Women Artists*, introduction by Leslie King-Hammond (New York: Midmarch Arts, 1995), p. vii.

9. *Gumbo Ya Ya*, p. 94.

10. Bontemps, *Forever Free*, p. 13.

11. Ibid., pp. 13–14.

12. Ibid.

13. *Since the Harlem Renaissance: 50 Years of Afro-American Art* (exh. cat.), essay and interviews by Joseph Jacobs (Lewisburg, PA: The Center Gallery of Bucknell University, 1984), p. 34.

14. Ibid., p. 37.

15. The use of quilting techniques in particular intercepts with the strategy of engaging in techniques associated with crafts by the art mainstream, as an unique expression of "women's art," specifically the art of women that was relegated to anonymity by art history. Faith Ringgold has noted, for example, how her "soft" sculptures in the early 1970s were called "dolls," allowing critics to dismiss them as "crafts" and "write them off that way." (*Since the Harlem Renaissance*, p. 208). This has been an issue with the women's art movement as a whole since the 1960s. See Lucy Lippard, *Get the Message? A Decade of Art for Social Change* (New York: E.P. Dutton, 1984), p. 98.

16. See *Beverly Buchanan ShackWorks: A 16-Year Survey*, with an interview with the artist by Eleanor Flomenhaft, and essays by Trinkett Clark and Lowery Stokes Sims (Montclair, NJ: The Montclair Art Museum, 1994).

17. Dinah Berland, "Artist Finds Magic in the Everyday Object, Individual," *Los Angeles Herald Examiner*, February 21, 1987, p. B2.

18. Jackson Jarvis, artist's statement in *Art as a Verb*, n.p.

19. Ibid.

20. Michael D. Harris, "Resonance, Transformation and Rhyme: The Art of Renée Stout," in *Astonishment and Power* (Washington, DC: The Smithsonian Institution Press for the National Museum of African Art, 1994), pp. 107–55.

21. Ibid., p. 154.

22. Samella S. Lewis. *The Art of Elizabeth Catlett* (Claremont, CA: Hancraft Books, 1984), pp. 97–98.

23. Bontemps, *Forever Free*.

24. Ibid.

25. Lucy R. Lippard, "Beyond the Pale: Faith Ringgold's Black Light Series," in *Faith Ringgold: Twenty Years of Painting, Sculpture and Performance, 1963–1983* (New York: The Studio Museum in Harlem, 1984), p. 22.

26. Freida High Tesfagiorgis, "Afrofemcentrism and Its Fruition in the Art of Elizabeth Catlett and Faith Ringgold," *Sage: A Scholarly Journal on Black Women*, vol. 4, no. 1 (Spring 1987), p. 26.

27. Albert Boime, *The Art of Exclusion: Representing Blacks in the Nineteenth Century* (Washington, DC: The Smithsonian Institution Press, 1990), p. xiii.

28. Judith Wilson in *Autobiography: In Her Own Image*, p. 15.

29. Ibid.

30. See Tesfagiorgis, "Afrofemcentrism," p. 28.

31. Amalia Mesa-Bains in conversation with the author, New York, October 25, 1995.

32. Deborah Willis, ed., *Picturing Us: African American Identity in Photography* (New York: The New Press, 1994).

33. Ward Williams, artist's statement.

34. *All the Women are White, All the Blacks are Men, But Some of Us are Brave: Black Women's Studies*, ed. by Gloria T. Hull, Patricia Bell Scott, and Barbara Smith (Old Westbury, NY: The Feminist Press, 1982), p. xvii.

35. *Since the Harlem Renaissance*, p. 36.

36. Adrian Piper, "The Triple Negation of Colored Women Artists," in *Next Generation: Southern Black Aesthetic* (Winston-Salem: Southeastern Center for Contemporary Art, 1990), pp. 15, 16. See also *All Women Are White* and *Changing Our Own Words*; Michele Wallace, *Invisibility Blues: From Pop to Theory* (London: Verso, 1990); and hooks, *Ain't I a Woman*.

37. bell hooks, *Art on My Mind: Visual Politics* (New York: The New Press, 1995).

38. Tesfagiorgis, "Afrofemcentrism," p. 25. This philosophy was previously discussed by the author in her essay "Afrofemcentric: Twenty Years of Faith Ringgold," in *Faith Ringgold: Twenty Years*, pp. 17–18.

39. Ibid., p. 25; Smith, "Black Feminist Theory."

40. Tesfagiorgis, *Faith Ringgold: Twenty Years*, p. 26.

41. Ibid.

42. Alice Walker, *In Search of Our Mothers's Gardens: Womanist Prose* (New York: Harcourt, Brace, Janovich, 1983), p. xi.

43. *Gumbo Ya Ya*, p. 134.

44. Tesfagiorgis, *Faith Ringgold: Twenty Years*, pp. 26–27.

45. Ibid., p. 26.

46. Ibid.

47. The author was the juror for the installation component of the festival.

48. See Richard Westamacott, *African American Gardens and Yards in the Rural South* (Knoxville: The University of Tennessee Press, 1992).

49. Kirsten P. Buick, "The Ideal Works of Edmonia Lewis: Invoking and Inverting Autobiography," *American Art*, vol. 9, no. 2 (Summer 1995): 12–13.

50. Emma Amos, "Artist's Statement," in *Emma Amos, Changing the Subject: Paintings and Prints, 1992–1994* (New York, Art in General, 1994), p. 3.

51. *Gumbo Ya Ya*, p. 298.

52. *Gumbo Ya Ya*, p. 120.

53. Betye Saar, "Installation as Sculpture," *The International Review of African American Art*, vol. 6, no. 1, p. 14.

54. See Saar, "Installation as Sculpture," p. 14; Howardena Pindell, "The Aesthetics of Texture in African Adornment," in *Beauty by Design*, exh. cat. (New York: The African American Institute, 1985), pp. 26–30; and Michael D. Harris, "Renaissance, Transformation and Rhyme," pp. 107–55.

55. Saar quoted in *Art as a Verb*, n.p.

56. Toni Morrison, *Playing in the Dark: Whiteness and the Literary Imagination* (Cambridge, MA and London: Harvard University Press, 1992), p. x.

57. Christopher Read, "Postmodernism and the Art of Identity," in *Concepts of Modern Art*, 3rd ed. (London: Thames & Hudson, 1993).

58. *Gumbo Ya Ya*, p. xv.

HAGAR'S DAUGHTERS:

Social History, Cultural Heritage, and Afro-U.S. Women's Art

. . . .

JUDITH WILSON

[T]hough Afro-American cultural . . . history commonly regards the late nineteenth and early twentieth centuries in terms of great men, as the Age of Washington and Du Bois . . . these were the years of the first flowering of black women's autonomous organizations.

Hazel Carby[1]

Du Bois convened his Fourth (and last) Pan-African Congress in 1927, in New York. Most of the 220 delegates represented American Negro women's organizations.

St. Clair Drake[2]

IN HER 1990 essay "Modernism, Postmodernism and the Problem of the Visual in Afro-American Culture," Michele Wallace complained eloquently about the absence of African Americans from prevailing accounts of modernism and the absence of women from counterhistories of African American modernism. While she persuasively argued "the interdependency [of] issues of ethnicity and sex" in the formation of an Afro-U.S. modernism, Wallace refrained from naming particular women whose art played that initiatory role.[3] A startling omission, this lack of specificity indicates how deeply hidden much of the history of black visual production remains.

Widespread reluctance to abandon conventional definitions of "modernism" in which "style" outweighs "content" has also impeded efforts to name women pioneers or precursors of an African American modernism. Detecting non-canonical brands of modernism and retrieving marginalized modernist histories requires a close scrutiny of the various socio-cultural contexts that determine both an art form and its content. Thus, the following essay outlines some of the social and artistic frames within which a key trope of U.S. black modernism—the cele-

bration of African identity—emerged. It also locates the earliest, significant appearances of this theme in the work of two African American women, Edmonia Lewis and Meta Vaux Warrick Fuller.[4]

In "The West and the Rest of Us," Stuart Hall has demonstrated the crucial, though frequently overlooked or under-examined, role of colonialism in the formation of modern European culture.[5] Increasingly, art historians are probing links between colonial politics and early modern art.[6] Yet, all too often, theorists of an African American modernism forget that the so-called "New Negro" came of age in the heyday of Western imperialism. Forgotten too are the ways in which early twentieth-century black cultural self-assertion was a product of nineteenth-century abolitionist and post-Emancipation anti-racist struggles that took place in an international context of colonial commerce, evangelism, exploration, and imperialist expansion.[7]

During the antebellum era, blacks in the United States saw Africa as the former home of captives imported illegally as late as 1858, as well as a focus of various African American colonization schemes and black Protestant missionary efforts.[8] Black abolitionists, ranging from Frederick Douglass to African American photographer James P. Ball, also recognized that European myths of African "barbarism" or "savagery" provided excuses for slavery.[9] After Emancipation and the brief period of federal protection under Reconstruction, African Americans faced a "red tide" of unprecedented anti-black violence and a program of systematic disfranchisement not unlike today's reversal of Civil Rights and Affirmative Action legislation. Then as now, the defense of African civilization not only staved off black despair, but also aimed to counter an ascendant "scientific" racism that licensed both Jim Crow in the United States and the European "scramble for Africa."[10]

The figures generally associated with the nineteenth-century African American emigration movement, the Negro missionary movement, and proto-Pan-Africanist (or "Ethiopianist") thought are male: shipowner Paul Cuffee, physician Martin R. Delany, and preachers Daniel Coker and Alexander Crummell, for example. At first glance, this situation simply seems to mirror the dominant culture's practice of gendering social spheres, with males assigned the public domain and females the private. The massive proliferation of an ideology celebrating "the angel of the house" as cultural guardian and moral compass for the careworn, ethically-challenged man of the world is a prominent feature of nineteenth-century Euro-American life.[11] A by-product of industrialization and the accompanying triumph of modern capitalism, the emergence of sex segregation as a social ideal coincided with an increased economic marginalization of middle-class white women.[12]

The disparities associated with race and class throughout American history, however, meant that even supposedly "elite" black households seldom matched the wealth of middle-class whites. Hence, few bourgeois black families could afford to completely exempt their female members from materially productive roles. Similarly, in sociopolitical contexts, the magnitude of African American oppression and the enforced scarcity of black political and social resources permitted black women a place in public life—as abolitionist speakers, Underground Railroad "conductors," and anti-lynching crusaders, among other activities—often begrudged their white counterparts.[13] This racial difference in the articulation of nineteenth-century codes of gender difference forms a crucial backdrop to the careers of black women pioneers in the visual arts.[14]

Nevertheless, it is striking that, in most histories of nineteenth- and early twentieth-century African America, political agency on the international stage appears to have been an almost exclusively male prerogative. In contrast, black women's toils seem to have been largely confined to domestic political arenas.[15] While Cuffee, Delany, Coker, and others were busy promoting a black exodus from the Americas, Harriet Tubman was conducting Southern slaves to freedom in the North, and Sojourner Truth and Frances Ellen Watkins Harper were touring the North and Midwest on abolitionist lecture circuits. After the Civil War, free black women like Charlotte Forten would promote literacy among the newly emancipated, Ida B. Wells would campaign against lynching, and near the century's close, Mary Church Terrell and Josephine St. Pierre Ruffin would launch a nation-wide movement dedicated to the social elevation and ideological defense of black women.[16]

Such conspicuous female activity in the public sphere clearly deviates from nineteenth-century bourgeois white gender ideals. Yet, ironically, the record of nineteenth-century black women's social activism replicates those norms metaphorically, through the excision of female presence from black world(ly) politics and the confinement of female voices to domestic (i.e., national) political agendas. Thus, the situation in the visual arts seems especially remarkable.[17] For there the first signs of an *international* black consciousness apparently issued from the hands of Afro-U.S. *women.*

Edmonia Lewis (fig. 1) was probably born in the early 1840s in or near New York State.[18] According to Marilyn Richardson, Lewis's father was an Afro-Caribbean, who may have come to the United States from Haiti. Her mother was a woman of part Chippewa descent. Both parents were dead by 1848, leading Lewis's teenaged brother to make boarding arrangements for the little girl, then go west to seek his fortune.[19] His success in the California gold fields eventually financed his sister's education, first at an abolitionist-run school in upstate New York, then at Oberlin College in Ohio.[20]

At Oberlin from 1859 to early 1863, Lewis is known to have studied drawing. There she is also likely to have had her first exposure to sculpture in the form of small plaster casts of "Greek and Roman classics."[21] Her previous schooling had already brought her in contact with abolitionism, but Lewis's first encounters with feminism probably took place at Oberlin, the first American college to admit blacks and the first to admit women.[22]

From Mary Wollstonecraft, the mother of feminism in the English speaking world, to Virginia Woolf, the

Figure 1 Portrait of Edmonia Lewis, photographer unknown, n.d.. The Schomburg Center for Research in Black Culture, The New York Public Library.

especially abolition and temperance.[26] The conjunction of abolitionism and feminism that she experienced in the Keep household would play a crucial role in Edmonia Lewis's subsequent career, determining the specific character of her art's references to African heritage.

. . .

One of the earliest photographic sessions, conducted in Detroit probably sometime [in] 1864 . . . yielded several telling images of [Sojourner] Truth. . . .

The obvious juxtaposition in the seated pose of her wide-eyed yet self-confident facial expression with the small yet prominent, sphinx-like wooden finial on her Victorian chair is perhaps a subtle allusion to an *Atlantic Monthly* profile . . . entitled "Sojourner Truth, The Libyan Sibyl," . . . published the year before (1863) by . . . Harriet Beecher Stowe. . . . From almost all historical accounts, Truth was ambivalent about Stowe's "Libyan Sibyl" label. . . . Still, as seen in subsequent printed broadsides advertising Truth's lectures and in [a] circa 1864 *carte-de-visite* photograph of her, Truth willfully engaged the symbolic reference to ancient oracles and/or Egyptian sphinxes, in service to her own ends.[27]

Two extant works by Edmonia Lewis hint that, through her sculpture, this artist sought to locate African American history and culture on a *world* stage. Both sculptures refer to Africa in ways that are consistent with a contemporaneous black folk theology in which Biblical references to Egypt and Ethiopia were meant to instill group pride and deflect white claims that the curse of Ham doomed blacks to servile status.[28] But both works can also be linked to the rhetoric and history of early black feminism, as we can see by the noted black abolitionist-feminist Sojourner Truth's exploitation of a related visual and literary symbolism during the same period.

In contrast to her associations with white feminist-abolitionists, which are well-known, Lewis's ties to black feminists of her day have received little attention.[29] As a result, only one or two clues to this neglected chapter of her history are currently available.[30] In an 1868 diary, a young black woman named Frances Rollin recorded her social life in post-bellum Boston's black and white former

mother of Anglophone literary modernism, advocates of women's rights continually stressed the need for female access to higher education.[23] At Oberlin, Edmonia Lewis was one of several female students who boarded with one of the college's trustees, Reverend John Keep, the man said to have "cast the deciding vote . . . to admit women and African Americans."[24] An Oberlin historian credits Keep with unsurpassed "service" on behalf of female education, temperance, and abolitionism at the college.[25] Keep's advocacy of female education is consistent with the support for women's rights shown by a number of nineteenth-century male progressives, black and white, as well as with the tendency of both female and male feminists to support other reform movements, abolitionist circles. Along with visits to such figures as William Wells Brown, Lydia Maria Child, Wendell Phillips, and William Cooper Nell, Rollin cryptically noted the following:

> May 9: . . . Went to Addie Howard's. Addie received today two photographs of Edmonia Lewis from Rome taken in her Studio dress.[31]

A member of a distinguished black Boston family, Addie Howard was one of two sisters who both became school principals, while their brother gained prominence as a physician. Her sister, Joan, "was the first colored young lady to enter [Boston's prestigious Girls High and Normal School] and to graduate from [what was then] the highest institution of learning in her native city." In 1893, as a member of the Board of Women Managers of the State of New York, Joan Howard would be one of the

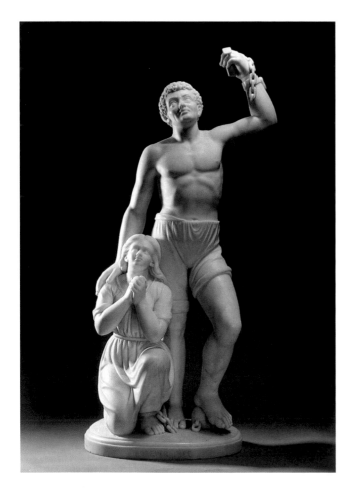

Figure 2 Edmonia Lewis, *Forever Free*, 1867, marble. Howard University Gallery of Art, Washington, D.C.

few blacks to serve in an official capacity in the organization of the Columbian Exposition—an event marked by discriminatory practices that sparked the founding of the national black women's club movement.[32]

In 1869, when Washington, D.C., black feminist Mary Ann Cary addressed the Colored National Labor Union convention, she cited "Miss Edmonia Lewis" first on a list of black women whose achievements demonstrated "a manifest desire to widen the boundaries" of black female activity.[33] Oblique and fragmentary as these references may be, they are highly suggestive—especially given the early stage of her career at which Lewis seems to have captured these black feminists' attention. Having taken up sculpting during her 1863–65 stay in Boston, where she gained some rudimentary training from portrait sculptor Edward A. Brackett, she initially produced only medallions and portrait busts, and would not attempt more ambitious full-figure works until she had settled in Rome in 1866.[34] Thus, Lewis would have produced only a handful of "major" works by the time Frances Rollin and Mary Ann Cary deemed her activities noteworthy—a situation that suggests an undocumented black feminist network that quickly circulated among its ranks any rumor of achievement on the part of contemporary Afro-U.S. women.

These speculations may or may not withstand further investigation. But the earliest surviving full-figure group by Lewis, her 1867 *Forever Free* (fig. 2), offers another set of clues that feminism and abolition were linked discourses informing this artist's work.

> In a patriarchal society, while masculine terms are routinely used to signify women as well as men, feminine terms are gender specific.
>
> Jean Fagan Yellin[35]

The subversive character of Lewis's Emancipation group is especially apparent when it is compared with works on this theme by her American contemporaries. In 1876, Thomas Ball, a prominent white American sculptor, completed his *Emancipation* (fig. 3) for the Freedmen's Memorial Monument to Abraham Lincoln, located in Washington, D.C.'s Lincoln Park. Ball had previously produced a slightly different version of this Emancipation group in 1865, two years before Lewis's *Forever Free*.[36]

The languages of costume, gesture, position, and pose differentiate the figures of Abraham Lincoln and the anonymous slave-on-the-brink-of-freedom in Ball's public monument. The Great Emancipator stands, while the soon-to-be freedman crouches—half kneeling, half poised to rise. Lincoln is fully and rather formally clothed. The African American is semi-naked—clad not in the tattered trousers of an actual nineteenth-century field worker, but in some neo-classical equivalent of what nineteenth-century Americans would have viewed as a "savage" or "barbaric" loincloth.

With one hand, Lincoln clutches a scroll (presumably inscribed with the Emancipation Proclamation), grasping a traditional emblem of the West's alleged cultural superiority—that is to say, its literacy. He raises his opposite hand over the crouching black in a gesture of priestly

Figure 3 Thomas Ball, *Emancipation* (Freedmens Memorial Monument to Abraham Lincoln), 1876, bronze, approx. 275 cm. Lincoln Park, Washington, D.C.

benediction that can be traced directly to familiar representations of Moses, who as the Hebrews' liberator and lawgiver perfectly embodies late nineteenth-century America's ambivalence about a black population it has released from slavery, but still wishes to control.[37] The gesture is equally familiar from images of Christ (for example, when he raises Lazarus from the dead). In contrast, both of the African American's hands flex in ways that emphasize brute strength—knuckles to the ground, supporting the weight of his crouching figure, in one case; fists clenched around a ring of his chain, in the other.

While Ball's image of a newly emancipated race graphically signals white benevolence and black passivity, white superiority and black inferiority, Lewis's sculpture advertises black (male) self-assertion, energy, and pride. Her upright and triumphant black male boldly displays his broken shackle and deftly balances himself by propping one foot on the discarded ball that once anchored his chains.

Depictions of slavery by black artists in America prior to Lewis are extremely rare. The few extant ones include Patrick Reason's 1835 *Kneeling Slave* (fig. 4). A graphic image meant to circulate widely and popularize the Abolitionist cause, Reason's print was based on a famous emblem of eighteenth-century British abolitionism, Josiah Wedgwood's jasper-ware medallion bearing the logo "Am I Not a Man and a Brother?" There is one major difference between Reason's image and the Wedgwood medallion, however. Reason's slave is a woman.

Indeed, according to Jean Fagan Yellin, she was the invention of female abolitionists in England, who began using her image as early as 1826, when she appeared on the cover of the First Report of the Ladies Negro's Friend Society of Birmingham, England. Enthusiastically embraced by American women abolitionists, black and white, when it appeared in this country in the 1830s, the female supplicant was reproduced in abolitionist women's poetry, needlework, and letterhead. This distaff version of the original anti-slavery icon would certainly have been familiar to Edmonia Lewis, since it had embellished the covers of three publications by her patron Lydia Maria Child.[38] As we will see, the abolitionist female supplicant lends Lewis's Emancipation group an especially subversive meaning.

Figure 4 Patrick Reason, *Kneeling Slave*, 1835.
National Afro American Museum and Cultural
Center, Wilberforce, Ohio.

Figure 5 Robert S. Duncanson, *Uncle Tom &
Little Eva*, 1853, oil on canvas, 97.2 cm × 69.2 cm.
Photograph © 1987 The Detroit Institute
of Arts, Gift of Mrs. Jefferson Butler and
Miss Grace R. Conover.

Among the few other images of slavery by antebellum black artists, we have a work derived from a literary source, Robert S. Duncanson's 1853 *Uncle Tom and Little Eva* (fig. 5). Instead of one of the highly charged scenes of white violence and black resistance that Harriet Beecher Stowe used to enlist the sympathies of her readers, Duncanson has chosen an idyllic pastoral tableau depicting a rare moment of racial harmony. Taken from the novel's twenty-second chapter, it shows the slave Tom and his angelic charge, Little Eva, "on a little mossy seat, in an arbor, at the foot of the garden" at sunset. Holding a Bible in one hand and pointing heavenward with the other, Eva is instructing Tom about the Christian promise of salvation in the afterlife. Stowe's subtext, however, is highly critical of the hypocrisy of whites who claim to be "Christians" while holding slaves and vaunting their own alleged cultural superiority over so-called "heathen" like the saintly, but unbaptized, Uncle Tom. Yet there is no trace of this caustic irony in Duncanson's painting.

If comparisons with the work of her black and white male contemporaries emphasizes the bold, self-assertive character of Lewis's depiction of the freed*man* in *Forever Free*, a combination of socio-historical contexts and art historical sources shed light on his companion, the kneeling slave woman. In 1866—the year before Edmonia Lewis produced *Forever Free*—the U.S. Congress adopted the Fourteenth Amendment, conferring citizenship on newly emancipated blacks. In doing so, however, language limiting the vote to male citizens was introduced into the Constitution for the first time.[39] With the passage of the Fourteenth Amendment, many white woman suffragists who had previously been staunch supporters of black Civil Rights became staunch enemies of a proposed Fifteenth Amendment that would extend voting rights to black men while continuing to deny the franchise to women of all races.

Publicly at least, the majority of Reconstruction-era black feminists seem to have conceded that, in the words of Frederick Douglass, while woman suffrage was "a desirable matter," obtaining the vote was a question of life and death for black males. For black men, Douglass argued, "disfranchisement means New Orleans, . . .

Memphis, . . . New York mobs. It means being driven from the work-shops and the schools."[40] Among black activists of the period, only one woman vocally demurred, the ex-slave itinerant preacher Sojourner Truth who, in an 1867 speech, declared that emancipation left "slavery partly destroyed, not entirely":

> There is a great stir about colored men getting their rights, but not a word about the colored women; and if colored men get their rights, and not colored women theirs, you see the colored men will be masters over the women, and it will be just as bad as it was before. So I am for keeping the thing going while things are stirring; because if we wait till it is still, it will take a great while to get it going again.[41]

That Lewis *may* have shared Truth's opinion of the campaign to enfranchise black men and not women is conceivable, given the sculptor's multiple associations with feminism at Oberlin; in Boston, as a recipient of technical advice from sculptor Anne Whitney, career guidance and support from abolitionist-feminist, Lydia Maria Child, and the patronage of feminist-abolitionist Maria Weston Chapman; in Rome, as a newcomer immediately welcomed into the feminist salon of actress Charlotte Cushman, as well as the circle of exceptionally independent women artists around Harriet Hosmer, and as the subject of reports in the leading feminist journal in the United States. A comparison of the parallel poses of the former bondswoman in *Forever Free* and the antislavery feminist icon, the female supplicant, reinforces a reading of Lewis's *Emancipation* group as the visual analogue of Sojourner Truth's characterization of emancipation without universal suffrage as "slavery partly destroyed, not entirely."[42]

. . .

O, ye daughters of Africa, awake! awake! arise!
Maria W. Stewart (1831)[43]

Two other works by Edmonia Lewis index a conjunction of gender-based concerns and transnational black identity in Afro-U.S. women's ideology at a surprisingly early date. As Patricia Hill Collins has observed, the speeches of Maria Stewart, a free-born New

Figure 6 Edmonia Lewis, *Hagar*, 1875. National Museum of American Art, Smithsonian Institution, Washington, D.C.

England abolitionist and "one of the first Black feminists," found a tradition of black women intellectuals' preoccupation with certain themes. Chief among these nineteenth-century black feminist leitmotifs was an awareness of black women's sexual abuse during slavery and as domestic workers in the post-Emancipation era, and of the rationalization of this abuse via myths of black female promiscuity.[44]

The 1875 sculpture, *Hagar* (fig. 6), of which Lewis apparently executed a now-lost version in 1869–70, refers to the Talmudic story of Abraham's Egyptian concubine. Because of his wife Sarah's barrenness, Abraham is divinely instructed to enlist the sexual services of the slave woman, Hagar, in order to perpetuate his line. When Hagar succeeds in bearing Abraham a son, Sarah's jealousy eventually leads to the bondswoman's expulsion into the desert. Only the intervention of an angel of the Lord prevents Hagar from perishing in the wilderness.

The period in which Lewis created this sculpture was one of mounting federal retreat from the battle to "reconstruct" a defeated, but largely unrepentant South. As a tenuous scaffold of newly erected black legal and political rights was torn or fell down, Southern white racists and their Northern apologists and facilitators sought to blame black setbacks on African Americans themselves. At a time when many white woman suffragists felt betrayed by and resentful of black male victories in gaining constitutional citizenship and voting rights, white feminists increasingly distanced themselves from the plight of black women—often hoping to gain Southern support for their own cause instead. Thus, while Southern anti-black terrorism was increasingly rationalized as a defense of white womanhood against the alleged lasciviousness of black males, black females were simultaneously being reviled as innately unchaste, immoral creatures, with the history of antebellum black concubinage held up as proof!

In this context, Lewis's use of the Judaeo-Christian story of Hagar must be seen as an allegorical defense of black womanhood. But Lewis's *Hagar* possesses another important dimension that, while reported by various authors, has not been fully appreciated—that is, the ideological significance of her African identity.[45]

Hagar isn't Edmonia Lewis's only depiction of a legendary Egyptian woman. In 1875, the same year she carved the aforementioned version of Hagar, Lewis produced a slightly larger than life-size statue entitled *The Death of Cleopatra*[46] (fig. 7). Both subjects were popular with nineteenth-century artists who had no ancestral ties to Africa. One such was Lewis's white compatriot and Roman neighbor, William Wetmore Story, whose 1869 *Cleopatra* (fig. 8) was displayed at the Philadelphia Centennial along with Lewis's work on the same theme.[47]

The difference between the two artists' treatment of the fabled queen's suicide is striking. Story's dying monarch slouches glamorously in resignation, her head propped listlessly on her palm and her brow furrowed in gloom. Although her massive frame and air of grave dignity convey both her former force of character and imperial might, the overall mood is one of defeat and despair.

In contrast, the upper torso of Lewis's dying sovereign arches back and her head is thrown up and over to one side in a particularly graphic description of the expiring monarch's death throes. While this results in a degree of natural fidelity that late nineteenth-century audiences seem to have found simultaneously fascinating and repulsive, it also rhymes with the body language of haughty defiance.[48] Thus, even in death, Lewis seems to say, the Queen of the Nile radiates the indomitable pride and wily independence that precluded her surrender to the Romans.

For Richardson, "Lewis's determination to convey the dignity and authority of her subject in the moment when she has abandoned all hope of rule in favor of a defiant response to powerlessness," is a function of the artist's identification with Cleopatra as a woman who, like the Biblical Hagar, was "between two cultures."[49] But the line of interpretation that most intrigues me is one that

Figure 7 Edmonia Lewis, *The Death of Cleopatra* (frontal view), 1875. The National Museum of American Art, Smithsonian Institution, Washington, D.C. Gift of the Historical Society of Forest Park, Illinois.

Figure 8 William Wetmore Story, *Cleopatra*, 1869, marble. The Metropolitan Museum of Art, New York. Gift of John Taylor Johnston, 1988.

links the Nile Valley to the Mississippi by way of countless black preachers, teachers, and ideologues, who in the bleakness of the Post-Reconstruction era invoked the splendors of ancient African civilizations as a beacon of hope to African Americans. This line seems to run directly from Lewis's dying Cleopatra to *Ethiopia Awakening* by Meta Warrick Fuller.

. . .

> Rome got her civilization from Greece; Greece borrowed hers from Egypt. . . . Civilization descended the Nile . . . as it came down from Thebes. Thebes was built and settled by the Ethiopians. . . . So we trace the light of civilization from Ethiopia to Egypt, to Greece, to Rome, and thence diffusing its radiance over the entire world.
>
> Pauline Hopkins (1902)[50]

Fuller's *Ethiopia Awakening* (fig. 9) offers tantalizing hints of the ideological context in which African American modernism in the visual arts emerged.[51] Born into Post-Reconstruction-era Philadelphia's black middle class,

Figure 9 Meta Vaux Warrick Fuller, *Ethiopia Awakening* (detail), 1915–21, bronze. James Weldon Johnson Collection, Beinecke Rare Book Library, Yale University, New Haven. Bequest of Grayce Fairfax Nail, 1970.

Meta Warrick initially trained at a local school of industrial arts. In 1899, she quit Philadelphia for Paris, where she would continue her study in various ateliers and at the Académie Colarossi for three years. In France, her talent as a sculptor was recognized by such figures as the prescient collector and dealer Samuel Bing, who exhibited her sculpture at his innovative shop, l'Art Nouveau. The great French sculptor Auguste Rodin was so impressed by the young American's "sense of form" that he invited her to bring work for his inspection free of charge.[52]

In Paris, Warrick not only rubbed shoulders with such precursors of European modernism as Rodin and Bing, but she also socialized with two prominent African Americans. The painter Henry Ossawa Tanner had left Philadelphia a decade before her and would remain in Paris until his death in 1937. Although she had previously met the young scholar and activist W. E. B. DuBois in the United States, Warrick would get to know him better during her stay in France. DuBois was there in 1900, in part to oversee the African American pavilion at the Paris Exposition, in part to attend the first Pan-African Conference, which took place in London that year.[53]

Warrick's older sister was married to the son of a distinguished black educator and politician, while her uncles included two journalists, one of whom—William Bolivar—was also a bibliophile and avid student of black history.[54] As a result of her association with DuBois, as well as her contacts with other prominent and 'race proud' African Americans who visited the French capital during the Exposition, along with her Philadelphia family's ties to the period's African American intellectual and political elite, it seems plausible that the young sculptor might have brought some early form of a Pan-Africanist agenda to her figure of Ethiopia. This possibility is particularly intriguing.

That she was open to such thinking is also suggested by an intersection of certain social traits and ideological currents in Warrick's biography that may be crudely mapped by focusing upon three ostensibly anomalous works she created between 1906 and 1921. In her doctoral thesis on Warrick, Judith Kerr writes that the majority of the artist's "portraits were of individuals . . . she knew personally."[55] Yet in a "study" *circa* 1906 entitled

The Comedian (subsequently lost in the disastrous 1910 fire that destroyed "nearly all" of her early work), Warrick depicted a popular black entertainer, George Walker, whom she may have seen on stage, but who did not sit for her.[56]

On two separate occasions Walker and his partner Bert Williams had earned themselves a permanent place in the history of American popular culture: in 1896, they launched the first in a series of African American dance crazes—the cakewalk—which Africanized the way much of the world moves to music in our century; and again in 1902, the pair brought one of the first black musical comedies, *In Dahomey*, to the Broadway stage.[57] Both *In Dahomey* and its 1903 successor, *Abyssinia*, are credited with enlarging the scope of black performance on the American stage by breaking the stranglehold of minstrel stereotypes on the theatrical representation of people of African descent.[58]

It was no accident that this 'new and improved' version of the theatrical Negro appeared at this time or that it had been imaginatively placed in African—rather than African American—settings. For, as Kerr observes, Williams and Walker's admiration for the real Dahomeans they had seen on display at San Francisco's 1893–94 Midwinter International Fair mirrored the sentiments of "black theatregoers like [Warrick, who] . . . were beginning to rediscover and appreciate their African roots."[59] In 1905, the year before Warrick is thought to have produced her Walker portrait, for example, Boston journalist Pauline Hopkins self-published *A Primer of Facts Pertaining to the Early Greatness of the African Race and the Possibility of Restoration by Its Descendants.*[60]

This African American recovery and valorization of African heritage figured centrally in a broad program of psycho-social "uplift" that was widely advocated by members of the black clergy, intelligentsia, and the Civil Rights movement at the turn of the century and in the years prior to World War I. Much as their counterparts in colonial Africa were utilizing evidence of past glory to project visions of future autonomy and prestige, educated African Americans regarded the newly discovered splendors of ancient Egypt, archaeological reports on periods of "Ethiopian" ascendancy in the Nile Valley, and medieval

Arab descriptions of mighty West African empires as potent sources of "pride in . . . Negro ancestry."[61]

In 1909, Meta Warrick married Solomon Fuller, a neuropathologist and psychiatrist born in Liberia, where his parents were government officials.[62] Four years later, the sculptor modeled a commemorative plaque in honor of Ethiopia's recently deceased emperor Menelik II. Like *The Comedian*, this plaster relief was one of the few works by Fuller to portray someone she didn't know.

In 1913, when she created her *Menelik II of Abyssinia*, only two African nations—Ethiopia and Liberia—were free of colonial rule. Of them, Ethiopia alone had enjoyed continuous rule by indigenous leaders for centuries. And thanks to Menelik II's utter rout of Italian forces in the Battle of Adua in 1896, Ethiopia was the only modern-day African nation to have repulsed a European army.[63] Thus, Ethiopia stood as a lone symbol of African autonomy at the height of the age of imperialism, serving as a beacon of hope to Africans and African Americans in the early twentieth century, as they began to imagine a postcolonial future.[64]

In other words, by the time she began executing her *Ethiopia Awakening*, Fuller had already moved from depicting an African American who used African models to redeem the black image in contemporary theater, to portraying an African sovereign whose defeat of a Western army seemed to herald the entire continent's liberation.

Figure 10 Daniel Chester French, *Africa*, 1904. New York Historical Society.

Additional circumstances seem to reinforce a Pan-Africanist reading of the 1915–21 work:

First, there is the Daniel Chester French sculptural group known as *Africa* (fig. 10). One of four groups produced between 1903 and 1907, each symbolizing a different continent in accordance with the conventional allegory of the four corners of the globe, it was created in 1904 and installed outside the United States Custom House in New York City.[65] As Albert Boime has pointed out, while French portrayed America as a "lively and alert" figure, "advancing to meet the challenge of the future," the patriotic white sculptor's personification of Africa "is almost caricaturely . . . slumped over in deep slumber."[66] Indeed, Freeman Henry Morris Murray, the African American author of a 1916 survey of American sculpture depicting blacks, cites a contemporary reference to this figure as "Ethiopia Asleep."[67]

Fuller probably was aware of both of French's Custom House figures and the comic designation for his *Africa* that Murray reports. In Paris, she had frequented the studio of Augustus Saint-Gaudens—America's chief practitioner of the Beaux-Arts style and Daniel Chester French's arch-rival for the period's major sculpture commissions in the U.S.[68] Freeman Murray, a cousin of Fuller's journalist/historian uncle, William Bolivar, had sent her the manuscript of his sculpture survey in late December 1914 or early January 1915, seeking a critical evaluation.[69] Thus, French's implicitly racist depiction of Africa as "Ethiopia Asleep" must be seen as a negative source for Fuller's *Ethiopia Awakening*—i.e., an artistic embodiment of the antiblack stereotypes and imperialist myths that Fuller's portraits of George Walker and Menelik II had attempted to counter.

Less certain, but nonetheless striking, is the possibility that a literary work by one of the forefathers of African independence may have served as a positive source of inspiration. In 1912, upon the death of the great Creole Pan-Africanist Edward Wilmot Blyden, Joseph Casely-Hayford, a member of the colonial-era Gold Coast's (today Ghana) Fanti elite, became Blyden's "intellectual heir," carrying the torch of "cultural nationalism in West Africa in the years between the two World Wars." Unlike Blyden, Casely-Hayford's "concern with the revaluation of African culture" was accompanied by "a militant anti-imperialism."

In the book he published in London in 1911, Casely-Hayford outlined a program of development led by "an African elite, in touch with both the Western culture and the traditional way of life." Central to this scheme was the cultivation of "a new consciousness of the traditional structures [of African society] and the heritage of the past" among this Western-educated African ruling class.[70] The title of the tome in which Casely-Hayford laid out this ambitious plan for political independence and a culturally organic approach to modernization was *Ethiopia Unbound.*

"One of Mrs. Fuller's most significant works is a life-size *Awakening of Ethiopia*, a semi-Egyptian figure emerging from a casing of swathing bands like an awakening mummy," wrote Alain Locke in 1936.[71] What I think Locke helps us see is that Fuller has allegorized an emergent Africa—or, to use the antique designation, "Ethiopia"— as a female mummy released from a millennial sleep and from the mortuary bands in which she was encased. In other words, Fuller has produced an image remarkably congruent with the title of Casely-Hayford's book—that is, an image of "Ethiopia (-in-the-process-of-becoming-) Unbound."

Ultimately, then, in order to trace the origins of an African American modernism in the visual arts, we must look beyond questions of mere formal invention to the more complex problem of merging specific ideological goals with an appropriate visual language. In broaching the subject of African heritage for the first time in the history of Afro-U.S. art, Edmonia Lewis, then Meta Warrick Fuller, anticipated the entire subsequent history of black artists' conscious struggle with questions of cultural heritage and racial identity in the United States. Thus, despite the obvious stylistic conservatism of both Lewis and Fuller's work, in their art we can trace the origins of African American modernism in the visual arts to an upsurge of politically-motivated identification with Africa's ancient Nile Valley civilizations and a conflation of this romantic attachment to ancient Egypt and Nubia with concern for modern Ethiopia's fate. In Lewis's case, this orientation seems to converge with certain strains of nineteenth-century black feminism. With Fuller, whose artistic activity was significantly curtailed by the demands of middle-class marriage and motherhood, a corresponding debt to feminism is less clear, although she was briefly associated with the black feminist journalist and author Pauline Hopkins.[72]

Operating as they did within the confines of an elite art form—academic sculpture—and according to hegemonic (that is to say, "Eurocentric") canons, Lewis and Fuller may seem profoundly alien to contemporary black women. Given the general "proletarianization" of black culture in the wake of black economic gains during the post–World War II era that enabled unprecedented levels of black participation in mass market modes of consumption, as well as the ideological reinforcement of that trend by the anti-elitistic rhetoric of late 1960s cultural nationalism, it may be difficult to see how Lewis and Fuller's work has any bearing on today's art by African American women. And finally, efforts to identify with these artistic pioneers may be further hampered by the degree to which they appear to be "exceptional" in both race and gender terms—of biracial (African and Native American) ancestry in the case of Lewis and of "mixed" ancestry in the case of Fuller (judging by her light skin), both escaped the patterns of early marriage and frequent childbearing typical of women of their day.

Yet Lewis and Fuller's biographies and their art historical fate exhibit problems that haunt black women artists to this day. Acknowledged in most surveys of African American art as among the earliest successful black sculptors in the United States, their lives and work are seldom analyzed in detail, their politics have largely been ignored, and their activities are seldom viewed as having influenced other artists or played a crucial role in art historical developments.[73] Thus, while these foremothers of contemporary African American women's art are frequently included in art history texts and shows, they

Figure 11 Lois Mailou Jones, *The Ascent of Ethiopia*, 1932, oil on canvas, 23½″ × 17¼″. Milwaukee Art Museum, Purchase, African-American Art Acquisition Fund, matching funds from Sue and Dick Pieper, with additional support from Arthur and Dorothy Nelle Sanders.

seldom share the spotlight with their male counterparts. Marginalized in this way, Lewis and Fuller's contributions to the formation of an "African American modernism" have been swept under the carpet. As a result, contemporary Afro-U.S. women artists, in turn, have been denied their rightful inheritance. Deprived of full knowledge of the female art historical continuum of which they are a part, they remain "Hagar's daughters" crying in the wilderness of cultural anomie.

NOTES

1. Hazel V. Carby, *Reconstructing Womanhood: The Emergence of the Afro-American Woman Novelist* (New York: Oxford University Press, 1987), pp. 6–7.

2. St. Clair Drake, "Hide My Face? On Pan-Africanism and Negritude," in *Soon, One Morning: New Writing by American Negroes 1940–1962*, ed. Herbert Hill (New York: Alfred A. Knopf, 1963), p. 99.

3. Michele Wallace, "Modernism, Postmodernism and the Problem of the Visual in Afro-American Culture," in *Out There: Marginalization and Contemporary Cultures*, Russell Ferguson, Martha Gever, Trinh T. Minhha and Cornel West (New York: The New Museum of Contemporary Art; Cambridge, MA: MIT Press, 1990), p. 46.

I use the neologism "Afro-U.S.," interchangeably with the more problematic (because it concedes to the pernicious, if pervasive, taxonomies of race) term U.S. black, in an effort to avoid the cultural imperialism involved in terminology that implies that the African-derived population of the U.S. is the *only* group of people of African descent in the Americas. A dislike for monotonous diction, however, sometimes leads me to revert to this troublesome use of the term "African American."

4. My use of the term "significant" here is a kind of shorthand for a distinction that can be made between works about which we no longer know, in part because they either were not exhibited at prominent sites or were not regarded as artistically noteworthy in their day, and works that gained sufficient attention in their time to enter the historical record.

5. Stuart Hall, "The West and the Rest of Us," in *Formations of Modernity*, ed. Stuart Hall and Bram Gieben (Cambridge: Polity Press, 1992), pp. 317–18.

6. For examples of recent art historical investigations of the colonial/modernist nexus, see Abigail Solomon Godeau's "Going Native: Paul Gauguin and the Invention of Primitivist Modernism," *Art in America*, vol. 77, no. 7 (July 1989): 118–129, 161. See also Patricia Leighten's "The White Peril and L'Art négre: Picasso, Primitivism, and Anticolonialism," *Art Bulletin*, vol. 72, no. 4 (December 1990): 609–30.

7. Roland Oliver and J. D. Fage, *A Short History of Africa* (New York: Penguin Books, 1990), pp. 115–24.

8. Charles J. Montgomery, "Survivors from the Cargo of the Slave Yacht Wanderer," *American Anthropologist*, vol. 10 (1908): 611–23; St. Clair Drake, *The Redemption of Africa and Black Religion* (Chicago: Third World Press; Atlanta: Institute of the Black World, 1970), pp. 41–43.

9. See Paul Gilroy's *The Black Atlantic: Modernity and Double Consciousness* (Cambridge, MA: Harvard University Press, 1993), pp. 59–60, for an illuminating analysis of the ideological implications of Douglass' defense of African humanity and denunciation of the modern erasure of African history in an ethnological lecture he delivered in various venues from 1854 on.

For a brief discussion of James P. Ball's celebration of African history and culture in his 1855 abolitionist panorama, see my "The Challenges of the 19th Century: Two Recent Landmark Publications on African American Production," *The International Review of African American Art*, vol. 12, no. 1 (1995): 57–58.

10. Kevin Gaines, "Uplift Ideology as Civilizing Mission: Pauline E. Hopkins on Race and Imperialism," in *Cultures of United States Imperialism*, ed. Amy Kaplan and Donald E. Pease (Durham, NC: Duke University Press, 1993), pp. 435–36.

11. Karen Sanchez-Eppler, "Bodily Bonds: The Intersecting Rhetorics of Feminism and Abolition," *Representations*, no. 24 (Fall 1988): 49.

12. Joy S. Kasson, *Marble Queens and Captives: Women in Nineteenth-Century American Sculpture* (New Haven: Yale University Press, 1990), p. 3. For a discussion of the economic basis of this shift and the specifically bourgeois character of the cult of true womanhood that emerged as a result, see Ronald T. Takaki, *Iron Cages: Race and Culture in 19th-Century America* (New York: Alfred A. Knopf, 1979), pp. 139–40. For an especially trenchant analysis of the racial parameters of this discourse, see Carby, *Reconstructing Womanhood*, pp. 23–30.

13. In this regard, it seems telling that the first American-born woman to have lectured in public was Maria W. Stewart, an African American who, in 1832 in Boston, delivered a series of lectures that were subsequently published in William Lloyd Garrison's abolitionist weekly, *The Liberator*. Conversely, the fact that the first white American women to speak publicly, Angelina and Sarah Grimké, did so in 1837 on behalf of the American Anti-Slavery Society is paradigmatic of the historical relationship of both nineteenth- and twentieth-century U.S. anti-racist and anti-sexist struggles. For a pioneer study of this parallel in the histories of the early woman's suffrage movement and the birth of contemporary feminism, see Sara Evans, *Personal Politics: The Roots of Women's Liberation in the Civil Rights Movement and the New Left* (New York: Alfred A. Knopf, 1979), especially p. 24.

14. A failure to fully grasp this distinction, in my opinion, lies at the heart of Kirsten Buick's oddly ahistoric reading of Edmonia Lewis's figures of women of color. Buick's claim that the Victorian cult of "true womanhood" extended undifferentially to black women and therefore determined Lewis's representations of gender, fails to take into account both the contested nature of dominant nineteenth-century gender ideals and the pivotal role of black women as symbols of the intersection of ethnic and sexual exploitation, as well as role models for white female political activists in the emergence of nineteenth-century feminism. Kirsten P. Buick, "The Ideal Works of Edmonia Lewis: Invoking and Inverting Autobiography," *American Art*, vol. 9, no. 2 (Summer 1995): 5–19. For a discussion of nineteenth-century black women's awareness of and responses to their exclusion from the ideology of true womanhood, see Carby, *Reconstructing Womanhood*, pp. 32–39. For a complex and subtly nuanced reading of the black woman's symbolic function in the discourses of feminist abolitionism, see Sanchez-Eppler, "Bodily Bonds."

15. This is not to say that black women failed to go abroad, a misconception that the European travels of Phyllis Wheatley, Ida B. Wells, Lucy Parsons, and Sarah Parker Remond belie. Yet to a startling degree, with the exceptions of Remond (who published a letter in the *London Daily News* protesting the anti-black bias of British reports on Jamaica's 1865 Morant Bay Rebellion) and Anna Julia Cooper (who delivered a paper on "The Negro Problem in America" at the first Pan-African Conference in 1900 in London), Afro-American women seem remarkably silent in the annals of nineteenth- and early twentieth-century black diasporic debates. Gilroy, *The Black Atlantic*, pp. 17–18. Dorothy B. Porter and Sarah Parker Remond, *Dictionary of American Negro Biography*, ed. Rayford W. Logan and Michael R. Winston (New York: W.W. Norton, 1982), p. 523. Mary Gibson Hundley, Anna Julia Cooper, *Dictionary of American Negro Biography*, p. 128.

16. For the foundation of the national black women's club movement and the anticipation of its concerns by the authors of female slave narratives, see Carby, *Reconstructing Womanhood*, pp. 61, 96, 116–117.

17. However, Hazel Carby's discussions of Victoria Earle Matthews who, in 1895 at the First National Conference of the Colored Women of America, delivered "a plea for black scholars to focus on and explore African history and the African ancestry of black Americans" in order to facilitate the production of "race literature," and the Ethiopianist fiction and nonfiction of Pauline Hopkins suggests that further investigation might recover a parallel phenomenon in black literature. See Carby, *Reconstructing Womanhood*, pp. 119–20, 155–62.

18. Based on circumstantial evidence, Bearden and Henderson place Lewis's birth "in the village of Greenbush, across the Hudson from Albany, New York" and repeat the July 14, 1845 birthdate given by James A. Porter. Richardson, relying on an obituary and other data pertaining to the artist's only known sibling, avoids specifying both Edmonia Lewis's birthplace and date. Her sources indicate, however, that Lewis's mother died in 1844, thus precluding the sculptor's birth the following year. Richardson also cites census data that suggests at least part of Lewis's early life was spent in Newark, New Jersey. Romare Bearden and Harry Henderson, *A History of African American Artists: From 1792 to the Present* (New York: Pantheon Books, 1993), pp. 54, 485, notes 3, 4. James A. Porter, *Modern Negro Art* (New York: Dryden Press, 1943), p. 57. Marilyn Richardson, "Edmonia Lewis' The Death of Cleopatra: Myth and Identity," *The International Review of African American Art*, vol. 12, no. 2 (1995), pp. 44, 52, notes 23, 24.

19. Richardson, "Edmonia Lewis' The Death of Cleopatra," p. 44. Bearden and Henderson trace the mother's ancestry to "an African American, John Mike, presumably a fugitive slave," who married a "Mississauga woman named Catherine" and explain that "[t]he Mississauga are a Chippewa (Ojibwa) band, who then lived on the Credit River Reserve, now the site of the city of Mississauga on Lake Ontario." Bearden and Henderson, *A History of African American Artists*, p. 54.

20. Bearden and Henderson, *A History of African American Artists*, p. 55. Richardson, "Edmonia Lewis' The Death of Cleopatra," p. 44.

21. Bearden and Henderson, *A History of African American Artists*, pp. 56, 60.

22. Geoffrey Blodgett, "John Mercer Langston and the Case of Edmonia Lewis: Oberlin, 1862," *The Journal of Negro History*, vol. 52, no. 3 (July 1968): 202.

23. Mary Wollstonecraft, *A Vindication of the Rights of Women* (London, 1792). Virginia Woolf, *A Room of One's Own* (London, 1929), and *Three Guineas* (London, 1938).

24. Bearden and Henderson, *A History of African American Artists*, p. 57.

25. Blodgett, "John Mercer Langston and the Case of Edmonia Lewis," p. 202.

26. For the prominence of progressive males of both races in the nineteenth-century women's rights movement, see Philip S. Foner, Preface, in Foner, ed., *Frederick Douglass On Women's Rights* (Westport, CT: Greenwood Press, 1976), p. ix. For the tendency of feminist-abolitionists to support temperance and label "themselves as universal reformers," see Sanchez-Eppler, "Bodily Bonds," p. 29.

27. From an 1831 pamphlet entitled *Religion and Pure Principles of Morality, the Sure Foundation on Which We Must Build* by Maria W. Stewart, excerpted in Bert James Loewenberg and Ruth Bogin, eds., *Black Women in Nineteenth Century American Life* (University Park: The Pennsylvania State University Press, 1976), p. 187.

28. St. Clair Drake, *The Redemption of Africa and Black Religion* (Chicago: Third World Press, 1970), pp. 47–49.

29. They include Lydia Maria Child, whose correspondence with and about Lewis is one of the primary sources of information about the artist; sculptor Anne Whitney, who is said to have provided Lewis with technical information "on handling clay" at an early stage of her career; Maria Weston Chapman, head of the Boston Female Anti-Slavery Society and the subject of one of the artist's early portrait busts; pioneer woman physician Dr. Harriot K. Hunt—"a friend of such leading feminists as Elizabeth Cady Stanton and Susan B. Anthony"—who commissioned Lewis to execute the monument for her tomb in Mount Auburn Cemetery; and Laura Curtis Bullard, who publicized Lewis's work in Rome in the pages of *The Revolution*, the feminist journal founded by Stanton and Anthony and subsequently purchased by Bullard, as well as in Frederick Douglass's *New National Era*. Bearden and Henderson, p. 62. Charlotte Streifer Rubinstein, *American Women Sculptors* (Boston: G.K. Hall, 1990), p. 56. Lydia Maria Child to Sarah Shaw, April 8, 1866, published in Benjamin Quarles, "A Sidelight on Edmonia Lewis," *The Journal of Negro History*, vol. 30, no. 1 (January 1945): 83. Bearden and Henderson, *A History of African American Artists*, pp. 62, 71, 488, nos. 87, 94.

30. Marilyn Richardson's forthcoming biography of Lewis should rectify this situation.

31. Frances Rollin diary in Dorothy Sterling, ed., *We Are Your Sisters: Black Women in the Nineteenth Century* (New York: W.W. Norton, 1984), p. 459. I owe this reference to Crystal Strickland, an undergraduate who assisted me in research on Lewis at the University of Virginia during Spring 1992.

32. Lawson Andrew Scruggs, *Women of Distinction: Remarkable in Works and Invincible in Character* (Raleigh, NC: L.A. Scruggs, 1893), pp. 156–58. Carby, *Reconstructing Womanhood*, pp. 4–5.

33. Mary Ann Cary in Sterling, *We Are Your Sisters*, p. 413.

34. According Lynda Roscoe Hartigan, Brackett's instruction was limited to the then "common practice" of lending "Lewis fragments of sculptures to copy in clay as exercises which he then critiqued." Hartigan, "Edmonia Lewis," in *Sharing Traditions: Five Black Artists in Nineteenth-Century America* (Washington, DC: National Museum of American Art/Smithsonian Institution Press, 1985), p. 88.

35. Jean Fagan Yellin, *Women & Sisters: The Antislavery Feminists in American Culture* (New Haven: Yale University Press, 1989), p. 9.

36. In the 1865 version, which is in the collection of the Montclair Art Museum in New Jersey, with his right hand Lincoln balances a shield on a stack of books surmounted by a partially unrolled scroll of paper, while the black man (whose costume includes a liberty cap) raises his right hand in a gesture that seems to serve only to advertise its grace. It is striking that, while the alterations seen in the later version give the work a greater discursive unity and visual economy, they also seem to enforce a greater disjunction between the character of the artist's black

and white subjects—a shift that is consistent with the impending demise of Reconstruction with the Hayes-Tilden Compromise of 1877.

37. My thanks to David Byron, a graduate student in the history of art at Yale, for pointing out the Mosaic reference and its double-edged character of law-giver/liberator during an October 25, 1995, methods seminar.

38. Yellin, *Women & Sisters*, pp. 10, 12–21. My thanks to Evan R. Firestone, director of the School of Art at the University of Georgia, for drawing my attention to the formal analogy between the pose of the female figure in Lewis's *Forever Free* and the abolitionist female supplicant image. Although Yellin also notes this similarity, she is at a loss to interpret its significance in Lewis's work, a loss I would ascribe to a failure to seriously probe the ideological implications of Lewis's biography.

39. S. Jay Walker, "Frederick Douglass and Woman Suffrage," *The Black Scholar*, vol. 4, nos. 6–7 (March–April 1973): 27.

40. Anonymous, "Equal Rights Convention for New York State, Albany, New York, November 20, 1866," *New York Tribune*, December 21, 1866, in Philip S. Foner, ed., *Frederick Douglass On Women's Rights* (Westport, CT: Greenwood Press, 1976), pp. 79–80.

41. Sojourner Truth, address delivered at the Convention of the American Equal Rights Association, New York City, 1867, in Gerda Lerner, ed., *Black Women in White America: A Documentary History* (New York: Vintage, 1973), p. 569.

42. Along the same lines though in less historically specific terms, Marilyn Richardson, who also notes the formal analogy between the anti-slavery icon and Lewis's kneeling ex-bondswoman, suggests "[h]er supplicating posture . . . posits a possibly ironic intention in the title of the piece"—i.e., *Forever Free*. Richardson, "Edmonia Lewis' The Death of Cleopatra," p. 50.

43. From an 1831 pamphlet entitled *Religion and Pure Principles of Morality, the Sure Foundation on Which We Must Build* by Maria W. Stewart, excerpted in Loewenberg and Bogin, eds., *Black Women in Nineteenth Century American Life*, p. 187.

44. Patricia Hill Collins, *Black Feminist Thought: Knowledge, Consciousness, and the Politics of Empowerment* (New York: Routledge, 1991), p. 4. Carby, *Reconstructing Womanhood*, pp. 61, 116.

45. In a 1972 catalogue essay for example, William Gerdts writes of Lewis's *Hagar*: "This Biblical figure, lost in the wilderness, was symbolic of the alienation of the Negro. Also, as with Cleopatra, Hagar was Egyptian, and to the nineteenth century Egypt meant Africa." William H. Gerdts, Jr., Introduction, *The White Marmorean Flock: Nineteenth Century American Women Neoclassical Sculptors*, exh. cat. (Poughkeepsie, NY: Vassar College Art Gallery, 1972), n.p.

A decade later, Charlotte Streifer Rubinstein labeled her *Death of Cleopatra* symbolic of Africa, but gives no indication of the sculptor's motive(s) for employing such symbolism. Hagar, Rubinstein declares, obviously refers to the position of black women in white society, an interpretation that points in the right direction, but remains unnecessarily diffuse.

In a 1990 study, Rubinstein attempts to historicize the African content of Lewis's *Death of Cleopatra*, noting that "[s]ince Egypt was symbolic of Africa and the African people, . . . this image may have been a response to the disappointment of the Reconstruction period, with its aborted dreams of equality."

Charlotte Streifer Rubinstein, *American Women Artists from Early Indian Times to the Present* (New York: G.K. Hall, 1982), pp. 80, 81. Rubinstein, *American Women Sculptors*, p. 55.

46. The seated figure measures 60 × 43 × 33 inches, according to Richardson, "Edmonia Lewis' The Death of Cleopatra," p. 37, caption.

47. In Rome, Lewis resided at No. 8A Via San Niccolo di Tolentino, the same street on which Story was located nearby in the Palazzo Barberini. Gerdts, *The White Marmorean Flock*, n.p. Dolly Sherwood, *Harriet Hosmer, American Sculptor, 1830–1908* (Columbia, MO: University of Missouri Press, 1991), pp. 258, 260. For the inclusion of Story's *Cleopatra* in the Centennial, see Bearden and Henderson, *A History of African American Artists*, p. 73.

48. The authors of an 1879 book on nineteenth-century art explained that *The Death of Cleopatra* was "not a beautiful work," because the effects of death are represented with such skill as to be absolutely repellent. Nonetheless they considered it "a very original and very striking" work that "could only have been produced by a sculptor of very genuine endowments." Clara E. Clement and Laurence Hutton, "Artists of the Nineteenth Century" (1879), cited by James A. Porter, Edmonia Lewis, in *Notable American Women 1607–1950*, ed. Edward T. James (Cambridge, MA: The Belknap Press of Harvard University Press, 1971), vol. 2, p. 398.

49. Richardson, "Edmonia Lewis' The Death of Cleopatra," p. 48.

50. Pauline Hopkins, "Famous Women of the Negro Race, 7 Educators," *Colored American Magazine*, vol. 5 (June 1902): 130, quoted in Carby, *Reconstructing Womanhood*, p. 156.

51. Fuller's *Ethiopia Awakening* is both "tantalizing" and extremely frustrating. Indeed, the problems of interpretation and contextualization surrounding this work are endemic to the study of Afro-U.S. artistic production and generally indicative of the sadly underdeveloped state of the field.

Virtually all the standard histories of African American art discuss the Fuller statue, with most authors assigning it special significance on the basis of either its technical assurance or its unprecedented African theme. Yet, the most basic facts about the piece—its title, date of execution, number of casts and alternate versions, and those works' mediums—are not yet firmly established. In her doctoral thesis on Fuller, Judith Nina Kerr, a social historian, lists a life-size bronze version of the figure (Schomburg Collection) and three 13¼-inch reproductions, located in the James Weldon Johnson Collection at Yale University's Beinecke Library, the Meta Warrick Fuller Legacy in Framingham, Massachusetts, and a private collection in Pennsylvania. Kerr dates the Schomburg piece "1915–21," but gives no indication of whether or not the same dates apply to the reproductions. The question is a particularly vexing one, because various sources give conflicting dates for *Ethiopia Awakening* (occasionally dubbing it *The Awakening of Ethiopia*) and illustrate different versions of it without identifying them as such. And, although Kerr does not list it, there appears to have been a bronze reproduction in the Schomburg Collection, as well as the life-size piece, the latter frequently being misidentified as "bronze," when it is probably plaster painted to look like bronze (a procedure Kerr notes Fuller used in another work, the undated *So-Big*. Obviously, any reading of an artwork that cannot be confidently dated or matched to textual references must be highly provisional, if not entirely conjectural. See Judith Nina Kerr, "God-given Work: The Life and Times of Sculptor Meta Vaux Warrick Fuller, 1877–1968," (PhD diss., University of Massachusetts, Amherst, 1986), pp. 204, 259–62, 428. Deborah A.

Deacon, "The Art & Artifacts Collection of The Schomburg Center for Research in Black Culture: A Preliminary Catalogue," *Bulletin of Research in the Humanities*, vol. 84, no. 2 (Summer 1981): 146–49, 228–29. For a few of the many examples of inconsistent identifications, dates and descriptions cited above, see Elsa Honig Fine, *The Afro-American Artist: A Search for Identity* (New York: Holt, Rinehart and Winston, 1973), p. 76. Alain Locke, *The Negro In Art* (1940; reprint, New York: Hacker Art Books, 1979), p. 31. David C. Driskell, *Hidden Heritage: Afro-American Art, 1800–1950* (Bellevue, WA: Bellevue Art Museum; San Francisco: The Art Museum Association of America, 1985), pp. 30, 37, fig. 19.

52. Kerr, "God-given Work," pp. 1–4, 27–32, 112–13, 117, 137.

53. "DuBois was in charge of assembling 'The Negro Section' of the Paris Exposition of 1900" and eventually received "the exposition's Gold Medal" for his efforts, according to Herbert Aptheker. Herbert Aptheker, ed., *The Correspondence of W.E.B. DuBois, volume 1, Selections, 1877–1934* (Amherst: University of Massachusetts Press, 1973), p. 45, n. 1.

Kerr, "God-given Work," pp. 67, 75–76, 80–81, 95–96, 99–101, 128. As early as 1897, in "The Conservation of Races," a paper delivered to the American Negro Academy, DuBois had urged U.S. blacks to assume "their just place in the van of Pan Negroism." But the author of these words would not put them into practice until 1900, when he participated in the first Pan-African Conference, held July 23–25, at Westminster Hall in London. It was there, in an "Address to the Nations of the World" calling for self-government in Britain's African and Caribbean colonies, DuBois uttered his oracular statement: "The problem of the Twentieth Century is the problem of the color line—the relation of the darker to the lighter races of men in Asia and Africa, in America and the islands of the sea." W. E. B. DuBois, "The Conservation of Races," in Julius Lester, ed., *The Seventh Son: The Thought and Writing of W.E.B. DuBois*, vol. 1 (New York: Vintage, 1971), p. 181. Sylvia M. Jacobs, *The African Nexus: Black American Perspectives on the European Partitioning of Africa, 1880–1920* (Westport, CA: Greenwood Press, 1981), pp. 55–57. Rayford W. Logan and Michael R. Winston, "William Edward Burghardt DuBois," in *Dictionary of American Negro Biography*, Logan and Winston (eds.), p. 197.

54. Groups like Philadelphia's Benjamin Banneker Institute, to which Warrick's "Uncle Billy" belonged, wed political debate with cultural 'uplift' by championing black literature, preserving historical documents, and building some of the earliest libraries of African American history. As Jacobs points out, such organizations "were part of the black history and protest movement" that emerged in the late nineteenth century "to promote dignity and racial pride" in response to "racism and prevailing white notions of black inferiority." Kerr, "God-given Work," pp. 39–41, 44. James G. Spady, "William Carl Bolivar"; George B. Tindall, "Francis L[ouis] Cardozo," and Roland B. Scott, "W[illiam] Warrick Cardozo," in Logan and Winston, *Dictionary of American Negro Biography*, pp. 50, 89–90. Jacobs, *The African Nexus*, p. 52.

55. Kerr, "God-given Work," p. 147.

56. The ca. 1906 date comes from Benjamin Brawley's 1918 article on Fuller. The assertion that "nearly all" of her early work was lost in the 1910 fire comes from James A. Porter. Brawley, "Meta Warrick Fuller," *The Southern Workman*, vol. 47 (January 1918): 26. Porter, *Modern Negro Art* (1943; reprint, New York: Arno, 1969), p. 78.

57. James Weldon Johnson, *Black Manhattan* (1930; reprint, New York: Atheneum, 1972), pp. 104–6. Lynne Fauley Emery, *Black Dance: From 1619 to Today*, 2d ed. revised (Princeton, NJ: Dance Horizons, 1988), p. 213. Brenda Dixon-Stowell, "Popular Dance in the Twentieth-Century," in Emery, pp. 351–52. Donald Bogle, "George Walker," in Logan and Winston, *Dictionary of American Negro Biography*, p. 624.

58. In ways too subtle to detail here, Huggins makes clear that, by today's standards, this "break" was a barely discernible hairline fracture. Yet, insofar as Williams and Walker succeeded in modulating the grotesquely exaggerated comedic style of black minstrelsy in which—as Walker put it—"colored performers . . . imitated the white performers in their make-up as 'darkies'," the celebrated duo *did* produce a space in which it was possible for some viewers to experience a degree of psychological identification that could begin to disrupt the alienating structures of contemporary racism. Nathan Irvin Huggins, *Harlem Renaissance* (New York: Oxford University Press, 1971), p. 281.

59. Kerr, "God-given Work," p. 146. Huggins, *Harlem Renaissance*, p. 282. Douglas Henry Daniels, *Pioneer Urbanites: A Social and Cultural History of Black San Francisco* (Philadelphia: Temple University Press, 1980), p. 226.

60. Kerr, "God-given Work," p. 239. Dorothy B. Porter, "Pauline Elizabeth Hopkins," in Logan and Winston, *Dictionary of American Negro Biography*, p. 326.

61. The reference to "Ethiopia" here reflects the ancient Greek translation of "Cush," the ancient Hebrew term for "Nubia." William R. Scott, *The Sons of Sheba's Race: African Americans and the Italo-Ethiopian War, 1935–1941* (Bloomington: Indiana University Press, 1993), p. 14. Ulysses Lee, "The A[ssociation for the] S[tudy of] N[egro] L[ife and] H[istory], *The Journal of Negro History*, and American Scholarly Interest in Africa," in Présence Africaine, ed., *Africa Seen by American Negroes* (Paris: Présence Africaine, 1958): 405–6. Jacobs, *The African Nexus*, p. 52.

62. Robert C. Hayden, "Solomon Carter Fuller," in Logan and Winston, *Dictionary of American Negro Biography*, p. 247.

63. Drake, *The Redemption of Africa and Black Religion*, p. 73. Jacobs, *The African Nexus*, p. 189.

64. As an indication of the scale of Afro-U.S. response to Ethiopia's victory at Adua, Jacobs reports that "every black paper extant today" published articles and editorials on the event. References to Adua as the "'Italian Waterloo'" in the *Cleveland Gazette* and, by contrast, to Menelik II as "the Napoleon of Africa" in *The Topeka State Ledger*, as well as the *Indianapolis Freeman*'s congratulatory editorial, which employed the characteristic idiom of U.S. boxing fans to proclaim, "'They hit 'em hard in Abyssinia!'" exemplify the jubilant African American reaction to Italy's defeat. Jacobs, *The African Nexus*, pp. 193–200. Scott, *The Sons of Sheba's Race*, p. 21.

65. Albert Boime, *The Art of Exclusion: Representing Blacks in the Nineteenth Century* (Washington, DC: The Smithsonian Institution Press, 1990), pp. 9, 12, figs. 1–7. Matthew Baigell, *A Concise History of American Painting and Sculpture* (New York: Icon Editions, 1984), pp. 189, 191, fig. 190.

66. Boime, *The Art of Exclusion*, p. 11.

67. Freeman Henry Morris Murray, *Emancipation and the Freed in American Sculpture: A Study in Interpretation* (Freeport, NY: Books for Libraries Press, 1972 [orig. 1916]), pp. 92–93.

68. Kerr, "God-given Work," pp. 77–79. Baigell, *A Concise History of American Painting and Sculpture*, pp. 187–89. Daniel M. Mendelowitz, *A History of American Art* (New York: Holt, Rinehart & Winston, 1970), p. 333.

69. Kerr, "God-given Work," pp. 212–14.

70. Abiola Irele, "Négritude and Nationalism," in Irele, *The African Experience in Literature and Ideology* (London: Heinemann, 1981), p. 104. Casely-Hayford's scheme is remarkably similar to that advocated by DuBois in his *Souls of Black Folk*, with its notion of a "talented tenth" destined to lead Afro-America, if not the entire black world, by virtue of its superior skills and training, but newly appreciative of black history and traditional black culture.

71. Published in 1936, *Negro Art: Past and Present* is the first survey of African American art history. Trained in philosophy at Harvard and at Oxford, where he was the first U.S. black Rhodes Scholar, its author Alain Locke taught philosophy at America's premier black college, Howard University, for thirty-five years and worked tirelessly to cultivate and promote African American achievement in the arts. Alain Locke, *Negro Art: Past and Present*, in Locke, *The Negro and His Music and Negro Art: Past and Present* (1936; reprint, Salem, NH: Ayer Company, 1991), p. 30. David Levering Lewis, *When Harlem Was in Vogue* (New York: Alfred A. Knopf, 1981), pp. 87, 117–18, 149–55. Michael R. Winston, "Alain Leroy Locke," in Logan and Winston, *Dictionary of American Negro Biography*, pp. 398–404.

72. Fuller contributed an art column to Hopkins magazine, *The New Era*, in February 1916. A subsequent pregnancy forced the artist to abandon the column after the journal's first issue, however. Kerr, "God-given Work," pp. 239–43.

73. In Lewis and Fuller's wake, African heritage was thematized in the work of countless Afro-U.S. artists during the mid-1920s to mid-1930s "Negro Renaissance." Along with references to tropical Africa in Aaron Douglas's illustrations for *The New Negro* (1925) and in some of the canvases Archibald Motley exhibited in his 1928 New Gallery show, imagery drawn from the ancient civilizations of the Nile Valley and the Horn figured in black cultural products ranging from the covers of the Urban League journal, *Opportunity*, and its rival, *The Crisis*, house organ of the NAACP, to epic pageants like the 1925 Hollywood Bowl performance of DuBois's "Star of Ethiopia." Alain Locke, ed., *The New Negro* (New York: Atheneum, 1969 [orig. 1925]), pp. 54, 56, 112, 128, 138, 228. Jontyle Theresa Robinson, "The Life of Archibald J. Motley, Jr.," in Jontyle Theresa Robinson and Wendy Greenhouse, *The Art of Archibald J. Motley, Jr.* (Chicago: Chicago Historical Society, 1991), pp. 11–13. See, for example, Albert Alexander Smith's drawing, *A Fantasy Ethiopia*, for the cover of the June 1928 issue of *Opportunity* and James Lesesne Wells's woodblock, *Ethiopia at the Bar of Justice*, illustrating a 1924 play of the same name, which appears on the cover of the November 1928 issue of *The Crisis*. Christine R. Gray, Introduction, *Plays and Pageants from the Life of the Negro*, ed. by Willis Richardson (Jackson: University of Mississippi Press, 1993 [orig. 1930]), pp. xxvii–xxviii, xxxiv–xxxv. W. E. B. DuBois, "Opinion: . . . The Pageant of the Angels," *The Crisis*, Vol. 30, no. 5 (September 1925): 217, cover ("A portrait in colors of Miss Ada Gaines, who played the part of Ethiopia in the pageant in Los Angeles").

While these works demonstrate Lewis and Fuller's prescience, they do not prove either woman was a direct influence on any of her successors. A 1932 canvas, Lois Mailou Jones' *The Ascent of Ethiopia*, however, has been described as a homage to Fuller's similarly named sculpture. In a 1990 article, Jones recalled having been "greatly inspired" by the older artist, whom she knew from summers at Martha's Vineyard, the Cape Cod retreat of New England's black middle class. Gail Gelbrud, Introduction, *A Blossoming of New Promises: Art in the Spirit of the Harlem Renaissance*, exh. cat. (Hempstead, NY: Emily Lowe Gallery, Hofstra University, February 5–March 18, 1984), unpag. Alvia J. Wardlaw, et al., *Black Art: Ancestral Legacy: The African Impulse in African American Art*, exh. cat. (Dallas, TX: Dallas Museum of Art, December 3, 1989–February 25, 1990), P. 159. Kathy Perkins, "The Genius of Meta Warrick Fuller," in *Black American Literature Forum*, Vol. 24, no. 1 (Spring 1990): 66.

ILLUSTRATIONS AND BIOGRAPHIES

....

JONTYLE THERESA ROBINSON

AMALIA AMAKI (b. 1949)

. . . .

Amaki's career encompasses many achievements: artist, curator, appraiser, speaker, writer, art critic, and teacher. She earned degrees in Journalism and Psychology at Georgia State University, in Photography at the University of Mexico, and received an MA in Modern American and European Art and a PhD in Twentieth-Century American Art and Culture from Emory University.

A distinct feature of her artwork is the use of digitally manipulated photographs or cards adorned with buttons, beads, and simulated pearls. These dynamic works, which feature black men, women, and children who have influenced her life and art, celebrate the African American cultural tradition.

SOUVENIR GAZE #2
wood, color photographs, buttons, simulated pearls, beads, and jewelry fragments
20" × 16"   1995

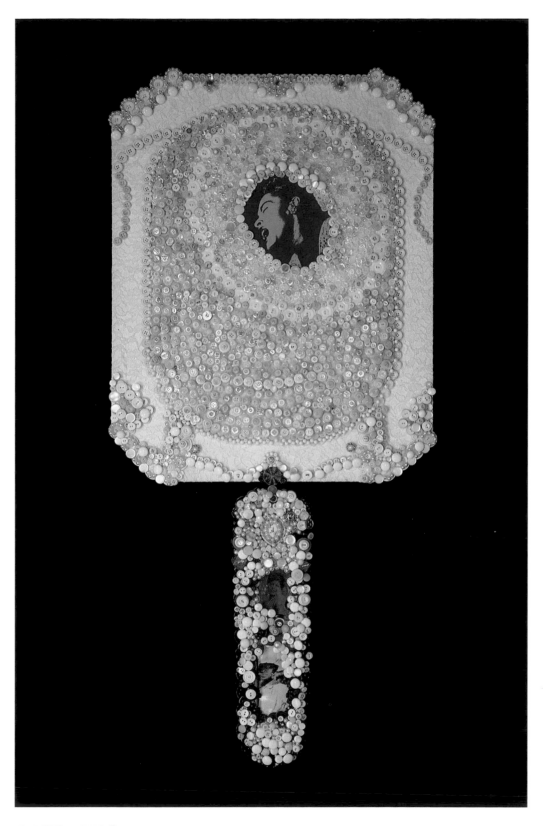

NUMBER 1 FAN #2
wood, cyanotype on cotton, buttons, simulated pearls, fabric, jewelry fragments, and color photographs
48″ × 30″   1995

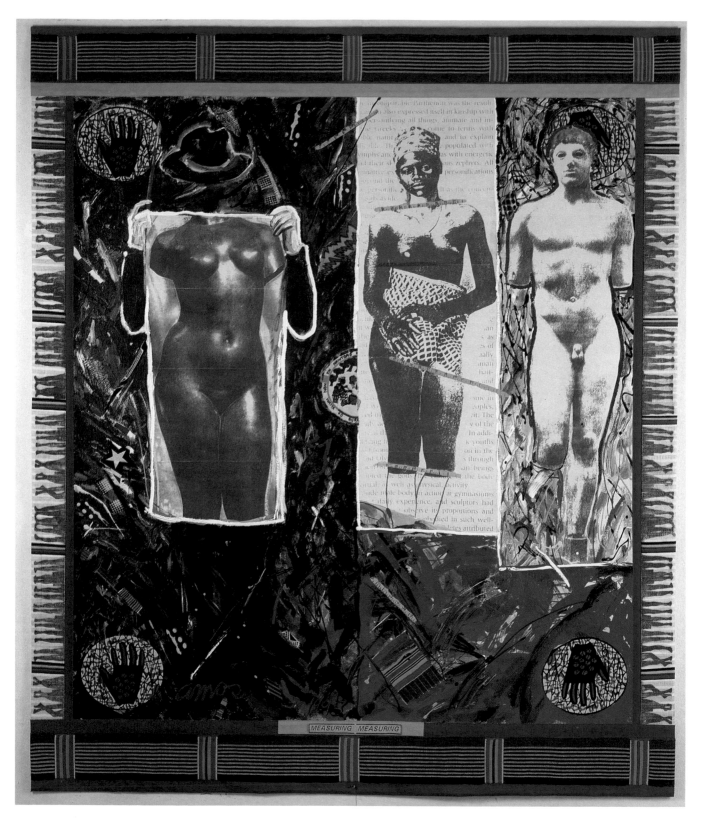

MEASURING MEASURING
acrylic on linen canvas, African fabric, laser-transfer photographs
84″ × 70″   1995

EMMA AMOS (b. 1938)

. . . .

Amos incorporates diverse mediums—painting, print-making, and weaving— which reflect the artist's "consciousness and respect for the history of the African American struggle and rich cultural heritage."[1] A native of Atlanta, Georgia, Amos received her BA from Antioch College and her MA from New York University.

While at New York University, Amos's dedication to the causes of African Americans, and especially African American artists, strengthened as she became a leader in establishing a "political identity for women artists of color and for women artists at large." In tune with gender politics, Amos's artwork reflects her concern for the mother-daughter bond and friendship, drawing upon her interpersonal and family relationships.

1. Moore, Sylvia and Dr. Leslie King-Hammond, eds., *Gumbo Ya Ya: Anthology of Contemporary African American Women Artists*, New York: Midmarch Arts Press, 1995.

TIGHTROPE
acrylic on linen canvas, African fabric, laser-transfer photographs of Mrs. Gauguin's breasts, *Two Tahitian Women with Mangoes* (reproduced in the four corners) 82″ × 58″   1994

BEVERLY BUCHANAN (b. 1940)

. . . .

Born in Fuquay, North Carolina, Buchanan was greatly influenced by the rural setting and especially the housing structures. These housing structures, or shacks, are featured in her sculpture and painting, depicting her consciousness of the socioeconomic dilemma of the Deep South and her fascination with rural architecture.

Educated at Bennett College and Columbia University, she received a Bachelor of Science degree in Medi-

cal Technology and a Master's degree in Parasitology and Public Health, respectively. Working in these fields, Buchanan applied her educational training as a medical technologist for the Veterans Administration and as a health educator.

Since 1963, Buchanan has been exhibiting her boundless skill through work in the mediums of drawing, painting, and sculpture.

4 SHACKS WITH BLACK-EYED SUSANS
oil pastel on paper
25½″ × 38″   1995

Courtesy: Steinbaum Krauss Gallery, New York City
Photographer: Adam Reich

BLUE LIGHTNING
oil pastel on paper
25½″ × 38″   1995

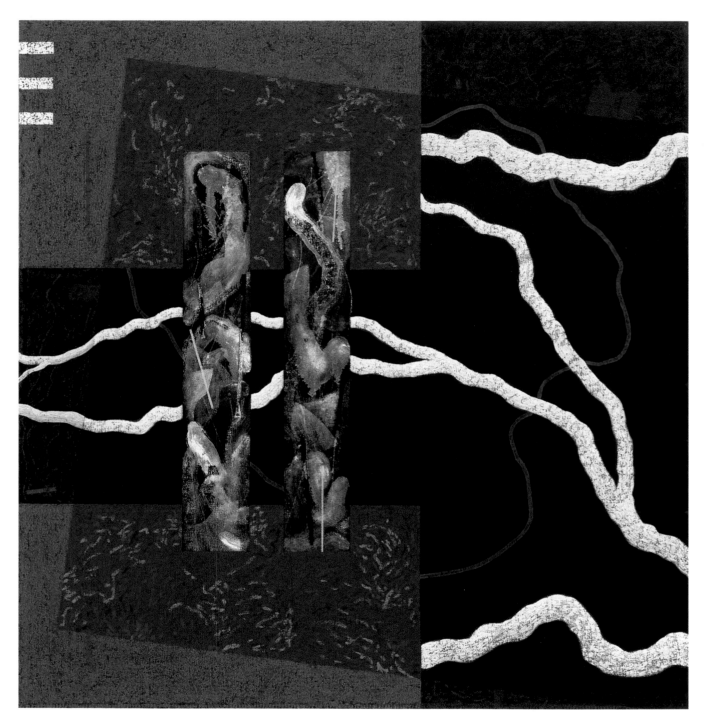

WINDOW VIEW-SCAPEOLOGY #9
oil on canvas
41″ × 40″   1995

WINDOW VIEW-SCAPEOLOGY #3
oil on canvas
40¾″ × 45½″   1995

Photographer: Manu Sassoonian

NANETTE CARTER (b. 1954)

. . . .

Carter began to paint as a child in Columbus, Ohio, and entered the artistic world very early in life. Later, she studied art at Oberlin College, where she received her Bachelor's degree. Notably, she spent her junior year during her undergraduate studies in Perugia, Italy, studying at L'Accademia di Belle Arti. In 1978, she earned her MFA from New York's esteemed Pratt Institute.

Carter employs a non-representational form of expression that is derived from her study of African art, Japanese prints, and Russian Constructivism. The influence of musical rhythms is also evident in her work, as she translates the subtleties of jazz into colorful visual melodies. Although her paintings are devoid of realistic images, they reflect her experiences as a black woman.

ELIZABETH CATLETT (b. 1915)

. . . .

Catlett's formal artistic training began during the Depression at Howard University where she earned her Bachelor of Science degree. She was privileged to study under such renowned African American artists as Lois Mailou Jones, James Porter, and James L. Wells. After graduating from Howard University, Catlett received her MFA degree from the State University of Iowa.

During Catlett's formative years, she mastered modernist and classical European techniques that greatly impacted her stylistic development. Moreover, inspired by Grant Wood, a painter who was instrumental in her aesthetic evolution, Catlett began to sculpt and paint images derived from her own experiences. For Catlett, this notion would translate into a desire to capture the lives of black people.

Catlett's prints and sculptures are simple and massive images that embody the soulful essence, magnificence, and painful struggle for self-determination of black people in America.

NORMA
gray marble with black grain
14½" × 9" × 12"   1994

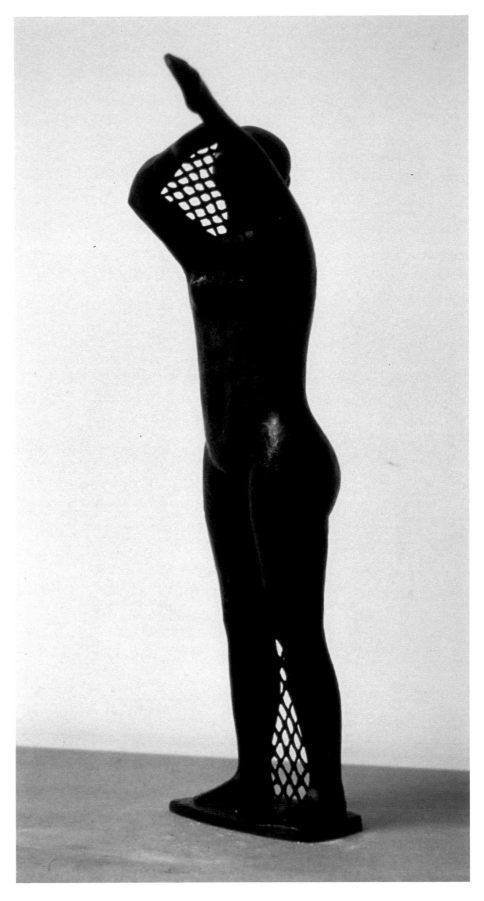

WEBBED WOMAN
bronze
38½″ high   1995

MAREN HASSINGER (b. 1947)

. . . .

Born in Los Angeles, California, Hassinger received her BA from Bennington College and her MFA at the University of California in Los Angeles.

She conveys her spiritual energy through all of her creative inventions and performances. Hassinger uses a phenomenal array of images to confront the viewer with iconographic tensions between nature and the industrialized world. She has organized numerous performances throughout Los Angeles county and New York, using her artwork as properties for theatrical exhibits.

For the exhibition, one of these maquettes will be constructed of metal and stand six feet high.

WEIGHT OF DREAMS #2
mixed media, maquette
6" high   1995

WEIGHT OF DREAMS
mixed media, maquette
6″ high   1995

Photographer: Tim Lee

CHARNELLE HOLLOWAY (b. 1957)

. . . .

Holloway's creations are deeply rooted in her knowledge of traditional African art. She began to study art at Spelman College in 1975, focusing her attention on life drawing. After receiving her BA in 1979, she received her MFA in jewelry design and silversmithing from Georgia State University.

Holloway's earliest work reveals her mastery of the medium of metal. Using a modernist style, she created simple and angular geometric shapes. Her later endeavors take on a more personal vision and disclose her beliefs about the black family, relationships, and spirituality.

FERTILITY BELT FOR THE CAREER WOMAN
repoussé *akua ba* doll, sterling silver, bronze, mixed media
8″ × 3½″   1995 (opposite)

WOMAN'S ARK
knurled maple, 17″ × 9″ × 9″   1995

FREIDA HIGH (b. 1946)

. . . .

Born in Starkville, Mississippi, High earned her BS in Art Education from Northern Illinois University, and her MFA in Studio Art focusing on graphics and painting and in Art History with a concentration in African and African American Art from the University of Wisconsin.

High's work shows her indomitable passion for her people and pays homage to African American survival. A writer as well as an artist, High serves as a catalyst for the preservation and uplift of African American culture.

RETURNING TO THE DOOR
OF NO RETURN
acrylic and sand on canvas
8' × 5'   1995

VARNETTE P. HONEYWOOD (b. 1950)

. . . .

Honeywood's art embraces an Afrocentric spirit, exploring themes through a variety of mediums—assemblage, collage, construction, charcoal drawing, acrylic painting, and mixed media. Born in Los Angeles, California, Honeywood received a BA from Spelman College and an MS in Education from the University of Southern California.

Honeywood uses bold colors throughout much of her artwork, symbolizing the beauty of African ancestry and African American contemporary life. With images rich in color and African allusions to the past, present, and future, Honeywood illustrates the diversity and complexity of black life while impugning racial biases and stereotypes.

THE CAREGIVER
acrylic on canvas
37″ × 52″   1995

LOIS MAILOU JONES (b. 1905)

. . . .

Lois Mailou Jones's achievements in the art world span over six decades. During this time, Jones "discovered a variety of individualized expressions of indigenous themes and personal styles."[1] Early in her career, Jones worked in the field of textile design, though she later triumphed as a much-recognized and appreciated painter.

Aesthetically, Jones's art is inspired by the varied elements of nature. Sparked by her interest in impressionism, it is this love of nature that marks her artistic origins and bolsters her captivating styles. Jones's stylistic approach focuses on design, form, and color. Her voyage to Haiti marked a turning point in her career, as she began to incorporate the vibrant color and abstract and linear forms that are boldly characteristic of Haitian and African art.

1. Moore, Sylvia and Dr. Leslie King-Hammond, eds., *Gumbo Ya Ya: Anthology of Contemporary African American Women Artists*, New York: Midmarch Arts Press, 1995.

CHANSON D' BAHIA
acrylic on canvas
40" × 29"   1989

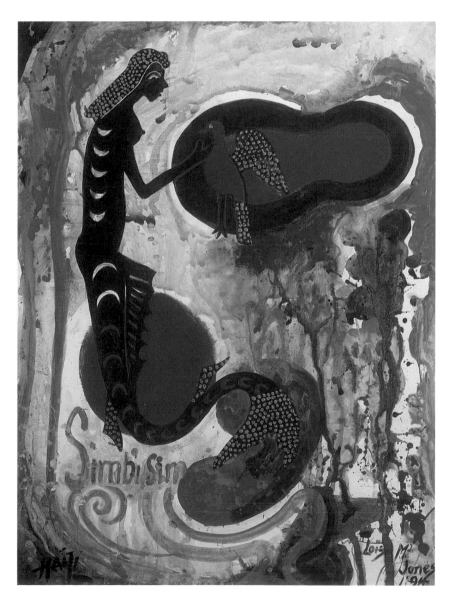

SIMBI, HAITI
acrylic on canvas
30½" × 24½"   1994

Photographer: Marvin T. Jones

STEPHANIE JOHNSON (b. 1952)

. . . .

Johnson studied theater at Emerson College earning her BFA, and received her MA in Interdisciplinary Art from San Francisco State University.

Her creative vision pays homage to her ancestors through multimedia presentations of photographs, sounds, and objects. Johnson's theatrical background as a lighting designer influences her installations in their dramatically vibrant displays of light, sound, and form.

Much of her art consists of historical revelations and evocations of her forgotten predecessors. Legitimizing the African American aesthetic tradition, Johnson's images oppose the processes of marginalization with respect to African American culture and encourage her audience to refute racist and sexist stereotypes.

A BOUQUET
light bulbs, steel tubes, steel boxes
7′ × 6′ × 2′   1995

Photographer: Andre Kreft

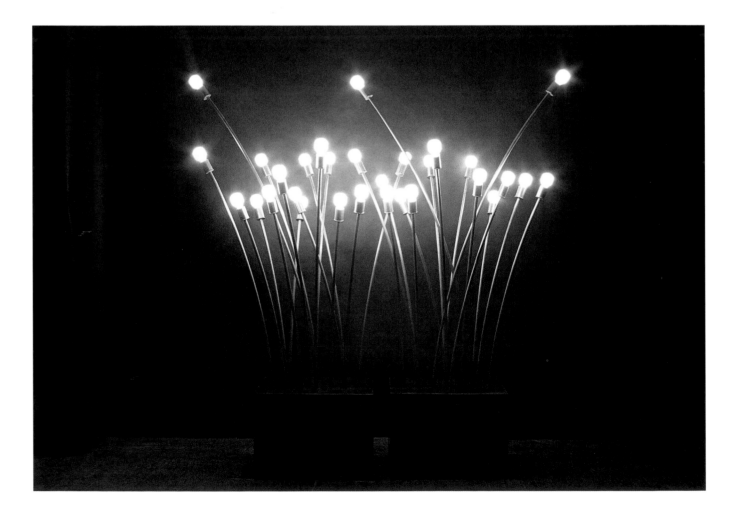

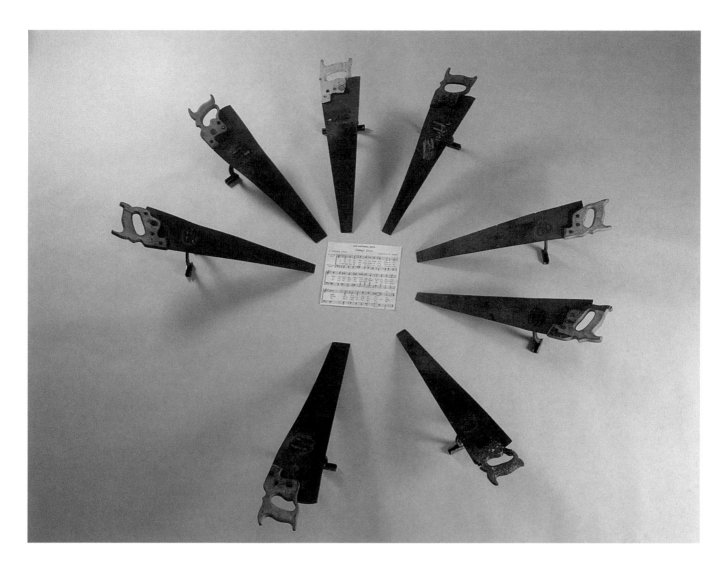

. . . WHEN WE SAY GOODBYE
IN MEMORY OF BROTHER LARRY
saws, horseshoes, sheet music
7′ diameter, 10″ deep   1995

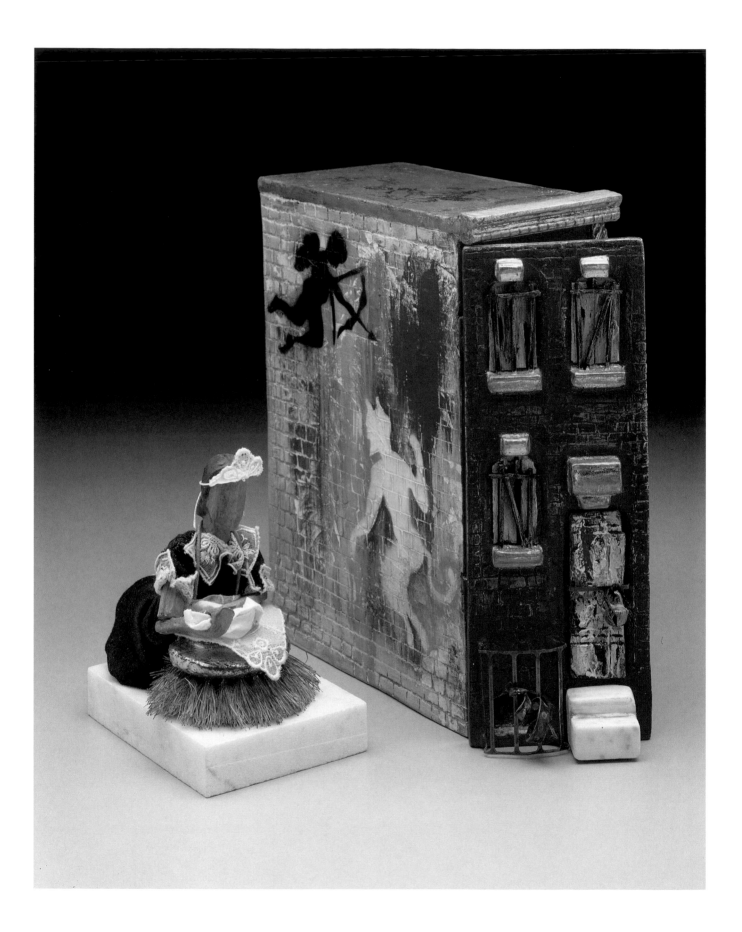

JEAN LACY (b. 1932)

· · · · · · · · · ·

Lacy received her BA in Art Education from Southern University in Baton Rouge, Louisiana. Her art is enriched with the imagery and collective spirit of all people of African descent. Lacy incorporates mixed media paintings, sculptures, and printmaking to visually elucidate the recurring themes of urban African life and experience.

Throughout her career, her artwork has been an expression of love for urban life and the myriad people in the African Diaspora. By aligning images of African antiquity with modern images of urban life, she illustrates a universal connection between people of African descent.

NOAH (BERT WILLIAMS/BILL
"BOJANGLES" ROBINSON)
animated music box
8½″ × 5½″ × 2½″   1986
Collection of Mani Jasiri Short and Alvia Wardlaw

Photographer: Thomas DuBrock

PRAYER FOR THE RESURRECTION OF A
ROW HOUSE IN BALTIMORE
mixed media construction with carved wooden doll
8½″ × 6½″, doll 4″ high   1995

Photographer: Tom Jenkins

VALERIE MAYNARD (b. 1937)

. . . .

A native of Harlem, Maynard studied painting, drawing, and printmaking at The Museum of Modern Art and the New School for Social Research in New York City. She received an MA in media, focusing on prints, collage, gouache, and sculpture from Goodard College in Plainfield, Vermont. An educator and an artist, Maynard has taught printmaking and sculpture at the Studio Museum in Harlem, Howard University, and abroad at the College of the Virgin Islands, St. Thomas.

Her sculpture displays a chiseled elegance characteristic of African art. Likewise, her lively prints, spray-painted acrylics on paper, and collages reflect the African aesthetic, vividly embodying a gamut of themes from a stalwart protest against institutionalized racism to the much-anticipated liberation of a political prisoner.

NO APARTHEID ANYWHERE
painting in three parts, overlapping
acrylic paint on oak tag
9′ × 3′   1995

GET ME ANOTHER HEART THIS ONE'S BROKEN
acrylic paint on oak tag
3′ × 4′8″   1995

HOWARDENA PINDELL (b. 1943)

. . . .

Born in Philadelphia, Pindell received her BFA from
Boston University and her MFA from Yale University.
Pindell delves freely into myriad creative realms, from
collage and painting to works on paper and video drawing. A virtuoso experimenter, she follows changing artistic trends and implements them into her work.

Pindell's achievements are not contained solely in
the field of art—she also expresses her inexhaustible talent through written scholarship, from catalogue texts to
articles on racism in the art world.

MANDELA WELCOME PARADE #1 (NEW YORK 1992)
(detail)

MANDELA WELCOME PARADE #1 (NEW YORK 1992)
acrylic, cibachrome, and gouache on museum board
15" × 42" × 3½"   1992–1995

HATHOR TEMPLE, VALLEY OF THE KINGS, EGYPT (1974)
acrylic, cibachrome, and gouache on museum board
20" × 16" × 3½"   1992–1995

Courtesy: G.R. N'Namdi Gallery, Birmingham, Michigan

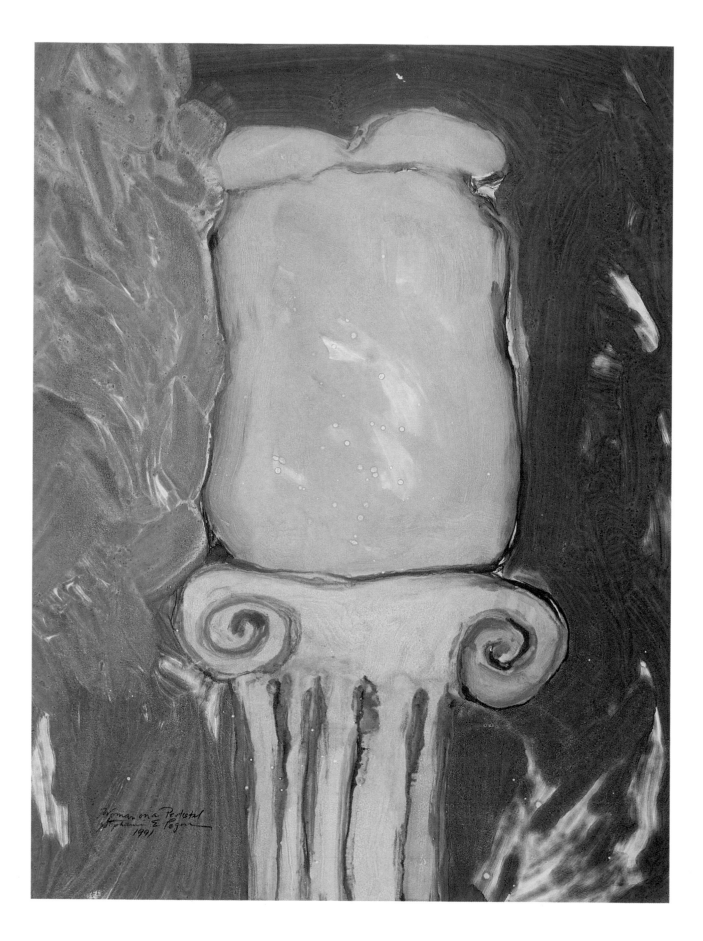

Woman on a Pedestal
Stephen E. Pogue
1991

STEPHANIE POGUE (b. 1944)

. . . .

Born in Shelby, North Carolina, Pogue earned her BFA from Howard University and her MFA in printmaking from Cranbrook Academy of Art in Bloomfield Hills, Michigan.

A teacher, artist, and curator, Pogue's artwork explores the fluctuation of emotion in coping with everyday life. In terms of style, the artist's choice of color stems from her studies and travels in India.

SELF-PORTRAIT:
VULNERABLE
Monotype
30″ × 22″   1989

Photographer: Joel Breger

WOMAN ON A
PEDESTAL
Monotype
30″ × 22″   1989

DEBRA PRIESTLY (b. 1961)

. . . .

Priestly studied at Ohio State University, earning her BFA in Painting and Drawing. Studying media with a concentration in painting, printmaking, and mixed media, she received her MFA in Painting and Printmaking from Pratt Institute in Brooklyn.

Inspired by music, quilts, the art of indigenous people, folk art, early Christian paintings, and the legacy of her family, Priestly creates with an acutely nostalgic eye. Alluding to her African ancestry and remembrances from childhood, Priestly's work pays homage to the lives of past generations and welcomes the future with joyful confidence.

PATOKA #11 BOAT
acrylic, canvas, pine on birch
32" × 48" × 4"   1994

PATOKA #3, LIGHTENING
acrylic, charcoal, pastel, paper, feather on birch
22″ × 22″ × 6½″   1992

Blackmelvet   A/P   Rachelle Pring

RACHELLE PURYEAR (b. 1947)

. . . .

A resident of Sweden since 1974, Puryear connects natural forms with abstract elements to build the thematic character of her spellbinding images. Puryear earned her BA from Trinity College in Washington, D.C., and her MA in African Art at Indiana University in Bloomington. Throughout college and graduate school, Puryear worked consistently in applied art corresponding with her art historical studies. Her main passion was printmaking, especially etching, with photography following at a close second.

During the late 1960s, Puryear's artwork was primarily abstract. In the mid-1970s, her love for photography, and especially her transition to Sweden, prompted a stylistic change—she began incorporating abstracted photographic images into her work. Creating in a naturalistic vein, Puryear continues to juxtapose photographic images and manually-created abstract elements.

CREVICE
silkscreen
40½″ × 22½″   1995

BLADVERKET (LEAFWORK)
silkscreen
31½″ × 21¼″   1995

BARBARA CHASE RIBOUD (b. 1939)

. . . .

Chase Riboud earned a BFA from a small art school aligned with Temple University in Philadelphia, where she not only studied the basic art requirements, but also medical drawing, anatomy, and dissection at the medical school. She received a MFA in sculpture from Yale University.

During her studies at Yale, the artist explored the key role of color in achieving artistic specificity. In her work, Chase Riboud promotes the use of color, utilizing its multi-hued power as a stabilizing force between race and art; she utilizes contrasting colors to show philosophical and social sameness between the races. Likewise, Chase Riboud's sculptures, a compilation of African and Western influences, are enigmatic expressions in that they attempt to unite diametric figures in order to erase division. She is known for combining materials not often used together to create powerful and complex visual works.

HARRAR OR MONUMENT
TO THE II MILLION
VICTIMS OF THE MIDDLE PASSAGE
(model)
33 × 11 × 8 cm
1993

TANTRA
gold, bronze, silk
190 × 100 × 60 cm   1993

MASTER'S TOOLS WILL NEVER DISMANTLE MASTER'S HOUSE • YOU GOTTA MOVE • BLACK IS BLACK AINT • UNITY DOES NOT EQUAL UNANIMITY •

BLACK MEN LOVING BLACK MEN • FREEDOM • BEEN IN THE STORM TOO LONG • TONGUES UNTIED •

MARLON RIGGS, TONGUES UNTIED, A PRINTED SPACE QUILT

WHAT HAPPENS TO A DREAM DEFERRED?

FAITH RINGGOLD (b. 1930)

. . . .

Born in New York City, Ringgold received both her BS in Fine Art and her MA in Visual Art from City College of New York. Through artwork, Ringgold celebrates her experiences as a woman of African descent in the United States. In her work, she focuses on painting, sculpture, performance, and quilt making, bombarding her viewers with images specific to her race, class, and gender.

During the 1960s, Ringgold painted works that reflected her involvement as an African American woman in the civil rights protests. The plight of black women was repeatedly emphasized in her poignantly feminist works. In fact, Ringgold's dedication to the African American struggle, along with her feminist views, inspired many of her works, especially her story quilts. The quilt, deeply embedded in the African American female tradition, became a palette on which Ringgold not only shares her talent as an artist, but also her experiences as a black woman.

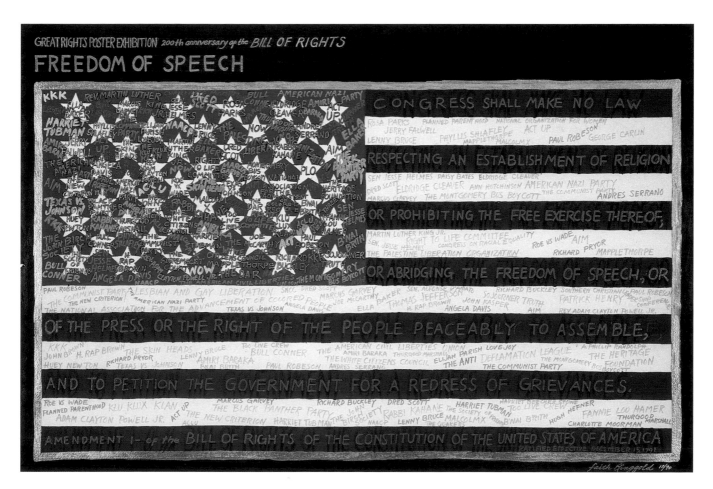

FREEDOM OF SPEECH
acrylic on paper
38″ × 45″ 1990

MARLON RIGGS: TONGUES UNTIED,
A PAINTED STORY QUILT
acrylic on canvas with pieced and quilted fabric,
fabric borders, and quotes given to Faith by Marlon
89″ × 59½″ 1994

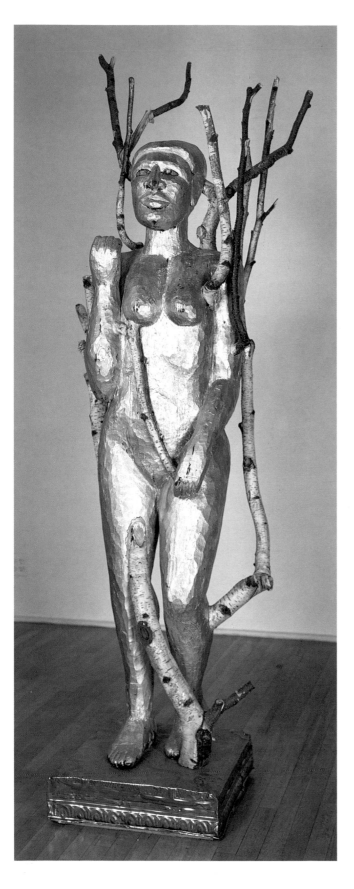

ALISON SAAR (b. 1956)

. . . .

The daughter of celebrated artist Betye Saar, Alison Saar inherited her mother's fondness for objects and stories. Saar earned her BA from Scripps College in Art History, with a focus on Afro-Caribbean art. She received an MFA from the Otis Art Institute of the Parsons School of Design in Los Angeles.

Saar's compulsion to collect objects is influenced by her European, Native American, and African ancestors. Working as an art conservator for her father, Saar was exposed to the art world and to influences from other cultures. By using random objects to make a captivating whole, she translates the collage aesthetic into an age-old African tradition, reintegrating past details into the present world. Saar excavates the extraordinary hidden properties of ordinary objects to erect an eclectic amalgam of accumulated history and visceral beauty.

CLEAN HOUSE
wood, tin, aluminum paint, and mirror
89″ × 28″ × 30″   1993

Courtesy: Phyllis Kind Gallery, New York City

BETYE SAAR (b. 1926)

· · · · · · · · · ·

Saar received her BA from the University of California in Los Angeles, in media with a concentration in painting, assemblages, and installation.

As a woman of African, Irish, and Native American descent, Saar recycles items from her mixed heritage along with the items of cultures far removed from her own and includes them in her assemblages and installations. She is not only influenced by her physical environment, but by various realms of spirituality, Vodun, palmistry, shamanism, and other philosophies of faith. She has explored the phenomena of spirituality throughout her life and, consequently, her works often have a mystical sensibility.

WATCHING
mixed media on metal
13½″ × 9½″   1995

Photographer: Steve Peck

P-MELON #1
glass beads, blown glass
11" × 14" × 8"   1995

Photographer: Kanui Takeno

JOYCE J. SCOTT (b. 1948)

. . . .

Scott received a BFA from Maryland Institute College of Art and earned an MFA in Crafts from the Instituto Allende in Mexico. A multi-talented creator, Scott works in myriad mediums—sculpture, jewelry, bead work, quilting, installation, and performance art. Her aggregation of distinct elements epitomizes the African aesthetic.

Scott exercises her artistic talent as a force of political commentary—the context of her energetic pieces runs the gamut from "the pleasures of roaming in cities at night"[1] to the pressures of social conformity and bias, to the evils of South African apartheid. Scott has been acclaimed for her expansive imagination and versatility in bead work.

1. Moore, Sylvia and Dr. Leslie King-Hammond, eds., *Gumbo Ya Ya: Anthology of Contemporary African American Women Artists*, New York: Midmarch Arts Press, 1995.

JAR WOMAN #4
beadwork, mixed media
49″ × 15″ × 15″   1995

LORNA SIMPSON (b. 1960)

. . . .

Simpson received her BFA in Photography from the School of Visual Arts in New York City and her MFA in Visual Arts from the University of California in San Diego.

Throughout her career, Simpson has retaliated against negative images of African American women through her conceptual photographs. Simpson draws on her own life and the experiences of all black women to poignantly express the significance of the African American female condition. Her acute awareness of the marginalization of black women and her extraordinary artistic talent grant her the tools to deconstruct the stereotypes of womanhood.

WIGS (detail)
thirty nine panels, 21 with photos and 18 with text, waterless lithography on felt, Edition 30
6' × 13.54' overall   1995

Courtesy: Rhona Hoffman Gallery, Chicago, Illinois

Dinner Party with boxer Harry Wills,
1926
James VanDerZee
Harry Wills aka "The Black Panther," boxer, businessman- sits with
seven other men and women, mostly women with champagne glasses raised as a
woman on his left makes a toast in his honor. There are three bottles of champagne,
a crystal decanter, a bottle of port, an arrangement of flowers and fruit, and before
each guest an untouched china place setting.

9 PROPS (detail)
nine duotone lithography on felt, Edition 30
14″ × 11″ each, 45″ × 35″ overall   1995

Courtesy: Sean Kelly Gallery, New York, New York

CARRIE MAE WEEMS (b. 1953)

. . . .

Weems tells the stories of her people through her own special lens. Following the example of writer and anthropologist Zora Neale Hurston, Weems excelled as a folklorist, receiving her MA in Folklore from the University of California at Berkeley. She earned her MFA in Photography from the University of California in San Diego.

Weems addresses identity and color consciousness in the African American psyche through her color prints. She includes text to supplement the visual content in her art, employing written anecdotes to describe, clarify, and explain her photographic images. Weems also uses text seemingly unrelated to the photograph as a means of exploring issues relevant to the black community such as class, physical appearance, patriarchy, and gender issues.

From the installation
FROM HERE I SAW WHAT HAPPENED AND I CRIED
(10 works) installation of monochromatic color photographs with
sand-blasted glass
26¾″ × 22¾″ each   1995

Courtesy: P.P.O.W. Gallery, New York, New York

PHILEMONA WILLIAMSON (b. 1951)

Born in New York City, Williamson received her BA from Bennington College in Vermont. Concentrating on the medium of painting, she earned an MA from New York University. After her graduate work, she taught at the Harlem School of the Arts, the Metropolitan Museum of Art, and other schools, serving as a visiting artist or faculty member.

Williamson's works conjure images of a dream state. She uses numerous shades of blue and her flat areas of color reflect Japanese-style painting. Swimming in an endless sea of color, Williamson's figures appear to be floating in a weightless expanse. Aligning young and old, past and present, Williamson celebrates the independence and magical uncertainty of art.

CAUTIOUS COLD
oil on linen
48″ × 60″ 1995

FIELD OF WATER
oil on linen
48″ × 60″ 1995

Spelman College, class of 1907. Spelman College archival photograph.

AFTERWORD

. . . .

PEARL CLEAGE

I AM always amazed that in the face of *magic*, there are those who will feel safe only by retreating to arenas where the spirit is expected to express itself exclusively through the intellect. It's not that I don't understand the impetus. *I do. Magic* is a powerful and mysterious thing, not without its own set of requirements for satisfactory engagement. The problem is, those requirements are rarely based on things that can be expressed in ways that are also magical, *transcendent*, embracing more than we see or touch or hear or taste or smell. *Magic* opens doors to things we always knew because we carry the code in our bones, passing it along as blood memory and the murmured dreams of ancestors.

Perhaps it is the undeniable presence of all those bones, and all that *blood*, that creates a discomfort capable of finding solace only in the consideration of questions like whether or not *race* or *gender* is of primary concern when finding oneself among conjure women. The translation and transformation of our black, female memories have, in truth, less to do with a struggle to answer such questions and more to do with understanding that it is as impossible to do so as it is to decide which is more important to the body, the lungs or the liver.

We were not, after all, brought here to make magic. We were brought here to make babies for sale and pick other people's cotton and keep another woman's house and not run screaming into the darkness when her hus-band kicked in our cabin door at midnight *just because he could.*

In the midst of such madness, we were not supposed to make art any more than we were supposed to love each other. We were supposed to work ourselves to death and take our stories to the grave, leaving behind a legacy no more akin to the rich complexity of human herstory than a mule or a chicken.

But those with such nefarious intentions did not know the power of our mothers and our grandmothers and *their* grandmothers and *their* great-grandmothers before them, all the way back across that watery trail of anguished African bones to the shores of the continent that surrendered us to the barbarity of this strange new world. They could not have known that, still marooned here all these years later, we would now defiantly produce a community of *sister artists* who can *tell the story straight* in a visual language as specific as their own shimmery individual ideas and images and styles but, somehow, as immediately familiar, and as *true*, as if we had shared their dreams.

Which brings us back to the *magic* connecting and sustaining us across barriers of race and class and age and gender, where the miracle of our shared, fragile, imperfect *humanity* allows us to view this amazing work and be consumed by it, scattering the ashes of our old selves into the winds of the change that means *growth*, and the growth that means *freedom*.

CHRONOLOGY

. . . .

JONTYLE THERESA ROBINSON

1619   African slaves, female and male, are brought to Jamestown, Virginia, aboard a Dutch ship. Three slave women are among the first group to arrive in America. Hundreds of thousands will join them. By 1860 slaves populate American states from Texas to Maine (including Arkansas, Tennessee, Kentucky, Missouri, and Illinois). Among their ranks are artisans who mold, sew, dye, weave, quilt, paint, carve, smith, and print. These artisans will have a double heritage, one that recalls Africa and one that acknowledges their involuntary journey to America.

1806   Sarah Mapps Douglass, artist and teacher, is born in Philadelphia, Pennsylvania (d. 1882).

1837   Harriet Powers, quiltmaker, is born a slave in Georgia (d. 1911).

ca. 1843   Mary Edmonia Lewis, sculptor, is born in Ohio or New York (d. after 1911).

1852   Sojourner Truth delivers her "Ain't I A Woman" address at the second National Women's Suffrage Convention in Akron, Ohio.

1855   Annie E. Anderson Walker, painter, is born in New York (d. 1929).

Anna Julia Cooper is born in Wake County, North Carolina, daughter of a slave mother and a white father. She authors (1892) the first feminist analysis of the condition of blacks and women (d. 1964).

1866   Sculptor Mary Edmonia Lewis creates *The Freed Woman and Her Child.*

1877   Meta Vaux Warrick Fuller, sculptor, is born in Philadelphia (d. 1968).

May Howard Jackson, sculptor, is born in Philadelphia (d. 1931).

1881   Spelman College is founded in Atlanta, Georgia, by two Northern white missionary women, Sophia B. Packard and Harriet E. Giles.

1890   Nancy Elizabeth Prophet, sculptor, is born in Warrick, Rhode Island (d. 1960).

1891   Alma Thomas, artist, is born in Columbus, Georgia (d. 1978).

1892   Augusta Savage, sculptor, is born in Green Cove Springs, Florida (d. 1962).

1895   Atlanta hosts the Cotton States and International Exposition and though not officially listed as an exhibit, it is believed that Harriet Powers's quilt *The Creation of the Animals* was part of the art exhibition.

Beulah Ecton Woodard, sculptor, is born in rural Ohio near Frankfort (d. 1955). Her one-woman exhibition of masks at the Los Angeles County Museum takes place September–October 1935.

1900   Nellie Mae Rowe, an Atlanta folk artist, is born (d. 1982).

Selma Hortense Burke, sculptor, is born in Mooresville, North Carolina (d. 1995).

1905   Artist Lois Mailou Jones is born in Boston, Massachusetts.

1917   Margaret Taylor Burroughs, artist and arts activist, is born in St. Rose Parish, Louisiana.

1929   Archibald John Motley, Jr., is the first artist of any race to receive front page coverage in *The New York Times* (see *The Art of Archibald John Motley, Jr.* by Jontyle Theresa Robinson and Wendy Greenhouse, Chicago: Chicago Historical Society, 1991).

1932   Augusta Savage establishes the Savage Studio of Arts and Crafts in Harlem, New York.

1933   Nancy Elizabeth Prophet becomes an instructor of art at Atlanta University.

1934   Nancy Elizabeth Prophet joins the faculty of Spelman College. She introduces sculpture into the curriculum and remains on the faculty for a decade.

1937   Augusta Savage is appointed the first director of the Harlem Community Art Center.

1939   The New York World's Fair commissions Augusta Savage's sixteen-foot structure *The Harp* inspired by "Lift Every Voice and Sing," a poem by James Weldon Johnson.

1941   In Chicago, Margaret Taylor Burroughs helps establish the South Side Community Art Center.

1959   The National Conference of Artists is organized at Atlanta University and has among its membership African American artists, art historians, and art educators.

1961   Margaret Taylor Burroughs (b. 1917) is the founder of the first African American history and culture museum in the United States, now the DuSable Museum of African American History in Chicago.

Elizabeth Catlett (b. 1915) delivers speech "Role of the Black Artist," which is later published in *The Black Scholar* in 1975.

1966   Kwanzaa, an African American holiday, is created by Dr. Maulana Karenga, a cultural nationalist, to celebrate African American culture.

Faith Ringgold is denied participation in the artist group Spiral.

1968   Alma Thomas has one-woman exhibitions at the Whitney Museum of American Art, the first by an African American woman, and at the Corcoran Gallery of Art.

"Contemporary Black Artists in America" exhibition opens in New York City at the Whitney Museum of American Art and includes the work of Betye Saar, Charles White, and Jacob Lawrence.

Faith Ringgold pickets Whitney Museum of American Art for its exclusion of black artists in its major exhibitions.

1970   WSABAL (Women Students and Artists for Black Art Liberation) is cofounded in New York by Faith Ringgold and daughter Michele Wallace as a response to Artist's Strike Against Racism, Sexism, Repression, and War (white male artists only). Ringgold successfully fought for the inclusion of Betye Saar and Barbara Chase-Riboud in the Whitney Biennial, which gave them the distinction of being the first black women ever in this exhibition.

"Where We At" black women artists' exhibition is held in New York City and has the distinction of being the first black women's art exhibition.

1971   Linda Nochlin's essay "Why Have There Been No Great Women Artists" is published in *Artnews* and signals the beginning of the feminist art movement.

1972   Faith Ringgold's mural *For The Women's House* is installed permanently at the Women's House of Detention on Riker's Island. The commissioned piece is intended to inspire the inmates.

Feminist Art Journal is founded.

A.I.R. Gallery, the first women's cooperative gallery, is founded in New York City. Howardena Pindell, founding member, leaves in 1975.

The Women's Caucus for Art (WCA) of the College Art Association is founded.

The Conference on Women in the Arts is held at the Corcoran Gallery of Art, Washington, D.C.

1975   The International Year of the Woman is designated by the United Nations conference held in Mexico City.

1976   "Women Artists 1550–1950" exhibition organized by Anne Sutherland Harris and Linda Nochlin opens at the Los Angeles County Museum of Art and is the first exhibition to survey women's art.

1980   The exhibition "Black Women Artists" opens at the Douglass College Art Gallery, Walters Hall, New Brunswick, New Jersey.

Marian Wright Edelman becomes the first black person and the second woman to chair the Spelman College Board of Trustees.

1981   "Forever Free: Art by African American Women 1862–1980" opens at the Center for the Visual Arts Gallery, Illinois State University, Normal, Illinois. It will travel nationally to five venues in Omaha, Nebraska; Montgomery, Alabama; Charleston, South Carolina; College Park, Maryland; and Indianapolis, Indiana. The catalogue that accompanies the exhibition reaches an even wider audience.

The Women's Research and Resource Center is founded at Spelman College with a grant from the Charles Stewart Mott Foundation and has the distinction of being the first women's center of its kind at a historically black college.

Alice Walker wins the Pulitzer Prize and the American Book Award for *The Color Purple*.

1983   *Sage: A Scholarly Journal on Black Women* is cofounded in Atlanta by Beverly Guy-Sheftall and Patricia Bell-Scott. Its "Artists and Artisans" issue is published in 1987.

The exhibition "Black Women on Paper" opens at the University of Wisconsin, Green Bay, and tours the nation.

1984   The first issue of the first black women's newspaper *Five Fifteen* is published.

1985   The exhibition "American Women in Art: Works on Paper" opens at the United Nations International Women's Conference in Nairobi, Kenya.

1986   *Radiance From the Waters: Ideals of Feminine Beauty in Mende Art* by Dr. Sylvia Ardyn Boone (d. 1993) is published by Yale University Press and provides an in-depth glimpse into the art and culture of the Mende women of Sierra Leone.

1987   Johnnetta B. Cole becomes the first black woman President of Spelman College.

    The exhibition "Black Women Artists 1987" opens at the Museum of the National Center of Afro-American Artists, Boston.

    Founding of the National Museum of Women in the Arts, Washington, D.C.

1988   The exhibition "1938–1988: The Work of Five Black Women Artists" includes Camille Billops, Margo Humphrey, Lois Mailou Jones, Howardena Pindell, and Faith Ringgold and opens at the Atlanta College of Art Gallery in collaboration with the National Black Arts Festival.

    The culmination of a seven-year statistical project by Howardena Pindell on museum exhibitions and current gallery representation of the 11,000 black, Asian, Hispanic, and Native American painters, sculptors, craftspersons, photographers, graphic designers, and architects who live and work in New York State. Report published in *The New Art Examiner,* March 1989.

1990   Feminist Art History Conference is held at Barnard College.

    The exhibition "Black Women in the Arts" opens at Montclair State College Gallery, Upper Montclair, New Jersey.

1991   Black Feminisms Seminar is hosted by Spelman College's Women's Center.

    Ground is broken on April 11 for the Camille Olivia Hanks Cosby Academic Center to be con-

structed with part of Bill and Camille Cosby's $20 million gift to the college in 1988.

1993   Carrie Mae Weems's one-woman exhibition opens at the National Museum of Women in the Arts in Washington, D.C. and tours the nation. She is the first African American to have a monographic exhibition at the museum since its opening in 1987, though other African American women artists have been included in group shows.

1994   *Theorizing Black Feminisms*, edited by Stanlie M. James and Abena P. A. Busia, is published by Routledge and includes an essay by Freida High W. Tesfagiorgis, "In Search of A Discourse and Critique/s That Center the Art of Black Women Artists" as well as one of her sculptures on the cover.

1995   United Nations International Conference on Women is held in Beijing, China and includes several art exhibitions.

    Elizabeth Catlett receives Honorary Doctor of Fine Arts from Spelman College.

    Carrie Mae Weems's one-woman show opens at The Museum of Modern Art in New York.

1996   "Bearing Witness" exhibition opens at the Spelman College Museum of Fine Art.

Biographical entries in this chronology were drawn from the following sources: Beverly Guy-Sheftall and Jo Moore Stewart (photo editor), *Spelman: A Centennial Celebration 1881–1981,* Atlanta: Spelman College, 1981; Sharon Harley, *The Timetables of African American History,* New York: Simon & Schuster, 1995; Faith Ringgold, *We Flew Over The Bridge: The Memoirs of Faith Ringgold,* Boston: Little, Brown and Company, 1995; Norma Broude and Mary D. Garrard, eds., *The Power of Feminist Art: The American Movement of the 1970s, History and Impact,* New York: Harry N. Abrams, 1994; The Network for African American Women and the Law, Adjoa A. Aiyetoro, Director, *Sisters' Voices from the United States;* and the resumes and catalogues of the twenty-five artists in this exhibition.

SELECTED BIBLIOGRAPHY

COMPILED BY BEVERLY GUY-SHEFTALL

EXHIBITION CATALOGUES

These exhibits focused on or included African Americans, African American women, and women artists or they were curated by African Americans, particularly women, and include essays by black art historians and critics, particularly women.

A Courtyard Apart: The Art of Elizabeth Catlett and Francisco Mora. Biloxi, MS: Mississippi Museum of Art, 1990.

The Afro-American Artist in the Age of Cultural Pluralism. Montclair, NJ: Montclair Art Museum, 1987.

Alexander, Margaret Walker. *Elizabeth Catlett.* Jackson, MS: Jackson State College, 1973.

Alpha Kappa Alpha Sorority. *Afro-American Women in Art: Their Achievements in Sculpture and Painting.* Greensboro, NC: Negro Heritage Committee, 1969.

Amos, Emma. *Hanging Loose at the Port Authority.* New York: Port Authority Terminal, 1984.

_____. *Resisting Categories/Finding Common Ground.* Newark, NJ: City Without Walls, 1995.

Amos, Emma, et al. *Progressions, A Cultural Legacy.* New York: The Clock Tower, 1986.

_____ et al. *You Must Remember This.* Jersey City, NJ: Jersey City Museum, 1992.

Art and Ideology. New York: The New Museum of Contemporary Art, 1984.

Art As A Verb: The Evolving Continuum, Installations, Performances, and Videos by 13 African American Artists. Essays by Leslie King Hammond and Lowery Stokes Sims. Baltimore: Maryland Institute College of Art, 1988.

Art in Washington and Its Afro-American Presence, 1940–1970. Washington, DC: Washington Project for the Arts, 1985.

Autobiography: In Her Own Image. Essays by Howardina Pindell, Judith Wilson, and Moira Roth. New York: INTAR Latin American Gallery, 1988.

Benberry, Cuesta. *Always There: The African American Presence in American Quilts.* Louisville: The Kentucky Quilt Project, 1992.

Benjamin, Tritobia Hayes. *The Life and Art of Lois Mailou Jones.* San Francisco: Pomegranate Artbooks, 1994.

Bibby, Deidre L. *Augusta Savage and the Art Schools of Harlem.* New York: The Schomburg Center for Research in Black Culture, 1988.

Black Art: Ancestral Legacy, The African Impulse in African-American Art. Dallas: Dallas Museum of Art, 1989.

Black Women in the Arts. Montclair, NJ: Montclair State College Gallery, 1990.

Blake, Nayland, Lawrence Rinder, and Amy Scholder, eds. *In A Different Light: Visual Culture, Sexual Identity, Queer Practice.* San Francisco: City Lights Books, 1995.

The Blues Aesthetic: Black Culture and Modernism. Washington, DC: Washington Project for the Arts, 1989.

Bontemps, Arna Alexander, and Jacqueline Fonvielle-Bontemps. *Forever Free: Art by African American Women 1862–1980.* Alexandria, VA: Stephenson, 1980.

Buchanan, Beverly. *ShackWorks: A 16-year Survey.* Montclair, NJ: The Montclair Art Museum, 1994.

California Black Artists. New York: The Studio Museum in Harlem, 1978.

Campbell, Mary Schmidt. *Harlem Renaissance: Art of Black America.* New York: The Studio Museum in Harlem and Harry N. Abrams, 1987.

Celebration: Eight Afro-American Artists Selected by Romare Bearden. New York: Henry Street Settlement, 1984.

Change: Over 100 Pounds Weight-loss Performance. New York: Bernice Steinbaum Gallery, 1987.

Coast To Coast: A Women of Color National Artist's Book Project. New York: Jamaica Art Center, 1988.

Constructed Images: New Photography. New York: The Schomburg Center for Research in Black Culture, 1989.

Contemporary Afro-American Photography. Oberlin, OH: Allen Memorial Art Museum, Oberlin College, 1983.

Contemporary Art By Women of Color. San Antonia: Guadalupe Cultural Arts Center and the Instituto Cultural Mexicano, 1990.

The Decade Show: Frameworks of Identity in the 1980s. New York: Museum of Contemporary Hispanic Art, 1990.

Dialectics of Isolation: An Exhibition of Third World Women Artists of the United States. New York: Asian Art Institute, 1985.

Diversity of Vision: Contemporary Works by African American Women. Minneapolis, MN: WARM Gallery, 1990.

Elizabeth Catlett, Works on Paper, 1944–1992. Hampton, VA: Hampton University Museum, 1993.

Emma Amos: Paintings and Prints 1982–92. Wooster, OH: The College of Wooster Art Museum, 1993.

An Exhibition of Black Women Artists. Santa Barbara, CA: Committee for Black Culture and the Center for Black Studies, 1975.

Faith Ringgold: Twenty Year Retrospective. New York: The Studio Museum in Harlem, 1984.

Fax, Elton, and Jeff Donaldson. *Elizabeth Catlett*. New York: The Studio Museum in Harlem, 1971.

Flomenhaft, Eleanor, ed. *Faith Ringgold: A Twenty-five Year Survey*. Hempstead, NY: Fine Arts Museum of Long Island, 1990.

Fragments of Myself/The Women: An Exhibition of Black Women Artists. New Brunswick, NJ: Douglass College Art Gallery, 1979.

Fry, Gladys-Marie. *Stitched From the Soul: Slave Quilts from the Ante-bellum South*. New York: Museum of American Folk Art, 1990.

Fusco, Coco. *Uncanny Dissonance: The Work of Lorna Simpson*. Hamilton, NY: Colgate University, 1991.

Golden, Thelma, ed. *Black Male: Representations of Masculinity in Contemporary American Art*. New York: Whitney Museum of American Art, 1994.

Grudin, Eva Ungar. *Stitching Memories: African American Story Quilts*. Williamstown, MA: Williams College Museum of Art, 1989.

Hall, Robert. *Gathered Visions: Selected Works by African American Women Artists*. Washington, DC: Anacostia Museum, 1992.

Hammond, Leslie King. *Nancy E. Prophet, Four from Providence: Black Artists in the Rhode Island Landscape*. Providence: Rhode Island College, 1978.

Hidden Heritage: Afro-American Art, 1800–1950. San Francisco: Art Museum Association of America, 1985.

Howardena Pindell: Painting and Drawings, A Retrospective Exhibition, 1972–1992. New York: ExhibitsUSA, Roland Gibson Gallery, Potsdam College, State University of New York, 1992.

Interrogating Identity. New York: Grey Art Gallery and Study Center, New York University, 1991.

Joyce J. Scott, Fearless Beadwork: Handwritings and Drawings from Hell. Rochester, NY: Visual Studies Workshop, 1994.

Joyce J. Scott: Images Concealed. San Francisco: San Francisco Art Institute, 1995.

Kirsh, Andrea, and Susan Fisher Sterling. *Carrie Weems*. Washington, DC: National Museum of Women in the Arts, 1993.

Leon, Eli, ed. *Who'd A Thought It: Improvisation in African American Quiltmaking*. San Francisco: San Francisco Craft and Folk Art Museum, 1987.

Lewis, Samella S. *The Art of Elizabeth Catlett*. Claremont, CA: Handcraft Studios, 1984.

McElroy, Guy C., et al. *Facing History: The Black Image in American Art 1710–1940*. Washington, DC: The Corcoran Gallery of Art, 1990.

Miller-Keller, Andrea. *Carrie Mae Weems/Matrix 115*. Hartford, CT: Wadsworth Atheneum, 1991.

9 Uptown. New York: Harlem School of the Arts, 1988.

Paintings,Sculpture and Prints of the Negro Woman by Elizabeth Catlett. Washington, DC: The Barnett Aden Gallery, 1947.

The Paul and Joyce Show. Baltimore: Maryland Art Place, 1987.

Piper, Adrian. *Pretend*. New York: John Weber Gallery, 1990.

Powell, Richard. *African and Afro-American Art: Call and Response*. Chicago: Field Museum of Natural History, 1984.

———. *The Blues Aesthetic: Black Culture and Modernism*. Washington, DC: Washington Project for the Arts, 1989.

Prints by Women. New York: Associated American Artists, 1986.

Prisoners of Image: Ethnic and Gender Stereotypes. New York: Alternative Museum, 1989.

Race and Representation: Art/Film/Video. New York: Hunter College Art Gallery, 1987.

Ritual and Myth: A Survey of African American Art. New York: The Studio Museum in Harlem, 1982.

Robinson, Jontyle Theresa. *VH-Decades: The Art of Varnette P. Honeywood*. Atlanta: Spelman College, 1992.

Rodriguez, Geno. *Artists of Conscience: 16 Years of Social and Political Commentary*. New York: Alternative Museum, 1991.

Schwarzer, Lynn, ed. *Lorna Simpson*. Hamilton, NY: Colgate University, 1991.

Scott, Joyce J. *I-CON-NOBODY/I-CON-O-GRAPHY*. Washington, DC: The Corcoran Gallery of Art, 1991.

Scott, Martha B. *The Art of Advocacy*. Ridgefield, CT: Aldrich Museum of Contemporary Art, 1991.

Selections: Six Contemporary African American Artists. Williamstown, MA: Williams College Museum of Art, 1989.

Shepherd, Elizabeth, ed. *The Art of Betye and Alison Saar: Secrets, Dialogues, Revelations*. Los Angeles: University of California, Wright Art Gallery, 1990.

Southern Women Artists. Columbia, SC: The Columbia Museum of Arts, 1990.

Tibol, Raquel. *Elizabeth Catlett*. Mexico City: Museo de Arte Moderno, National Institute of Fine Arts, 1970.

Tradition and Conflict: Images of A Turbulent Decade, 1963–1973. New York: The Studio Museum in Harlem, 1985.

Trippi, Laura. *And 22 Million Very Tired and Very Angry People*. San Francisco Art Institute, 1991 (Emma Amos installation).

Uhuru: African and American Art Against Apartheid. New York: City Without Walls Gallery, 1988.

Uncommon Beauty in Common Objects: The Legacy of African American Craft Art. Wilberforce, OH: Afro-American Museum & Cultural Center, 1993.

Weems, Carrie Mae. *Family Pictures and Stories: A Photographic Installation*. San Diego: Alternative Space Gallery 1984.

———. *Then What/Photographs and Folklore*. Buffalo, NY: CEPA Gallery, 1990.

Willis-Thomas, Deborah, and Howard Dodson. *Black Photographers Bear Witness: 100 Years of Social Protest*. Williamstown, MA: Williams College Museum of Art, 1989.

The Wisconsin Connection: Black Artists Past and Present. Madison: Memorial Union Galleries, University of Wisconsin, 1987.

Women Choose Women: An Exhibition Organized by Women in the Arts. New York: New York Cultural Center, 1973.

BOOKS

A Documentary History of Women Artists in Revolution. Pittsburgh, PA: KNOW Press, 1971.

Barnett, Alan W. *Community Murals: The People's Art*. Philadelphia: Art Alliance Press; New York: Cornwall Books, 1984.

Bearden, Romare, and Harry Henderson. *A History of African American Artists From 1792 to the Present*. New York: Pantheon Books, 1993.

Benamou, Michel, and Charles Caramella, eds. *Performance and Postmodern Culture*. Madison, WI: Coda Press, 1977.

Betterton, Rosemary, ed. *Looking On: Images of Femininity in the Visual Arts and Media*. New York: Pandora, 1987.

Brincard, Marie-Therese. *Beauty by Design: The Aesthetics of African Adornment*. New York: The African American Institute, 1984.

Broude, Norma, and Mary D. Garrard, eds. *The Expanding Discourse: Feminism and Art History*. New York: HarperCollins, 1992.

———. *Feminism and Art History: Questioning the Litany*. New York: Harper & Row, 1982.

———. *The Power of Feminist Art: The American Movement of the 1970s, History and Impact*. New York: Harry N. Abrams, 1994.

Chase, Judith Wragg. *Afro-American Art and Craft*. New York: Van Nostrand Reinhold, 1971.

Chase Riboud, Barbara. *Echo of Lions*. New York: William Morrow, 1989.

———. *Egypt Nights*. 1994.

———. *From Memphis and Peking*. New York: Random House, 1974.

———. *Portrait of a Nude Woman as Cleopatra*. New York: William Morrow, 1987.

———. *The President's Daughter*. New York: Crown Publishers, 1994.

———. *Sally Hemmings*. New York: Viking Press, 1979.

———. *Valide*. New York: William Morrow, 1986.

Collischan, Judy. *Lines of Vision: Drawings by Contemporary Women*. New York: Hudson Hills Press, 1989.

Dannett, Sylvia. *Profiles of Negro Womanhood*. Yonkers, NY: Educational Heritage, 1964.

Dent, Gina, ed. *Black Popular Culture: A Project by Michele Wallace*. Seattle, WA: Bay Press, 1992.

Driskell, David. *Two Centuries of Black American Art*. Los Angeles: Los Angeles County Museum of Art; New York: Alfred A. Knopf, 1976.

Driskell, David, et al. *Harlem Renaissance: Art of Black America*. New York: The Studio Museum in Harlem and Harry N. Abrams, 1987.

Fax, Elton C. *Black Artists of the New Generation*. New York: Dodd Mead, 1977.

Ferguson, Russell, et al. *Discourses: Conversations in Postmodern Art and Culture*. Cambridge, MA: MIT Press, 1990.

———. *Out There: Marginalization and Contemporary Cultures*. Cambridge, MA: MIT Press, 1990.

Ferrero, Pat, Elaine Hedges, and Julie Silber. *Hearts and Hands: The Influence of Women and Quilts on American Society*. San Francisco: Quilt Digest Press, 1987.

Ferris, William, ed. *Afro-American Folk Art and Crafts*. Boston: G.K. Hall, 1983.

Fine, Elsa Honing. *The Afro-American Artist: A Search for Identity*. New York: Holt, Rinehart and Winston, 1973.

———. *Women and Art: A History of Women Painters and Sculptors from the Renaissance to the 20th Century*. Montclair, NJ: Allanheld and Schram, 1978.

Goldberg, Rosalee. *Performance Art: From Futurism to the Present*. New York: Harry N. Abrams, 1988.

Gumbo Ya Ya: Anthology of Contemporary African American Women Artists. New York: Midmarch Arts, 1995.

Guy-Sheftall, Beverly, ed. *Words of Fire: An Anthology of African American Feminist Thought*. New York: The New Press, 1995.

Harris, Ann Sutherland, and Linda Nochlin. *Women Artists 1550–1950*. New York: Alfred A. Knopf, 1976.

Heller, Nancy G. *Women Artists: An Illustrated History*. New York: Abbeville Press, 1987.

Henkes, Robert. *The Art of Black American Women: Works of Twenty-four Artists of the Twentieth Century*. Jefferson, NC: McFarland & Company, 1993.

Hess, Thomas B., and Elizabeth C. Baker, eds. *Art and Sexual Politics*. New York: Collier, 1971.

Hess, Thomas B., and Linda Nochlin, eds. *Woman as Sex Object; Studies in Erotic Art*, 1730–1970. New York: Newsweek, 1972.

Hine, Darlene Clark, ed. *Black Women in the U.S.: An Historical Encyclopedia*. Brooklyn, NY: Carlson Publishing, 1993.

hooks, bell. *Art on My Mind: Visual Politics*. New York: The New Press, 1995.

———. *Black Looks: Race and Representation*. Boston: South End Press, 1992.

Igoe, Lynn Moody. *250 Years of Afro-American Art: An Annotated Bibliography*. New York: R.R. Bowker Company, 1981.

Illustrated Biography of Black Photographers, 1940–1988. New York: Garland Publishing, 1989.

Interviews with Women in the Arts. New York: Tower Press, 1976.

Jones, Virginia Watson. *Contemporary American Women Sculptors*. Phoenix, AZ: Oryx, 1986.

Ladislas, Bugner, ed. *The Image of the Black in Western Art*. 4 vols. New York: William Morrow, 1976.

Lerner, Gerda, ed. *Black Women in White America: A Documentary History*. New York: Pantheon Books, 1972.

Lewis, Samella S. *African American Art and Artists*. Berkeley and Los Angeles: University of California Press.

———. *Art—African American*. New York: Harcourt Brace Jovanovich, 1978.

Lewis, Samella S. and Ruth Waddy. *Black Artists on Art*. 2 vols. Los Angeles: Contemporary Crafts, 1969–71.

Lippard, Lucy R. *From the Center: Feminist Essays on Women's Art*. New York: E.P. Dutton, 1976.

———. *Get the Message? A Decade of Art for Social Change*. New York: E.P. Dutton, 1984.

———. *Mixed Blessings: New Art in Multicultural America*. New York: Pantheon Books, 1990.

———. *The Pink Glass Swan: Selected Feminist Essays on Art*. New York: The New Press, 1995.

Locke, Alain. *Negro Art: Past and Present*. Washington, DC: Associates in Negro Folk Education, 1936.

———. *The Negro in Art*. Washington, DC: Associates in Negro Folk Education, 1940.

Loeb, Judy, ed. *Feminist Collage: Educating Women in the Visual Arts*. New York: Columbia University Teachers College Press, 1979.

Lorde, Audre. *Sister Outsider*. Trumansburg, NY: Crossing Press, 1984.

Miller, L. F., and S. S. Swensen. *Lives and Work and Talks with Women Artists*. Metuchen, NJ: Scarecrow Press, 1981.

Moss, Kathlyn, and Alice Sherer. *The New Beadwork*. New York: Harry N. Abrams, 1992.

Moutoussamy-Ashe, Jeanne. *Viewfinders: Black Women Photographers*. New York: Dodd, Mead & Company, 1986.

Munro, Eleanor. *Originals: American Women Artists*. New York: Simon and Schuster, 1979.

Nochlin, Linda. *Women, Art, and Power and Other Essays*. New York: Harper & Row, 1988.

Pollack, Griselda. *Vision and Difference: Femininity, Feminism and Histories of Art*. New York: Routledge, 1988.

Pollack, Griselda, and Rozsika Parker. *Old Mistresses: Women, Art, and Ideology*. New York: Routledge and Kegan Paul, 1981.

Porter, James. *Modern Negro Art*. New York: Dryden Press, 1943.

Raven, Arlene. *Crossing Over: Feminism and Art of Social Concern*. Ann Arbor, MI: UMI Research Press, 1988.

Raven, Arlene, ed. *Art in the Public Interest*. Ann Arbor, MI: UMI Research Press, 1989.

Raven, Arlene et al., eds. *Feminist Art Criticism: An Anthology*. New York: Icon Editions, 1991.

Ringgold, Faith. *Aunt Harriet's Underground Railroad in the Sky*. New York: Crown Publishers, 1992.

———. *Dinner at Aunt Connie's House*. New York: Hyperion Books, 1993.

———. *Tar Beach*. New York: Crown Publishers, 1991.

———. *We Flew Over the Bridge: The Memoirs of Faith Ringgold*. Boston: Little, Brown, 1995.

Robinson, Charlotte. *The Artist and The Quilt*. New York: Alfred A. Knopf, 1983.

Robinson, Hilary, ed. *Visibly Female: Feminism and Art Today*. New York: Universe Books, 1988.

Roth, Moira, ed. *The Amazing Decade: Women and Performance Art in America, 1970–1980*. Los Angeles: Astro Artz, 1983.

Rubinstein, Charlotte Streifer. *American Women Artists from Early Indian Times to the Present*. Boston, MA: G.K. Hall, 1982.

Seigel, Judy, ed. *Mutiny and the Mainstream: Talk That Changed Art, 1975–1990*. New York: Midmarch Arts, 1992.

Starks, Barbara, et al., eds. *African American Dress and Adornment: A Cultural Perspective*. Dubuque, IA: Kendall/Hunt Publishing Co., 1990.

Thompson, Robert Farris. *Flash of the Spirit: African and Afro-American Art and Philosophy*. New York: Random House, 1983.

Ugwu, Catherine, ed. *Let's Get It On: The Politics of Black Performance*. Seattle, WA: Bay Press, 1995.

Vlach, John Michael. *The Afro-American Tradition in the Decorative Arts*. Cleveland, OH: Cleveland Museum of Art, 1978.

Wahlman, Maude Southwell. *Signs and Symbols: African Images in African American Quilts*. New York: Studio Books, 1993.

Wall, Cheryl A. *Women of the Harlem Renaissance*. Bloomington: Indiana University Press, 1995.

Wall, Cheryl A., ed. *Changing Our Own Words: Essays on Criticism, Theory, and Writing by Black Women*. New Brunswick, NJ: Rutgers University Press, 1989.

Wallace, Michele. *Invisibility Blues: From Pop to Theory*. London: Verso, 1990.

Williams, Ora. *American Black Women in the Arts and Social Sciences: A Bibliographical Survey*. Metuchen, NJ: Scarecrow Press, 1978.

Willis, Deborah, ed. *Picturing Us: African American Identity in Photography*. New York: The New Press, 1994.

Witzling, Mara, ed. *Voicing Our Visions: Writings by Women Artists*. New York: Universe Books, 1991.

ARTICLES

Amos, Emma. "Contemporary Views on Racism in the Arts." *M/E/A/N/I/N/G: Contemporary Art Issues* 7 (May 1990).

———. "Do's and Don'ts for Art Students." *Heresies*, vol. 25 (1990).

———. "Juicy Overflowing Studios: Questions Too Rude to Ask Older Artists." *Art and Artists* (November 1982).

———. "Do's and Don'ts for Black Women Artists," *Heresies; A Feminist Publication on Art and Politics*, vol. 15 (1982).

"Appreciating Art on All Levels: Joyce Scott's Bead Sculpture." *The Art of Seeing*. Edited by Paul Zelanski and Mary Pat Fisher. Englewood Cliffs, NJ: Prentice Hall, 1994.

Benner, Susan. "A Conversation with Carrie Mae Weems." *Art Week*, vol. 23 (May 7, 1992): 4–5.

Bloomfield, Anna. "New History: Beverly Buchanan, Mel Edwards, Maren Hassinger." *Art Papers* (November/December 1990).

Brown, Kay. "Where We At Black Women Artists." *Feminist Art Journal*, vol. 1 (April 1972).

"Carrie Mae Weems/Matrix 115, Wadsworth Atheneum." *Journal of the Print World*, vol. 14 (Spring 1991): 49.

Catlett, Elizabeth. "The Role of the Black Artist." *The Black Scholar*, vol. 6 (June 1975):10–14.

———. "The Negro People and American Art." *Freedomways*, vol. 1 (1961): 74–80.

Conwill, Houston. "Interview with Betye Saar." *Black Art: An International Quarterly* (Fall 1979): 13–14.

Cullen, Countee. "Elizabeth Prophet: Sculptress." *Opportunity* (July 1930): 205.

Doniger, Sidney, Sandra Matthews, and Gillian Brown, eds. "Personal Perspectives on the Evolution of American Black Photography: A Talk with Carrie Weems." *Obscura*, vol. 2 (Spring 1982): 8–17.

Erickson, Peter. "Seeing White." *Transition*, vol. 5, no. 3 (Fall 1995): 166–85.

Failing, Patricia. "Black Artists Today: A Case of Exclusion." *Art News*, vol. 88, no. 3 (March 1989): 124–31.

Goldman, Shifra. "Six Women Artists in Mexico." *Women's Art Journal*, vol. 3, no.2 (February 1982): 1–9.

Gomez, Jewelle. "Showing Our Faces: A Century of Black Women Photographed." *In a Different Light*. Edited by Nayland Blake et al., 1995.

Gouma-Peterson, Thalia. "Elizabeth Catlett: The Power of Human Feeling of Art." *Woman's Art Journal*, vol. 54 (Spring/Summer 1983).

Gouma-Peterson, Thalia, and Patricia Mathews. "The Feminist Critique of Art History." *Art Bulletin*, vol. 69 (September 1987): 326–57.

Hamilton, Meg. "Interview: Joyce J. Scott." *Art Papers*, vol. 17 (January/February, 1993): 34.

Heartney, Eleanor. "Carrie Mae Weems." *Art News*, vol. 90 (January 1991): 154–55.

Herzog, Melanie. "Elizabeth Catlett in Mexico . . ." *International Review of African American Art*, vol. 11, no. 3 (1994).

Hoover, Velma J. "Meta Vaux Warrick Fuller: Her Life and Art." *Negro History Bulletin* (March/April 1977): 679.

James, Curtia. "Interview with Maren Hassinger." *Art Papers* (January/February 1994): 6–8.

Johnson, Ken. "Maren Hasinger at Soho 20." *Art in America* (May 1990): 244–45.

Jones, Kellie. "Howardena Pindell." *Artist and Influence*, vol. 9 (1990): 112–28.

———. "In Their Own Image." *Artforum*, vol. 29 (November 1990): 133–38.

Kelley, Jeff. "The Isms Brothers: Carrie Weems at SFAI." *Art Week*, vol. 23 (May 7, 1992): 4.

Lippard, Lucy. "Catalysis: An Interview with Adrian Piper." *From the Center: Feminist Essays on Women's Art*.

———. "Floating Falling Landing: An Interview with Emma Amos." *Art Papers* (November/December 1991): 13–16.

Mercer, Kobena. "Black Art and the Burden of Representation." *Third Text*, vol. 10 (Spring 1991): 61–78.

Mercer, Kobena, et al. "Sexual Identities: Questions of Difference." *Undercut*, vol. 17(Spring 1988): 19–30.

Nemser, Cindy. "The Women Artists' Movement." *Feminist Art Journal*, vol. 2 (Winter 1973–74): 8–10.

Nochlin, Linda. "Why Have There Been No Great Women Artists?" *Art News* (January 1971): 22–39, 67–71.

Novick, Brent. "Maren Hassinger." *International Review of African American Art*, vol. 6 (1984): 34–41.

O'Grady, Lorraine. "Olympia's Maid: Reclaiming Black Female Subjectivity." *Afterimage*, vol. 20 (Summer 1992): 14 ff.

Piper, Adrian. "The Joy of Marginality." *Art Papers*, vol. 14 (July–August, 1990): 12–13.

———. "The Triple Negation of Colored Women." *Next Generation: Southern Black Aesthetics*. Southern Center for Contemporary Art, 1990.

Pindell, Howardena. "Art (World) and Racism: Testimony, Documentation and Statistics." *Third Text*, vol. 3, no. 4 (Spring–Summer 1988): 157–90.

———. "Covenant of Silence: De Facto Censorship." *Third Text*, vol. 11 (Summer 1990): 71–90.

Pierre-Noel, Lois Jones. "American Negro Art in Progress." *Negro History Bulletin* (October 1967).

Raven, Arlene. "Feminist Rituals of Re-Membered History: Lisa Jones, Kaylynn Sullivan, Joyce Scott." *Women and Performance*, vol. 7 (1988–89): 23–41.

Scott, Joyce. "Carrying On." *Spirit, Space and Survival: African American Women in Academe*. Edited by Joy James and Ruth Farmer. New York and London: Routledge, 1993.

Searle, Karen. "Migrant Worker for the Arts: Joyce Scott." *Ornament*, vol. 15 (Summer 1992): 46–51.

Shortal, Helen. "Getting a Bead on Sexism and Racism: Artist Joyce Scott Uses Traditional Materials in Decidedly Untraditional Ways." *In These Times*, Chicago, October 23, 1991.

Sims, Lowery Stokes. "Aspects of Performance in the Work of Black American Women Artists." *Feminist Art Criticism: An Anthology*. Edited by Arlene Raven, Cassandra L. Langer, and Joanne Frueh. New York: HarperCollins, 1991, pp. 207–25.

———. "HEAT and Other Climatic Manifestations: Urban Bush Women, Thought Music, and Craig Harris with the Dirty Tones Band." *High Performance*, vol. 45 (Spring 1989): 22–27.

———. "The Mirror/The Other: The Politics of Esthetics." *Artforum* (March 1990): 111–15.

———. "The New Exclusionism." *Art Papers*, vol. 12 (July/August 1988): 37–38.

———. "19th Century Black Women Artists." *The Black Arts Magazine* (January 1978): 32.

———. "Third World Women Speak." *Women Artists News* (December 1978): 1–10.

Tesfagiorgis, Freida High. "Afrofemcentrism and Its Fruition in the Art of Elizabeth Catlett and Faith Ringgold." *Sage: A Scholarly Journal on Black Women*, vol. 4 no. 1 (Spring 1987): 25–29.

————. "In Search of a Discourse and Critique/s That Center the Art of Black Women Artists." *Theorizing Black Feminisms*. Edited by Stanlie M. James and Abena P. A. Busia. New York: Routledge, 1993.

————. "Interweaving Black Feminism and Art History: Framing Nigeria." *Callaloo*, forthcoming 1996.

Thompson, Mildred. "Amalia Amaki/Liz Hampton." *Art Papers* (November/December 1994).

Wardlaw, Alvia. "Call and Response: The Art of Jean Lacy." *American Visions*, vol. 8 (December/January 1994).

Willis, Deborah. "Photobiographers," *International Review of African American Art*, vol. 11, no. 3 (1994): 39–42.

Wilson, Judith. "Beauty Rites: Towards an Anatomy of Culture in African American Women's Art." *International Review of African American Art*, vol. 11, no. 3 (1994): 11–17.

————. "Down to the Crossroads: The Art of Alison Saar." *Third Text*, vol. 10 (Spring 1990): 25–44.

————. "In Memory of the News and of Ourselves: The Art of Adrian Piper." *Third Text*, vol. 16/17 (Autumn/Winter 1991): 39–64.

————. "Optical Illusions: Images of Miscegenation in Nineteenth and Twentieth Century American Art." *American Art*, vol. 5 (Summer 1991): 89–107.

————. "What Are We Doing Here: Cultural Difference in Photographic Theory and Practice." *S.F. Camerawork Quarterly*, vol. 17 (Fall 199): 27–30.

White, Clarence, "Amalia Amaki: American Reminiscences, Buttons, and Blues." *Art Paper* (May/June 1994).

PERIODICALS

These journals are useful in a consideration of African American and/or women artists. Some are defunct, but back issues are available in libraries.

Afro-American Art History Newsletter. New York, edited by Judith Wilson.

Artists and Influence. Hatch-Billops Collection. New York, NY (1981–present).

Callaloo: A Black South Journal of Arts and Letters. Charlottesville, University of Virginia.

Chrysalis: A Quarterly. Los Angeles (1977–1980).

The Feminist Art Journal. Brooklyn, NY (1972–1977).

Fire! A Quarterly Devoted to Younger Negro Artists. Westport, CT, Negro University Press (1970).

Heresies: A Feminist Publication on Art and Politics. New York (1977–1993).

The International Review of African American Art.

Sage: A Scholarly Journal on Black Women. Atlanta: Sage Women's Educational Press (1984–).

Third Text. London, Kala Press.

Upfront. New York, P.A.D.D. (Political Art Documentation/Distribution).

Womanart. Brooklyn, NY (1976–).

Woman's Art Journal. Knoxville, TN (1980–present).

Women Artists Newsletter/Women Artists New (1975–1991).

SPECIAL ISSUES OF PERIODICALS

Art Papers. "The Black Aesthetic Issue." (November/December 1985).

————. "Multicultural Issue." (July/August 1990).

Cultural Critique. "The Nature and Context of Minority Discourse." Nos. 6, 7 (Spring/Fall 1987).

Discourse. "She, The Inappropriate(d) Other." No. 8 (Winter 1986–87).

————. "On Ethnography and the Politics of Representation." No. 11 (Spring 1988).

Feminist Review. "Difference: A Special Third World Women Issue." No. 25 (Spring 1987).

Heresies. "Racism Is the Issue." No. 15 (1982).

————. "Women in Theatre and Perfomance," vol. 5, no. 1 (1984).

————. "Women and Activism," vol. 5, no. 4 (1984).

————. "Third World Women: The Politics of Being Other." No. 8 (1979).

Ikon. "Art Against Apartheid." No. 5–6 (Winter/Summer 1986).

International Review of African American Art. "Art in Public Places." Vol. 7, no. 2 (1987).

————. "Women Artists." (December 1990).

Sage: A Scholarly Journal on Black Women. "Artists and Artisans." Vol. 4, no. 1 (Spring 1987).

Screen. "The Last 'Special Issue' on Race." Vol. 29 (Autumn 1988).

Third Text. (Summer 1992).

LIST OF ILLUSTRATIONS

Entries that are asterisked do not appear in the Exhibition.

INDEX

. . . .